Hoops

THE AMERICAN WAYS SERIES

 AmericanWays

General Editor: John David Smith
Charles H. Stone Distinguished Professor of American History
University of North Carolina at Charlotte

From the long arcs of America's history, to the short timeframes that convey larger stories, American Ways provides concise, accessible topical histories informed by the latest scholarship and written by scholars who are both leading experts in their fields and polished writers.

Books in the series provide general readers and students with compelling introductions to America's social, cultural, political, and economic history, underscoring questions of class, gender, racial, and sectional diversity and inclusivity. The titles suggest the multiple ways that the past informs the present and shapes the future in often unforeseen ways.

CURRENT TITLES IN THE SERIES

HOOPS

A Cultural History of Basketball in America

Thomas Aiello

ROWMAN & LITTLEFIELD
Lanham • Boulder • New York • London

Published by Rowman & Littlefield
An imprint of The Rowman & Littlefield Publishing Group, Inc.
4501 Forbes Boulevard, Suite 200, Lanham, Maryland 20706
www.rowman.com

86-90 Paul Street, London EC2A 4NE, United Kingdom

British Library Cataloguing in Publication Information Available

Library of Congress Cataloging-in-Publication Data
Names: Aiello, Thomas, 1977- author.
Title: Hoops : a cultural history of basketball in America / Thomas Aiello.
Description: Lanham, Maryland : Rowman & Littlefield, 2021. | Series: The
    American ways series | Includes bibliographical references and index. |
    Summary: "From its nineteenth-century roots to its position today as a global
    symbol of American culture, basketball has been a force in American society.
    This book presents the first cultural history of the sport from the street to the
    highest levels of professional men's and women's competition, chronicling the
    relationship between the sport and American society"— Provided by publisher.
Identifiers: LCCN 2021027497 (print) | LCCN 2021027498 (ebook) | ISBN
    9781538147115 (cloth) | ISBN 9781538199947 (paper) | ISBN 9781538148563
    (epub)
Subjects: LCSH: Basketball—United States—History. | Basketball—Social
    aspects—United States.
Classification: LCC GV885.7 .A54 2021 (print) | LCC GV885.7 (ebook) | DDC
    796.3230973—dc23
LC record available at https://lccn.loc.gov/2021027497
LC ebook record available at https://lccn.loc.gov/2021027498

∞™ The paper used in this publication meets the minimum requirements of
American National Standard for Information Sciences—Permanence of Paper for
Printed Library Materials, ANSI/NISO Z39.48-1992.

Dear Basketball,
From the moment
I started rolling my dad's tube socks
And shooting imaginary
Game-winning shots
In the Great Western Forum
I knew one thing was real:

I fell in love with you.
—Kobe Bryant

Contents

Prologue

Robin walked into the bedroom where her husband was quietly watching basketball. It wasn't their bedroom; it belonged to the host of the party they were attending. But the game was on. He turned to her when she came into the room. "Two minutes ago the Knicks are ahead fourteen points and now they're ahead two points," he said.

His wife, trying to coax him back into the common rooms of the party, was incredulous. "Alvy, what is so fascinating about sitting around watching a bunch of pituitary cases stuff a ball through a hoop?"

"What is fascinating is that it's physical," he told her. "You know, that's one thing about intellectuals: they prove that you can be absolutely brilliant and have no idea what's going on."

Alvy Singer's colloquy in *Annie Hall* was played for laughs, but it laid bare two competing misconceptions about the game: those who didn't watch basketball were dismissive of the game's athletic draw to the majority of its fans, and those who did watch it often enjoyed its physicality and competition without understanding the broader cultural and historical context in which it existed. One of the reasons for such disconnects is that there has never been a full cultural history of the game from its founding to the twenty-first century—taking into account both college and professional versions, Black and White, women and men. While the historiography of basketball is vast and important, a broad history of the game has never been attempted.

Hoops: A Cultural History of Basketball in America is that attempt. It argues that the game has existed in a reciprocal relationship with the broader culture that has surrounded it, both embodying conflicts over class, race, and gender, and serving as a public theater for them. Intersections of race and gender in particular have proven to be axes upon which the game has turned. *Annie Hall*, for example, was first released in April 1977. Less than eight months later, on December 9, 1977, the Los

Angeles Lakers played the Houston Rockets. During a fight on the court, Laker forward Kermit Washington turned in the heat of the scrum and punched an onrushing Rudy Tomjanovich, shattering Tomjanovich's skull, almost killing him. It gained national attention for a professional basketball league, the NBA, that often found itself in the public eye only when controversy came its way.

That night was the culmination of a long descent from the founding of a late nineteenth-century amateur game designed to improve the strength and morals of its players. It had developed from there through high school gymnasiums, college pep rallies, and the fits and starts of professionalization. It was a playground game, an urban game, tied to all the caricatures that were associated with urban culture. It struggled with integration and representations of race. It struggled with the influence of gambling and corruption. As a game early played by women, often to the scorn of cultural critics who saw it as a gateway to barrenness, lesbianism, or both, basketball also struggled with the gendered assumptions of a patriarchal society negotiating those assumptions about a group never granted full equality. And often, in the 1970s, it struggled with fights. Kermit Washington's punch of Rudy Tomjanovich was an inflection point of so many of those struggles. Washington was Black, Tomjanovich White. The violence of basketball was emblematic of its urban associations.

Basketball would not lose those urban associations in the decades to come, but after 1977, the trajectory of the sport would move in a different direction, often playing on such associations to build its popularity. When Washington punched Tomjanovich, the NBA Finals, the culmination of the league season, was aired on television on tape delay. In the decades that followed, the game would grow to unprecedented heights, building on the marketing of its star players who were tightly regulated to ensure they would not punch each other again. It was a difficult task, one that failed most infamously in November 2004 when a fan in Detroit threw a drink on an Indiana Pacers player, generating a brawl between players and fans that became pilloried as "Malice in the Palace."

Still, despite the bumps along the way, the trajectory of basketball after 1977 was decidedly upward. The NBA Finals moved from tape delay to live in primetime, becoming one of the most watched events on the sports calendar. The NCAA tournament's Final Four moved to play its games in massive football venues. The Amateur Athletic Union, which participated in the early amateur emphasis of the game, became the gatekeeper of player success prior to college recruitment. The women's game, shunted to the sidelines for so long, became a powerful economic and cultural driver in its own right at both the collegiate and professional level. Most importantly, in the decades after Washington's punch, basketball became a cultural force in the country, its influence seeping into film, music, dance, and fashion. It is a core element of hip-hop, which itself is a celebration of the urban cultural forms so castigated in earlier generations.

Basketball's cultural role in American history has morphed substantially since its founding in the 1890s, but its relevance has only grown. *Hoops* tells the story of that cultural relevance, of the reciprocal relationship between basketball and the society that received it. It makes the case that the game has used the very signifiers of its difference and illegitimacy, turned them on their head, embraced them, and used them to celebrate difference and gain mainstream legitimacy, a revolutionary cultural act whose influence is still felt today. Its fascination, despite Alvy Singer's protestation, is more than physical. Basketball's growth from 1891 to 2020 was a cultural revolution.

The attempt at a comprehensive history of any cultural revolution contains within it an inherent contradiction. In an effort to spread a study's scope to encompass 130 years, investigating in particular the intersections of a game with race, gender, and corruption concerns, that comprehensivity counterintuitively and of necessity forces choices about which events to include in a limited space. In this account, for example, John Havlicek doesn't steal the ball, Willis Reed doesn't walk out of the locker room in the seventh game of the 1970 NBA Finals, Allen Iverson doesn't lead the 76ers to two Finals appearances, and Reggie Miller doesn't score 8 points in nine seconds in the Eastern Conference playoffs. Hampton University doesn't upset Iowa State in 2001, Valparaiso doesn't upset Ole Miss in 1998, Chaminade doesn't upset the Virginia Cavaliers in 1983, and the University of Maryland, Baltimore County, doesn't upset them in 2018. The development of important ancillary games like wheelchair basketball and Paralympics competition is not part of this story, either.

The narrative does, however, tell the story of the game, providing a contextual overview for those not familiar with the history of basketball and connecting the often segregated dots of previous scrutiny for those who are. The choices about what to include are entirely my own, but when taken together they paint a portrait of a game and a culture that made the moments not included possible, that made it possible for a young Kobe Bryant to roll his father's tube socks, shooting imaginary game-winning shots in the Great Western Forum. So many others, including players, coaches, and fans, had similar experiences, finding moments in the game that served as intersections with their turbulent lives, breeding in them a similar devotion that allowed them in some form or another to tell basketball, in their own way, "I fell in love with you."

I

Muscular Christianity

IN 1888, James Naismith was a slight and meager freshman at McGill University, arriving as he had from rural Northern Ontario, thin and lonely in his new surroundings. While studying in his dormitory one night, two upperclassmen arrived at his door. "Naismith," said one, "we have been watching you for some time, and we see that you never take part in any of the activities. You spend too much time with your books." He was surprised that popular, athletic students would talk to him at all, much less try to give him advice. Naismith politely expressed his gratitude for their suggestion but assured them that he had strength enough for studying, and such was the only strength he needed.

Their interest was surprising to a young loner who often felt out of place, and despite his original reluctance, it stuck with him. "Late that night, when I finished my studies and lay on my bed, I began to wonder why those two fellows had seen fit to spend their time in giving advice to a freshman," he remembered. "The more I thought, the more clearly to my mind came the realization that they were doing it purely for my own benefit. I determined that the next day I would go over to the gymnasium and see what they were doing." It was a transformative moment for the young student. "From that time to the present I have been engaged in physical work both in the gymnasium and on the athletic field."

That time was spent most readily at McGill on the football field. "For seven years I played without missing a game," Naismith remembered, but it was a problem for him socially. The theology major discovered that his peers believed football to be "a tool of the devil," and that "some of my comrades gathered in one of the rooms one evening to pray for my soul." It was a defining moment for the young student, the frustrating reality that sports and Christian faith were seen by some to be incommensurate. Others, however, disagreed.

The Young Men's Christian Association was founded in London in 1844, emphasizing the need for a healthy physical life in conjunction with a healthy spiritual life. In 1851, London hosted the Great Exhibition of the Works of Industry of All Nations, beginning the trend of world's fairs that would dominate much of the second half of the nineteenth century, and the YMCA's presence at the event led to the creation of chapters across Europe and North America.

Exercise was part and parcel of the Victorian project of antebellum reform, a movement that also emphasized temperance and abolition and ultimately became the cradle that fostered the YMCA. Physical health, it was argued, was a fundamental part of mental health, of moral and spiritual health. It was the age of Sylvester Graham, hawking his special Graham crackers to reduce the temptation of appetites that could cause temporary pleasure but long-term bodily and spiritual harm. That kind of educational bent to much of the rhetoric surrounding reform would necessarily redound to students benefiting from the new push for public education. Horace Mann, the educational reformer behind much of that push in the antebellum era, argued that physical fitness should be part of a core curriculum. Colleges soon followed suit. Of course, the other main home of American education in the antebellum period was the home—the domestic sphere. That being the case, mothers were accountable for helping their families maintain sound minds and bodies, as well. Antebellum reformer and spokesperson for domesticity Catharine Beecher published *Course on Calisthenics for Young Ladies* in 1832, advocating physical exertion for spiritual growth.

At the same time, however, animal blood sports like cockfighting also proved exceedingly popular, moving on a decidedly different track than the exercise proselytized by Beecher, Mann, and others. The division between those two standards of play meant that for all the blood and guts of lower-class amusements, a new attitude in the middle and upper classes was able to ensconce itself as standard dogma: sports for the Victorian middle and upper classes could be a moral force, a source of self-discipline. If played properly, sports didn't have to be part of those appetites that worried Sylvester Graham so much and led so many cockfighting enthusiasts astray. Sports could actually control them.

The transcendentalists would pick up on this interpretation of sport as a method of self-improvement. Ralph Waldo Emerson argued that "archery, cricket, gun and fishing-rod, horse and boat are all educators, liberalizers, and so are ... swimming, skating, climbing, fencing, riding, lessons in the art of power." Walt Whitman's *Leaves of Grass* stated that "if anything is sacred the human body is sacred.... And in man or woman a clean, strong, firm-fibred body, is more beautiful than the most beautiful face."

Victorian attitudes were a combination of a new business ethic spurred by the post–revolutionary capitalist economy and the new evangelical Christianity spurred by the Second Great Awakening, a loose series of revivals between the 1820s and 1840s. The new theology it generated tied economic prosperity to spirituality, abandoning much of the Bible's poverty doctrine and replacing it with an American ideal of optimism and effort. It was a culture of faith, work, and unlimited possibility, and it would help expand the country, aided in large part by a corresponding transportation revolution that paralleled its budding industrial counterpart and created the possibility of a nationwide sporting infrastructure. New roads, canals, and railroads led to further urbanization. In the fifty years following 1820, American cities grew faster than ever before or since.

Urbanization, in turn, led to the vices feared by Graham and others. In the half-century before the creation of basketball, athletic morality claims did not stop more violent animal blood sports like cockfights, dogfights, and bull-baiting from dominating in the shadows of the new American cities among working-class enthusiasts who reveled in the brutality and melodrama of such contests. It was a revolt against much of the rhetoric of the dominant national moral reforms, one that took a decidedly classist hue. The Victorians were associated with the new post–revolutionary middle class, the manufacturing class that grew between old money capitalists and the factory workers who reveled in the violence of blood sports. So when Graham and other activists emphasized the virtue of restraint, they did so because of the fine line the new theology walked between spiritual growth and financial ambition, but also because they wanted to draw a different sort of line between themselves and the working-class devotees of cockfights.

And so those same attitudes that brought the Victorians to attack working-class sports—the desire for self-improvement, hard work, self-control—now served to defend the reformed versions of sports preached by Catharine Beecher and Ralph Waldo Emerson. By the 1850s, the alliance of morality, religion, and sport became known as "muscular Christianity," as ministers and laypeople made consistent sports-as-moral-authority arguments. One of the most important "muscular Christians" was Thomas Wentworth Higginson, editor of the *Atlantic Monthly*. His 1858 essay, "Saints and Their Bodies," argued that ministers were weak. He asked why the cloistered, scrawny minister was glorified. If ministers were the representatives of God, their bodies should be proper temples of God. Health and strength were paramount. It was how you built a nation. It was how you built a religion. Strength, health, discipline, success, and godliness—they were all the same thing, all part of a larger whole.

In making that case, the muscular Christians, like the rest of the Victorian moralists, claimed sports for themselves. But only a certain kind of sport. Theirs was clearly different from the lower-class version, one that emphasized the strenuous life over and against temporary pleasure; self-improvement and testing over personal expression and fame; duty over impulse.

At the same time, though, the Victorians also used "sports," weighted as that word was with masculinity, to provide them with a sense of masculinity of their own. The Victorians were the authors of the ideals of discipline, order, and productivity, but they were also the authors of the domestic sphere and were pilloried as effete by so many of the working-class blood sport enthusiasts who saw their emphasis on morality in athletics as another form of social control. One could not be a dandy, after all, and still maintain his masculinity. So sports guided middle-class Victorians as a form of compensation and education.

"The object of education," argued the *Spirit of the Times* in 1857, "is to make men out of boys. Real live men, not bookworms, not smart fellows, but manly fellows." In 1852, for example, Harvard faced Yale in a crew race. It was an informal contest, but it was the first American intercollegiate game. Other northeastern schools would follow, usually competing in crew. Soon, however, the contests would expand to other sports, and it was this climate, this combination of body and spirit, into which the American YMCA was born.

Its original purpose in the United States had been to offer spiritual guidance and practical assistance to young men flooding nineteenth-century cities—working-class products of the new urbanization and industrialization. It was after the Civil War when this began to change, and the US YMCA began to offer courses in "physical culture"—mostly exercise and gymnastics.

When the group's pivot away from that original mission began—when coursework and Victorian ideals came into the YMCA—that lower-class clientele began to change. Now white-collar workers, businessmen, skilled workers, the middle and upper classes, were the main users of the YMCA. By 1892, YMCA membership had grown to a quarter million. It had 348 gymnasiums across the country.

There was similar organizational growth in Canada, and Naismith made his way to the Montreal branch to speak with the leader there. He told him a story about a football game at McGill where a frustrated teammate was cursing loudly at their opponents, before apologizing to his theology-major teammate for using profanity in his presence. It struck him, he told the YMCA director, that "there might be other effective ways of doing good besides preaching." The director agreed and told Naismith about a school in Springfield, Massachusetts, that was working specifically at the intersection of moral and athletic development. After he finished his degree, the new graduate decided to attend. It was there that he met Luther Halsey Gulick Jr.

Gulick was one of the leaders of the YMCA movement, an advocate of the "strenuous life" who argued for his own version of "muscular Christianity." Spiritual life, he argued, rests on the equal development of the mind and the body. Gulick would also lead the Boy Scouts movement and the Playground Association of America. He cofounded the American Campfire Girls with his wife.

In the 1890s, Gulick teamed with G. Stanley Hall of Clark University to develop an evolutionary theory of play that became incredibly influential in the early twentieth century. Humans had developed an impulse to play during evolution, they argued. Everyone mimicked the broader stages of human evolution in every phase of their lives. In early childhood, play activities were kicking and squirming as an infant, running and throwing when the child got a bit older. These actions corresponded to the play of our primal ancestors. Between ages seven and twelve, the track, field, and tag games of children corresponded to the hunting instinct and individualistic actions acquired during the presavage stage of human development. Older boys then developed complex group games like baseball or football, which essentially acted as a combination of that earlier hunting instinct and a new instinct of cooperation, corresponding to the savage development where natives hunted in groups and subordinated their will to the leadership of a chief.

Each person recapitulated the history of humanity through sports, which made sports essential to proper physical, moral, and neural growth. Since team sports in particular required teamwork, self-sacrifice, obedience to a leader, and loyalty, they were an unparalleled opportunity for growth. "These qualities appear to me," said Gulick, "to be a great pulse of beginning altruism, of self-sacrifice, of that capacity upon which Christianity is based."

It was a theory that would have broad consequences for the structure of the YMCA movement. It encouraged the creation of special institutions for boys to supervise their play, for example. It preferenced activity over spirituality or intellectualism, making the YMCA, despite its emphasis on morality, increasingly secular. It also subsumed the ethnic, religious, and class differences of boys to a more universal experience of maturation. Finally, the evolutionary theory of play served to segregate the sexes, an almost inevitable outgrowth of comparing individual development to human social development. Males and females acquired distinct propensities over the course of human evolution, so the theory went, and those of females were geared toward the home and family. "So it is clear," wrote Gulick in 1920, "that athletics have never been either a test or a large factor in the survival of women; athletics do not test womanliness as they test manliness."

His gender biases were matched by his racial ones. "The Anglo-Saxons are the only peoples who have developed team games," he argued, clearly seeing his evolutionary theory of play as part of the larger social Darwinist project of sociologists like Herbert Spencer. "We are an Anglo-Saxon people," he wrote. "The chief interests and activities of the young of all races, and of the higher animals, center about play," but "the characteristics of the Anglo-Saxon" were where "the highest life must show itself." Thus it was that even before Naismith put pen to paper to define his new game, its potential existed at the fraught intersection of race, class, and gender, which would continue to bear upon its progression for the next 130 years.

Whatever his racial and gender bias, however, it was under the leadership of Gulick, working out of the YMCA Training School in Springfield, that the YMCA moved from gymnastics to competitive sports. There he took Naismith under his wing, along with other students like fellow theology graduate Amos Alonzo Stagg, who would become influential in the development of collegiate football. Along with anatomy and motor skills, Gulick's YMCA also taught a course in the psychology of play—in that class, in 1891, he asked students to experiment with new games that could be played in the confined space of gymnasiums. The group generally understood that team games utilized balls and that the larger the balls, the more translatable the game could be to all potential players. Games with smaller balls, like baseball or tennis or golf, for example, required more equipment that made exercise cost prohibitive for a large portion of the clientele to whom the YMCA catered. "We needed some sort of game that would be interesting and could be played indoors," remembered Naismith. "It was a seminar in psychology, and one day in discussing inventions Dr. Gulick made this statement: 'There is nothing new under the sun, but all new things are simply a re-combination of the factors of existing things.'" He wanted "a new game to exercise our students, a competitive game, like football or lacrosse, but it must be a game that can be played indoors." Even more important were the Victorian mores that served as the motivating force of the YMCA itself. "It must be a game requiring skill and sportsmanship, providing exercise for the whole body and yet it must be one which can be played without extreme roughness or damage to players and equipment."

Naismith devised a game that combined features of others he had grown up with in Canada. His would combine the passing and jump ball of rugby; the use of a goal, as in lacrosse; and a soccer-shaped ball that would be large enough to ensure that other equipment would not be necessary. He had also, as a child in Ontario, played a game called "duck on a rock," and from it he borrowed the concept of "a goal with a horizontal opening high enough so that the ball would have to be tossed into it, rather than being thrown." After the school janitor found him two peach baskets, Naismith nailed them to each end of the gymnasium, ten feet high. He drew up thirteen original rules, the class divided into teams, and they played the first basketball game. "The invention of basketball was not an accident," Naismith remembered. "It was developed to meet a need. Those boys simply would not play 'Drop the Handkerchief.'"

Naismith walked down to the Armory Street YMCA and posted the thirteen sparse rules on the bulletin board. Players couldn't run with the ball; it could only be advanced by passing and could only be held in the hands without using the body to help control it. "No shouldering, holding, pushing, tripping, or striking in any way the person of an opponent shall be allowed." Violation would constitute a foul, and two fouls would disqualify a player until a goal was made. A foul with intent to injure would lead to disqualification, and if a team committed three consecutive fouls without one charged to their opponents, it would count as a goal against the offenders. There would be two fifteen-minute halves, with five minutes to rest between them. "The side making the most goals in that time shall be declared the winners."

Skeptical students who had served as guinea pigs for their instructor's various starts and stops in sport invention were mildly incredulous. "Huh!" said Frank Mahan, a student from Tennessee. "Another new game." Naismith begged their indulgence. This would surely be his last effort. The players divided up, nine players per side, and began the experiment. In that first game, the only goal came from a midcourt shot, leaving the gymnasium's janitor to climb a ladder to retrieve the ball. Cutting out the bottom of the baskets fixed that cumbersome problem and play at Armory Street became more common. Though disqualification for excessive fouling was chronic in those early days as players struggled to manage the rules, the new game was popular. To protect themselves, many began wearing padded football pants as a makeshift uniform, and soon spectators began arriving to watch. Female teachers from nearby Buckingham Grade School would come to the gym to watch during their lunch break and eventually asked if they, too, could play.

Graduates of women's colleges in the late nineteenth century had experience with sports. Calisthenics of the antebellum era had given way to actual competitive games for women who chose to attend the university. Swimming and tennis provided women new outlets for their competitiveness and creativity, but male paternalistic commentary was divided as to its efficacy. Some assumed that strenuous female activity would damage a woman's internal organs, making them unfit for childbirth. Others, however, argued that the strength gained from sports gave women a leg up in the new job markets that were opening for them.

Female advocates, meanwhile, championed sports as a way for women to escape the domestic sphere.

The 1890s were the age of the New Woman. The early Victorian female ideal was a plump, round-faced woman with rich, gaudy dresses. The New Woman, made popular by the magazine illustrations of Charles Dana Gibson, was tall, slender, and athletic. She dressed practically, not ornately. She exercised, worked, and pushed the boundaries of the paternalistic norms that circumscribed life for so many in previous generations. Women of the 1890s were working, playing in public, and dressing less and less like former conceptions of ladies. And in December 1891, soon after men began experimenting with Naismith's new game, they would experiment with it, as well. Naismith organized the teachers into teams and taught them the game. He was, however, a creature of his time and a student of Gulick. Basketball, he argued, "has also been found valuable for girls and women, as there are few games which they can play that are not a strain on the nervous system rather than on bodily functions." The game was "peculiarly adapted for giving health without involving severe mental strain." Five years later, the first women's intercollegiate basketball game was played between students at Stanford and the University of California, Berkeley. There was gender segregation from the game's inception—women still had to cover themselves while playing to align with Victorian moralistic norms; male spectators were even barred from watching the Stanford-Cal game—but basketball was, even in its earliest days, just as much a game for women as it was for men.

Or at least the game that would become basketball. In December 1891, Naismith's invention had no name, but early the next year, after students returned from the Christmas holiday, Mahan asked what the game would be called. The original skeptic had grown fond of the game. He first suggested Naismith-ball, but after the instructor demurred, he pointed out its rudimentary makeshift goals, nailed as they were ten feet above the floor. "Why not basketball?"

The official publication of Springfield's YMCA Training School, the *Triangle*, was distributed to YMCAs around the world, and in January 1892 the paper published Naismith's rules, even before it had a formal name, spreading what it called "A New Game" far and wide and fostering play in a variety of countries. The new rules did not include

such basics as how many players to include in games. The first attempt
in Springfield featured nine players per side, and that was the form that
dominated early efforts, but Naismith envisioned it as one in which any
number could participate. That permissiveness, however, could prove
problematic. Cornell University became the first college to take up the
game but played it as a mass contest with twenty-five players per side.
When the fifty players running on the gymnasium floor threatened the
stability of the building, administrators decided it was best to ban the
game from campus.

The first public basketball game is a contested issue, some sources cit-
ing a February 12, 1892, contest between Central YMCA and Armory
Street in Springfield, a 2–2 tie witnessed by roughly one hundred spectators. Others reference a March 11, 1892, contest between students and
instructors at the YMCA Training School. The students defeated their
instructors 5–1 in that game, despite the fact that the instructor team featured Naismith, Stagg, and Gulick himself. In those contests, each basket made counted for one point and no one dribbled. But dribbling soon
became part of the game, instituted at least by 1894.

Basketball would quickly become incredibly popular and would ultimately draw thousands of new recruits to the YMCA. Branches across
the country began playing the game in earnest, reporting a surge in attendance and membership in response to basketball. The YMCA in Hartford, Connecticut, established a five-team league that drew an average of
more than five hundred fans to each contest. YMCA branches also began
playing one another, teams earning a following that only increased the
game's popularity.

In so doing, it would take a far different trajectory than football. Football was developing in colleges, and therefore was revitalizing the upper-
middle and upper classes—the sorts of people who could afford to attend
colleges. Basketball, taking hold in YMCAs, became a creature of urban
kids, those people whom the evolutionary theorists of play wanted to fix
and develop. It was a way to Americanize immigrants. An outlet for the
working poor, the lower-middle and lower classes. But at the same time,
basketball was a game that Victorian moralists could see as okay—one that
wasn't "a tool of the devil" that required prayer groups for its enthusiasts.

There were, however, far more people packing urban industrial
hubs than there were attending the schools of the Ivy League, and the

popularity of their new game was not the result of a desire for physical and spiritual discipline. More and more people were playing, but more and more of them were playing despite not caring about or understanding the evolutionary theory of play or "muscular Christianity."

The growth of cities was integral to the new game's popularity, as were the class divisions it clearly fostered. In 1860, roughly 20 percent of Americans lived in cities. By 1900, it was 40 percent. In 1860, six million people lived in cities. In 1890, it was twenty-two million. From 1878 to 1893, per capita income rose by 35 percent, but real wages rose by only 20 percent. The rich were getting richer, and they practiced economist Thorstein Veblen's "conspicuous consumption," only exacerbating the class consciousness bred by employment abuses made possible by lack of regulation. It was a cold reality that ultimately led to the development of American unions: the Knights of Labor founded in 1869 and the American Federation of Labor in 1886.

Technology also played a role. In 1878, the first gasoline engine was patented, and the first cars appeared in the 1890s. In 1909, Henry Ford built his Model T, its success facilitated by factories that featured mechanized mass-production techniques, which often meant replacing skilled workers with machines and employing unskilled workers at cheaper wages. But it also meant hundreds of thousands of new jobs, and with union influence, people were likely to find more free time than they would have in the 1870s or prior.

But this new industrial age impacted more than just its wage workers. It grew a new white-collar business class, new millionaires who worked to make sports like horse racing respectable to Victorian mores. It also made American products uniform, gave people more options, and thus increased a tendency toward American consumerism. In 1876, John Wannamaker opened the first department store in Philadelphia. Montgomery Ward and Sears, Roebuck developed catalog shopping. Woolworth's and A&P made chain stores popular. Spectator sports would take advantage of this new consumerism. Baseball games routinely sold out, charging up to fifty cents for entry. It was during the Gilded Age that sports sections grew in American newspapers. Gilbert Patten wrote young adult novels featuring his fictional protagonist, college football star Frank Merriwell. The emphasis on exercise by the Victorians led people to begin spending disposable income on sporting goods like bicycles. Albert Spalding, one of the founders of baseball's National League, left the game to produce and distribute sports books and equipment. Sports in the Gilded Age, then, became profitable commodities. There were national rules, regulatory bodies, uniform schedules. Sports in the era became big business.

That new paradigm, more than anything else, allowed sports to interact with other social institutions. Those Ford assembly lines, for example, were so valuable to the American economy not just because they made cars, but because they exacerbated the rubber, glass, and steel industries. Similarly, when a sports event came to town, hotels, restaurants, railroads all benefited. Stadium construction meant jobs. Sports brought a level of interconnectivity to the industrializing country. It served as a unifying force around which people could order a changing world. At the same time, however, much of the consumerism that drove such changes was anathema to the Victorian mindset that believed in muscular Christianity.

This presented Gulick and the YMCA with a dilemma. As early as 1894, one of the leading YMCA publications wondered, "Is Basketball a Danger?" Basketball "could never and should never be allowed to take the place of all other exercise in the gymnasium," admonished an article in the *New Era*. Branch directors complained that those who emphasized basketball "neglected their regular body-building work and would show up just in time for games." Such competition fostered jealousy, rivalry, and a shirking of other responsibilities. Spectators were rowdy and misbehaved. Arguments over officiating led to fights. Many branches began limiting access to basketball to those who regularly attended other YMCA classes. Others shut it down entirely.

Basketball's popularity continued to rise, but it threatened to take over as a spectator sport—to make YMCAs into athletic clubs rather than places of learning and muscular Christianity. To try to fix the problem, YMCAs created the Athletic League of North America, which joined with the Amateur Athletic Union (AAU) and tried to regulate basketball, setting and formalizing rules and trying to provide a broader structure for the phenomenon as well as the game. Founded in 1888, the AAU was developed as an umbrella organization to organize amateur athletic contests—to celebrate pure competition devoid of the professionalism that brought ruin to players and fans. But it failed at protecting the muscular Christianity mission of the YMCA. By 1905, YMCA teams played basketball games with other competitors, including colleges and athletic clubs. YMCA teams won national championships and other tournaments. The Buffalo German YMCA team won the 1904 Olympic gold medal when basketball was included in the St. Louis games.

All of the game's new competitive popularity was to the dismay of Gulick, who expressed relief when the Buffalo team finally went pro. By that time, however, basketball had passed a Rubicon. Despite Gulick's best efforts, YMCAs began to go the way of other competitive organizations. They tended toward rivalry, specialization, even star treatment of the best athletes. But in 1911, the YMCA would experience a renaissance of its original founding principles. Henry F. Kallenberg, Gulick's replacement at Springfield, instituted a comprehensive sports program that would fit with those original ideas of muscular Christianity. He severed the YMCA's ties with the AAU and focused on reaching "the mass of young men and boys, discourag[ing] prize winning and overtraining."

The bent toward amateurism led to the newfound popularity of tennis, golf, and polo, amateur sports that required a club membership of one kind or another. Thus, they solved every Victorian problem in one fell swoop. They taught amateur values. They shunned the violence of lower-class sports. And they had a built-in system for ensuring that only those of a certain class and breeding would be able to participate, as entry fees and high walls eliminated the unwelcome from club grounds. Basketball's trajectory, however, was aimed at a different group. The leaders of the YMCA sought to instill those values, not to revel in them.

Of course, not all of those wealthy advocates of amateur athletics would end up so effete. Theodore Roosevelt was from a rich New York family, but found cultural worth in the rough games of the working class. He saw in them not a wallowing in lower-class values, but a celebration of masculinity. And as an advocate of "race science," like Gulick, he believed in the necessity of that virile masculinity to ensure a satisfactory population base. He pointed to ancient Greece and Rome and other grand dynasties of history, arguing that they all had violent sports. They made the country strong. "If you are rich, and are worth your salt," he said, "you will teach your sons that though they may have leisure, it is not to be spent in idleness. . . . We do not admire the man of timid peace. We admire the man who embodies victorious effort; the man who never wrongs his neighbor, who is prompt to help a friend, but who has those virile qualities necessary to win in the stern strife of actual life." He called this concept "the strenuous life," and it served as a counter to that common nineteenth-century Victorian ideal, a possible bridge, like basketball, between the class differences in how sports and the values they instilled were conceived—a sign that the times, in fact, might be changing.

Of course, the major event of the second decade of the twentieth century, like basketball itself, also involved rivalry and specialization. World War I would require much of its soldiers, but it would also give them a lot of free time. When John J. Pershing led an American force to capture Pancho Villa in 1916, the troops caused a scandal by drinking and womanizing while not in the field. That couldn't be the case in World War I, especially with Woodrow Wilson declaring that the country's purpose was to "make the world safe for democracy." The YMCA would use its influence in the conflict, as well. "I hope that sports will be continued," said Wilson, "as a real contribution to the national defense." Naismith had left Springfield in 1895, moving to Denver to earn a medical degree before moving in 1898 to the University of Kansas to head the school's education department. But he would always maintain an association with the YMCA. He went on sex education speaking tours during the war to warn soldiers about venereal disease. Twelve thousand YMCA workers went overseas in 1917 with the troops when the United States finally entered the war.

After the war's conclusion, the threat of Bolshevism convinced US leaders to temporarily keep troops in Europe. Worried about a Pancho Villa–like reputation problem on the continent, the YMCA organized a vast series of athletic competitions, the American Expeditionary Forces championships, which again brought basketball across the ocean, this time in a formal, organized form. They also fielded teams in what would become known as the Inter-Allied Games, the Military Olympics, in Joinville, France, in summer 1919. Even though much of France had been destroyed, and even though the war had killed more soldiers than any other in history, more than half a million spectators came to watch the surviving soldiers compete for their various countries at the conclusion of the conflict.

And so the YMCA created new sports, served the country, and tried to maintain the moral lessons of sports while dealing with lower-class sports fans. Thus, it served to bridge the twentieth-century gap that had developed during the nineteenth-century Victorian morality push. It was the YMCA that made that gap irrelevant. And it was World War I that killed Victorianism. Sports could now be lower-class and moral, and basketball, situated as it was at the intersection of those realities, was poised to take advantage of that new mindset.

2

Professionalizing the Amateur Game

THE NEXT STEP taken from the amateur ideal of muscular Christianity was to play for paying spectators, and for the players themselves to earn a share of the proceeds. Professionalization was a decided rejection of the moral push of the YMCA, and it occurred just a few short years after the game's invention. When moving beyond the bounds and facilities of the association, players had to rent gymnasium space, and in turn needed to charge admission to spectators to recoup the losses. When there was profit left over after a game, it was split between the players deemed to be the hosts, the "home team," the advent of pay-for-play.

There were several competitors for the first professional basketball game. Early pro Ed Wachter claimed that a game at the Fox Opera House in Herkimer, New York, in 1893 was the first, when locals challenged a team from Utica. After paying the venue for rights to use the space, the remaining funds were passed around among the teams. In 1895, there was a contest between the Syracuse YMCA team and a group of self-described professionals from Rochester. While there is no evidence of pay-for-play in this game, the description of the Rochester team by a YMCA publication as "professional" led many to speculate. In 1896, in Trenton, New Jersey, a game between locals at the Masonic Hall, calling themselves the Trenton Basket Ball Team, and the decidedly amateur Brooklyn YMCA netted enough money to pay the rental fee and still provide each member of the home team roughly $5. The Trentons, as they were known, usually have pride of place in such discussions, but whatever claim is ultimately correct, it is clear that there was a legitimate and sustained turn from amateurism in the years immediately following basketball's creation.

It was a trend that corresponded with the dominant culture of the Gilded Age. In 1860, about one in five people lived in cities. By 1900, it was two in five. Chicago had 50,000 residents in 1850; 500,00 in 1880; and 1.7 million in 1900. As the physical space and geography of cities also grew, residents could no longer walk to all their destinations within the city. Therefore, streetcars, made possible by railroad engineering and electric power, moved people from place to place. Immigrants and rural laborers coming to the cities for work moved into cramped, stuffy tenement buildings, while white-collar businessmen and owners built giant homes and created the gilding of the Gilded Age. Meanwhile, a growing middle class that felt threatened by the presence of both groups moved to the outskirts of town, creating suburban communities.

The growth of urban industrial hubs grew the broader economy, but that growth came with tangible costs. One was the widening gulf between rich and poor. From 1878 to 1893, per capita income rose by 35 percent, but real wages rose by only 20 percent. The rich were getting richer. In 1860, there were three hundred millionaires. In 1892, there were four thousand. And they practiced "conspicuous consumption," collecting global treasures and building palaces in which to put them. It was a proto-capitalism that beautified American cities while sharpening a growing class consciousness among those unable to enter the homes of the wealthy.

Class consciousness continued to grow in 1893, two years after basketball's invention, when the bankruptcy of the Reading Railroad initiated a stock market collapse, the Panic of 1893, which plunged the economy into a severe four-year depression. By the end of the year, 491 banks and 15,000 other businesses failed. By mid-1894, the national unemployment rate was more than 15 percent.

But industry still dominated. The first automobiles appeared in the 1890s, as mass production pushed a burgeoning new consumerism. In 1876, for example, John Wanamaker opened the first department store in Philadelphia. Wanamaker's sold products from a variety of different producers, offering them cheaply because its owner made a profit from volume sales. Department stores like Wanamaker's and others that followed modeled themselves after the new museums funded by wealthy conspicuous consumers, decorating interiors ornately to make the experience more pleasant for customers. Meanwhile, companies like Montgomery

Ward and Sears, Roebuck developed thick catalogues that were shipped all over the country, offering anything one could find in urban environments like Philadelphia. And the Great Atlantic and Pacific Tea Company (A&P) and Woolworth's developed extensive systems of food and dry goods stores built in both cities and large towns, using the expanding railroad systems to keep the stores' shelves stocked.

The chain store, along with mail-order catalogs and department stores, were all made possible by mass production. Standardization became the norm. And when manufacturers produced basically the same product, companies needed new ways to convince people to buy them. Advertising at that time became an industry in itself, with agencies creating marketing campaigns featuring icons like Aunt Jemima and the Quaker man featured on boxes of Quaker Oats. Advertisers used printed catalogs, booklets, posters, cigarette cards, and other means to let people know about new products. But their most prominent method of advertising was the magazine. By the mid-1890s, almost half the pages of America's most popular magazines were taken up by advertisements.

Magazines became the dominant form of American episodic entertainment in the Gilded Age. At the same time, yellow journalism became the main form of reporting the news in American daily newspapers, using, along with scandal headlines and populist editorials, sports journalism to sell newspapers to an increasingly impoverished readership. And the professional sport they promoted most was baseball.

When baseball's National League was founded in 1876 by William A. Hulbert and Albert Spalding, the organization played to all the swirling concerns represented by the Victorians and the YMCA. Any team that wanted membership had to be in a city with a population of at least seventy-five thousand. The league banned Sunday games, prohibited liquor at the ballpark, and charged fifty-cents admission. That attempt at propriety, however, would get the league into trouble. In 1877, for example, four Louisville players were expelled for taking bribes. Philadelphia and New York were expelled for failing to travel to late-season road contests. Cincinnati was kicked out for playing on Sunday and continuing beer sales.

It was the first real attempt at a professional league organization, and it portended the kinds of trouble that basketball would find two decades later. The National League's strong hand would inevitably lead to revolt.

In 1881, six teams formed the American Association to compete for dollars and fans with the National League. It was known derisively as "the Beer Ball League," partly because four of the six teams had brewers in their ownership groups, but mostly because they decided to compete with the National League by moving away from Victorian respectability: it sold liquor at games and held games on Sunday. It only charged twenty-five cents for entry. And it was successful. It wasn't long before the American Association was luring players away from the older National League, another foreshadowing for professional basketball efforts.

Of course, the most tangible sign of baseball's coming-of-age was the World Series. The American Association collapsed in 1891, the year of basketball's invention, and in its place, in 1893, a new league arose—the Western League, led by Byron Bancroft "Ban" Johnson, who railed against the National League and promised to take all its best players. It began playing games in 1894, and six years later, in 1900, it changed its name to the American League, moving most of its teams into larger markets. It was clear what Johnson wanted: direct war with the National League.

He got it. In 1903, his success led the two leagues to sign the National Agreement of 1903. They agreed to recognize each other's reserve clauses. They created a National Commission to serve as a three-member judicial body to resolve disputes. And they created a championship. Pennant winners from each league agreed to play a "World Championship" nine-game series, so as to judge which league was the best for that season. The first World Series was won by the American League's Boston Pilgrims, who defeated the National League's Pittsburgh Pirates.

Boxing, too, had made its way to professionalization in that period. Its success grew from the decidedly non-Victorian tavern scene, the most important of which was Harry Hill's Saloon on Bleeker Street in New York, known as "the last resort of a low class of prostitutes, and the ruffians and idlers who support the prize ring." Hill himself became famous as a promoter, boxing referee, and patron of boxing talent. But this was also the age of the athletic club, where private establishments sprang up with sport as a specific motive. These clubs practiced "high class" boxing, where the wealthy took boxing lessons to learn what they called "the manly art." It was this scene that created the first national amateur boxing championships. The clubs set a number of rounds for bouts, developed weight classifications and divisions, and offered purses for winners. Finally, they adopted the Marquis of Queensberry rules, requiring gloves, limiting rounds to three minutes, and formally establishing a faster-paced, commercially appealing product. The changes provided the impression of less violence and an air of semi-Victorian respectability.

The poster child for this new era in boxing, the greatest star of his day and the original sports hero of the postbellum period, was John L. Sullivan. Born in Boston to poor Irish immigrant parents, Sullivan discovered boxing in the 1870s and rose to become the heavyweight champion and the most famous athlete in America. And he took advantage of the opportunity. He went on nationwide tours, offering $1,000 to anyone who could stay in the ring with him for four rounds. In 1892, the year after basketball's invention, Sullivan took on James J. Corbett in New Orleans, a match billed as the biggest of the century. Every major daily newspaper in the country reported on the event without condemnation, papers that had originally railed against violence and blood sports. It was, in other words, the first real Victorian championship. Corbett, for his part, had gone to college and been a bank clerk to make ends meet. He was known as "Gentleman Jim." Corbett knocked out Sullivan in the twenty-first round. Boxing had adapted to the new professional environment.

Hence, sports in the Gilded Age became profitable commodities. National rules, regulatory bodies, and uniform schedules turned sports into big business. Horse racing in the 1890s saw more than $200 million change hands every year, baseball more than $10 million a year.

Though basketball was still in its infancy, the prospects for professionalization that followed from the success of sports like baseball and boxing led many to make the effort. Baseball had shown the way for league organization, and boxing had proven that games associated with the effluvium from industrialization and urbanization could move deftly into the mainstream. The most influential of the early professional basketball teams hailed from Trenton, New Jersey, credited by many with playing the first professional game in the sport. The team from Trenton was poised to take advantage of the new sport's profitability, becoming a charter member of the first professional organization, the National Basketball League (NBL), founded in 1898. With teams ranging from New York to Delaware, the league began its run in Philadelphia, with the Trenton team, now calling itself the Trenton Nationals, winning the first contest against the local Hancock Athletic Association in front of roughly nine hundred paying customers. The Nationals would win the championship that first season in a six-team league, three based in Philadelphia and three from New Jersey. Only four teams survived the season, but in its second year, the league seemed to gain stability with teams like the New York Wanderers, Bristol Pile Drivers, and Camden Electrics proving to be successful ventures. They were still, as of yet, no match for the Nationals, however, who also won the split-schedule second season.

Split schedules were common in early professional sports without a glut of teams. Seasons were divided in half, the first-half winner and second-half winner playing for the league championship. In the 1899–1900 season, however, Trenton managed to win both halves.

The following season didn't have a split schedule, but the modest but growing popularity of professional basketball led the league to expand to a thirty-two-game schedule. For 1901–1902, it expanded to forty games. What seemed at first to be a signpost of solidity, however, was instead an example of overreach. The following season returned to a split schedule, with two of the league's eight teams folding before the season's first-half conclusion. The Camden Electrics would take the championship in what was ultimately a chaotic season. The disorganization led only five teams to agree to play the next season, and two of those dropped out in December. The league officially and controversially disbanded in January 1904, hurt feelings, recriminations, and even one lawsuit in its wake.

Before the NBL folded, it was joined by another, the Philadelphia Basket Ball League, in 1902. The eight-team circuit witnessed several teams come and go in its seven seasons, but lack of travel and accommodation costs in an organization that played in the cloister of one city kept it relatively stable, with the exception of its failed and final 1908–1909 campaign. The geography that allowed it to flourish for several years in Philadelphia, however, was a hindrance when it came to growth and broader appeal outside city limits.

Meanwhile, another professional league formed in western Pennsylvania and eastern Ohio in 1906, with teams in Pittsburgh, McKeesport, Canton, East Liverpool, Uniontown, and other medium-sized markets. Despite a controversy at the conclusion of its first season stemming from East Liverpool's refusal to play a championship series with Pittsburgh because the two sides couldn't agree on officials to referee the contests, it survived for five more seasons, playing schedules that included as many as seventy-two games. Teams had a difficult time remaining profitable, however, and the 1911–1912 season ended with only four surviving entrants. A brief attempt at a 1912–1913 campaign failed after several early exhibition games.

On the other side of Pennsylvania, the Eastern Basketball League (now spelling the sport's name as one word rather than two) rose to replace the Philadelphia Basket Ball League, beginning in 1909 with teams from New Jersey, smaller eastern Pennsylvania hubs, and Philadelphia. Teams from Camden, Trenton, Atlantic City, Wilkes-Barre, Harrisburg, Reading, and Scranton played against those from the big city in an organization that lasted until 1923, with the exception of the 1918–1919 season, which disbanded as a result of World War I. Also founded in 1909, the Hudson River League featured teams from White Plains, the Catskills, Yonkers, Schenectady, and Poughkeepsie. Its two feature teams were the Paterson Crescents, formed in 1902 and already a well-established commodity, and the Troy Trojans, which included among its stars Ed Wachter, one of the most dynamic players of his day, credited with inventing the fast break.

Hudson River only lasted three seasons, felled by infighting over the reelection of controversial league president Albert Saulpaugh after its 1910–1911 campaign. Several of Saulpaugh's supporters, including Troy, which had won both Hudson River titles, left the group and began a rival, the New York State Basket Ball League. Its first season proved successful, leading players from Hudson River teams to abscond to the new organization and all but leave the former in ruins. Troy would dominate that first New York State season, making three championships in a row for the squad, but the league would become more competitive and survive until 1923, minus two seasons from 1917 to 1919, eliminated because of the war. The Pennsylvania State League and the Interstate Basket Ball League also competed for space in the crowded markets of Pennsylvania, New York, and New Jersey in the late 1910s.

The 1920s were dominated by the Metropolitan Basket Ball League and the American Basketball League. The Metropolitan began in 1921 with teams from Brooklyn, Manhattan, and Patterson, but soon expanded to include teams throughout New York and New Jersey. The league's

stars were Benny Borgmann and Joe Brennan, who would remain two of
the game's most prominent players in the decade.

Then there was the American Basketball League (ABL), founded in
1925 and lasting in its original form until 1931. It represented the first
real expansion of the professional game, moving beyond the bounds of
New York, New Jersey, and Pennsylvania to a wider section of the country. Teams in Boston, Baltimore, Cleveland, Detroit, Chicago, Toledo,
and Washington, DC, broadened professional basketball and its appeal
to a wider swath of potential fans. Founded by Joseph Carr, president
of the recently formed National Football League (NFL), the new group
sought to make basketball a national game. NFL team owners like
George Halas, Max Rosenbloom, and George Preston Marshall owned
teams in the ABL, and that organizational prowess led the league to success in the second half of the 1920s, only to fold in 1931 in the face of the
Great Depression.

The efforts of the Metropolitan League and the ABL were given suc-
cor by the economy of the 1920s. Though World War I put most professional basketball on hold in 1918, it would ultimately be a boon to
the sport. World War I obviously had its problems, but it had, for the
most part, been good for the American economy. Corporations consoli-
dated. Productivity rose. The economy struggled from 1919 to 1921, as
the country switched from a wartime to a peacetime footing, but with
that exception, America was doing well. From 1922 to 1929, the country's
gross national product grew at an annual rate of 5.5 percent, rising from
$149 billion to $227 billion. Real wages rose 15 percent, and the unemployment rate never rose above 5 percent.

Spurred by that growth, people began spending. By 1929, as many
as seven million Americans owned stock, most of them of middle-class
means. Cars, clothing, and other expensive commodities were purchased
at the highest rates in history. To help facilitate these purchases, car
dealers, home appliance salesmen, and other merchants began offering
installment plans. Advertising generated people's willingness to purchase
items they couldn't even afford. The same audiences would similarly
respond to the mass-marketing of celebrities, most prominently in sports.

The 1920s were the age of the sports hero. It was the age of every hero.
The decade gave birth to the movie star, the comic book hero, and police
dramas on radio. Sports would play a major role in this hero culture. In

baseball, there was George Herman "Babe" Ruth. In boxing, William Harrison "Jack" Dempsey, White, and Jack Johnson, Black. In football, there was Harold "Red" Grange. In golf, Robert T. "Bobby" Jones. In tennis, William T. "Big Bill" Tilden. Professional basketball marketed such stars as Benny Borgmann and Joe Brennan, along with several others.

This advertising and spending culture bred the first sports pitchmen and promoters, such as George "Tex" Rickard and Jack "Doc" Kearns. It created hyperbolic journalists and radio broadcasters such as Grantland Rice and Graham McNamee. And all of them sold athletes as the be-all and end-all of hero culture. The sports heroes they sold served a compensatory cultural function in American society. They helped the public compensate for the erosion of Victorian values, the powerlessness that came with the change bred by World War I. Society was becoming more and more complicated. Success, it seemed, now came from playing bureaucratic games. Sports heroes provided a model for many who saw them as becoming successful without giving in to bureaucratic pressure. They were defense mechanisms against a changing world. It was a code of immediate success, a new ideal driven by the optimism that similarly drove credit purchases and middle-class investment in the stock market. "It is some comfort for the little man who has become expelled from the Horatio Alger dream," explained historian Leo Lowenthal, "who despairs of penetrating the thicket of grand strategy in politics and business, to see his heroes as a lot of guys who like or dislike highballs, cigarettes, tomato juice, golf, and social gatherings—just like himself."

The professional basketball team that perhaps embodied that attitude more than any other was the Original Celtics, who barnstormed throughout the nation from 1914 to 1930, only occasionally as part of one of the established professional leagues that served as their own form of bureaucracy. After the New York Celtics disbanded during World War I, the core of that team, reorganized by promoter James Furey in 1918, combined with new players from the city and called themselves the Original Celtics. The team traveled the country, playing as many as two hundred games a year. During the 1922–1923 season, the Celtics amassed a record of 193 wins, 11 losses, and 1 tie.

Furey offered his players consistent contracts that did not depend on the gate the team drew on any given night, the first individual contracts in the game. They played team defense, defenders switching onto ball-handlers if they entered a given zone, unlike the individual man-to-man defenses before them. In the hands of the Celtics, basketball was a different game. "It isn't how many goals you get," said Celtics star Johnny Witte, "it's how good you are without the ball that determines how good a basketball player you are." The team invented the pivot play and changed the way people developed offenses. They also originated another staple of the modern game. "As soon as the first foul was called against them," remembered rival promoter Lou O'Neill, "all five of them charged the referee, demanded to know if they were getting a jobbing, where he got off to call such a foul, and so on." It was common behavior for Celtics players. "They played in so many strange courts, and with even stranger officiating, that they had to protect themselves right from the start by jumping the referee."

It could be rough going. Perhaps the most intimidating venue for the Original Celtics was Brooklyn's Prospect Hall, crowded with fans. "It seemed as though they were hanging from the rafters. And the guys in the rafters thought nothing of throwing a bottle at you when you were trying to shoot a foul," remembered Dutch Dehnert. "That was bad enough, but the fellows sitting on the sidelines would trip you up when you were going down the court. They were holy terrors." They were holy terrors, but they were also simply an extreme version of what the Celtics faced in venues all over the country.

The Celtics teams of the early 1920s were led by Henry "Dutch" Dehnert and Nat Holman, whose star turns benefited from the celebrity culture of the decade. Dehnert played basketball in neither high school nor college, turning pro at age nineteen and essentially learning on the job. Holman came from a different background, a former star for New York University, where he earned a master's degree. At the height of his playing career and throughout the Celtics star run, Holman simultaneously coached the City College of New York team. They served as their own form of basketball's Queensberry rules, combining urban self-promotion with the amateur tradition to generate a new popularity for the team and the game. Dehnert and Holman were joined by players like Joe Lapchick, considered by many to be the best center of the age, and John Beckman, an offensive forward nicknamed "the Babe Ruth of basketball."

That kind of star power made the Celtics a threat to any league that didn't include them, and the nascent ABL's Joe Carr banned his teams from playing games against the barnstorming celebrities after the 1925 season, worrying that the beatings the Celtics administered to ABL squads would diminish the league. It was a blacklisting that caused the team to lose many lucrative exhibition opportunities. Adding insult to injury, team owner James Furey was indicted that summer for embezzlement. The financial pressure and the exhibition ban ultimately gave the Celtics little choice but to sign with the ABL. While the team's star power brought fans to arenas and ensured that the best players in the country would want to be part of the league, it was a bitter pill for the Celtics to swallow. They expressed their bitterness on the court, winning the ABL championship for both the 1926–1927 and 1927–1928 seasons. The team disbanded in December 1929, less than two months after the stock market crash that helped usher in the Great Depression. The ABL itself would soon follow.

Early professional leagues like the ABL were plagued with financial difficulties, with players who often jumped from team to team and league to league in search of better contracts. Teams themselves proved willing to change league affiliations when better opportunities came around. The motion not only led to organizational instability but hurt the popularity of the professional game at a time when baseball and football had stable league play and championships. And both mattered. Organization and championships provided fans with an overarching narrative that made individual games a form of episodic entertainment, like the magazines read by so many, leading to a satisfactory conclusion at season's end. Just as readers would be reluctant to engage a serial novel without confidence that the concluding chapters would be published, sports enthusiasts needed surety to invest themselves in professional basketball. The longstanding, popular baseball and the fledgling but growing NFL had that surety. Professional basketball in its first three decades didn't, and it suffered as a result.

The pro game was a rough endeavor. Headbutting defenders was allowed, as were two-handed discontinued dribbles, allowing players to indiscriminately charge the basket. The ball in those first games was larger than the modern version, leather covering an inflatable bladder and tied with laces, which made careful dribbling a necessity, as bouncing the ball on its laces could send it careening left or right. If the teams were not living up to Naismith's standard, however, neither were the spectators. Hometown fans accosted visitors with hat pins and cigar butts, leading most venues to erect fencing around the court. Players routinely shoved opponents into what quickly became known as "the cage." The ball never went out of bounds; it bounced off the cage and remained in play. Officials only awarded free throws when fouls occurred during a shot attempt. All other fouls led to in-bounding passes with a player pressing his back against the cage to pass the ball, making him vulnerable to angry fans. Referees often avoided the hard play by officiating from outside the cage. "The pro game was mostly an exercise in brute force and dirty tricks that appealed only to the most bloodthirsty of sports fans," explains sportswriter Charley Rosen. "Old-timers compared it to ice hockey played on wood and without skates."

That violence served as the line of demarcation between professional basketball and its college counterpart, which hewed to the earlier amateur tradition. It was a difference that often drew a different type of fan to professional contests, but it did draw fans. So the professional game soldiered on during the hard years of the Great Depression.

The ABL, for example, reformed in 1933. Financial exigency, however, kept it from covering the entirety of the Midwest as it had in its first incarnation. Instead, the league focused its energies on the East Coast, including teams from New York and New Jersey before spreading to Connecticut and Pennsylvania, then south to include representatives from Delaware, Maryland, and Washington. Any further expansion seemed unlikely, if not impossible. In 1929, for example, before the roar of the Roaring Twenties finally and definitively quieted, the estimated national income was $83 billion; by 1932, it was $39 billion. In 1929, there were 513 American millionaires. In 1932, there were 20. In 1929, average per capita income was $1,475; in 1932, it was $1,119. Three percent of the labor force, 1.6 million people, were unemployed in 1929. By 1933, that number had grown to 12.8 million, a full 25 percent of workers. In the first four years of the Depression, more than nine thousand banks closed. When jobs and disposable income for potential paying customers were scarce, operating costs necessarily diminished and travel and its related expenses to midwestern cities quickly became unrealistic.

But travel in the northeastern corridor was still possible, and desperate people were desperate for diversions from the crushing poverty that surrounded them. Thus, the ABL soldiered on. Philadelphia owner Eddie Gottlieb, who headed the Philadelphia Warriors in the league's first incarnation, acknowledged that the Depression had been a contributing factor to its early demise, but also worried that fans were not yet ready for the game as played by the pros. "We had big buildings and players on monthly salaries and we stretched from New York to Chicago," he said, "but we were just three or four years ahead of our time." Three or four years had passed since its first effort, and in the ABL's new incarnation, Gottlieb's Philadelphia SPHAs dominated the standings.

Gottlieb was a Ukrainian immigrant active in Philadelphia's Jewish community, one that was devoted to the new sport. Basketball's growth mirrored the growth of the Jewish population in the early twentieth century. Millions of Jews, predominantly from Eastern Europe, fled anti-Semitism for cities like New York, Philadelphia, and Boston, and de facto segregation in the North ensured that the community would be close-knit. Basketball was a principal means of assimilation, with few complicated rules and no expensive equipment. After the birth of the YMCA, the Young Men's Hebrew Association grew as a Jewish version of the organization, with educational, religious, and athletic programs for the growing urban population. "Every Jewish boy was playing basketball," explained Harry Litwack. "Every phone pole had a peach basket on it. And every one of those Jewish kids dreamed of playing for the SPHAs." Its influence among Jewish players associated the game with supposed Jewish culture in many circles, and while anti-Semitism sometimes accompanied that association, its ubiquity ensured that overt expressions of Judaism were possible if not encouraged in professional basketball play.

Gottlieb's SPHAs embodied that reality. "The SPHAs were to Philadelphia what the Original Celtics were to New York," Bill Himmelman explained. The team's name came from the South Philadelphia Hebrew Association, but unlike the original Victorian association ideals, it was a decidedly professional enterprise. The SPHAs were founded in 1917 and played in a variety of Philadelphia associations through the 1920s, as well as the Eastern Basket Ball League. "We played in a lot of dance halls in those early years," Gottlieb said. "It was basketball, then dancing. A very nice Saturday evening for yourself and your date. We used to let the girls in for free, because you couldn't have a dance after the game without the girls. We had no trouble getting the guys to pay for the basketball game when they heard that news." During the team's stint in the original ABL, Gottlieb renamed them the Warriors, but they were always the SPHAs to the locals, and when the league reformed, the team would dominate it.

Of course, there was some strategy in the name change while playing for a league that went throughout the Midwest. "We would have the Jewish star on our jerseys, and it took courage to do that," explained Jerry Fleishman. "The Jewish star on the jerseys got us into trouble. We got into fights, but we got out of it. We were proud to represent the Jews, who were supposedly the weak ones. But we could handle ourselves." A Jewish presence wasn't foreign to fans and players in eastern cities, however, so the SPHAs reverted to their original name, printing it in Hebrew on the front of team jerseys.

The SPHAs were the dominant squad of the 1930s. They won three of the new ABL's first four championships, then won four more before the end of World War II, seven total titles in twelve seasons from 1933 to 1945.

The third of those titles came in 1937. That same year, a new organization developed to fill the professional basketball void in the Midwest, since the SPHAs' ABL no longer extended its reach that far. The National Basketball League was organized by General Electric, Firestone, and Goodyear as a Rust Belt advertising vehicle. Teams from larger cities like Chicago, Detroit, and Indianapolis joined others from Fort Wayne, Akron, Buffalo, Oshkosh, Toledo, and Sheboygan. While teams from Akron won the NBL's first three championships, the Oshkosh All-Stars proved the most consistent, appearing in the league's first five championship series and winning two. Oshkosh starred Leroy "Cowboy" Edwards, a former consensus All-American from the University of Kentucky who shocked the basketball world by leaving college early after two successful seasons to pursue a professional career.

After the All-Stars' run, the Fort Wayne Zollner Pistons and Sheboygan Red Skins dominated in the mid-1940s, their success ultimately eclipsed by the Rochester Royals later in the decade. Fitting the advertising impetus of the league's creation, the Zollner Pistons were named for their owner, Fred Zollner, whose company made pistons. Zollner, however, was also a legitimate basketball pioneer who cared about the sport and would continue, even after his team's twilight, to support the professional game. Sheboygan, meanwhile, was led by star guard Buddy Jeannette, who worked in a defense plant in Rochester during the war and commuted to Sheboygan and other Red Skins game locations every weekend. His dominance, even with such hindrances, would spark the team's success. Meanwhile, Rochester's own team was waiting in the wings, boasting Al Cervi, Red Holzman, and Bob Davies, three players who would ultimately join the basketball hall of fame.

The Royals won the league title in 1946 but lost the championship series the next two seasons. In 1947, they were bested by the Chicago American Gears, who were carried to the championship by their star rookie center from DePaul University, George Mikan. Mikan would become the biggest star of the age, a six-foot, ten-inch behemoth who would fundamentally shift the game to one dominated by big men. He rebounded over defenders, blocked shots, and had an ambidextrous hook shot that was virtually indefensible. Ultimately, the game would adjust to him, the later NBA widening the foul lane, introducing a goaltending rule, and adding a shot clock just to counter the advantage provided by his size and talent. Back in 1946, however, the lanes were narrow, there was no shot clock, and Mikan tended the goal better than anyone else.

Maurice White, who owned the American Gears, thought he found the goose who laid the golden egg, and so pulled the Gears from the NBL to form his own league, the Professional Basketball League of America. It was a venture fraught from the beginning and quickly collapsed, leaving Mikan to sign with a new NBL team, the Minneapolis Lakers, a new club formed from the ashes of the now defunct Detroit Gems. The Lakers would win the title that season, Mikan's second in a row, prompting yet another league jump, Mikan's new team absconding for another infant league, the fledgling Basketball Association of America, forerunner of an even larger, more successful organization: the National Basketball Association.

3

The Negro Leagues

ON A COLD NIGHT in 1934, a bus carrying the barnstorming New York Renaissance Five stopped at a restaurant in the Midwest. The Depression had killed the various attempts at White league organization across the northern states, but it had not killed the popularity of perhaps the best team of the decade, which continued to schedule profitable dates throughout both the Northeast and the Midwest. When the team got off the bus, the players were stopped by the restaurant owner. They explained that they just wanted something to eat. "Sorry," he told them. "We don't serve niggers."

It was a common occurrence for most Black residents in the country prior to World War II, including those residents outside the South, and in particular for those whose living kept them on the road, a particularly precarious position for traveling Black basketball teams that often found themselves in towns that refused them restaurant and hotel service, even as White fans packed gymnasiums to watch them play. Of course, that kind of structural racism was also common within the game played by the Rens.

Basketball began as a decidedly White endeavor, but any project begun as an attempt to build the muscular Christianity of the nation would ultimately have to consider those in dispossessed groups flooding northern urban industrial hubs to find jobs, those of the lower classes who represented a mission field for middle-class Victorians hoping to shape sports in their own image. The Young Men's Hebrew Association was able to translate such messages to the Jewish population with teams like the Philadelphia SPHAs, but education at the intersection of physical and moral values would also be present in the curricula of African American institutions.

The bulk of the Black population in the decade following basketball's invention still lived in the South, but the numbers were slowly beginning to shift. In response to voting restrictions, segregation, convict lease, and extralegal violence like lynching, many Black southerners decided to flee the region in 1916 in what is known as the Great Migration. It lasted until 1970. Still, however, the migration began in piecemeal fashion, with Black southerners in those early decades moving to Africa or the American West just as often as they moved to northern urban industrial hubs, many taking advantage of the 1862 Homestead Act that granted 160 acres of free federal land to those who would settle the land and farm on it for at least five years. Among those opposed to such escapes was Frederick Douglass. In 1879, he insisted that the South was the place for Black Americans to be. "Not only is the South the best locality for the Negro on the ground of his political powers and possibilities, but it is best for him as a field of labor. He is there, as he is nowhere else, an absolute necessity." So, some of that migration actually happened within the South itself, as rural Black farmers moved to urban hubs within the region to find jobs. Atlanta, Richmond, and Nashville grew large and significant Black neighborhoods, as did Washington, DC.

Working at the crossroads of muscular Christianity and the growth of Black urban residency in Washington, DC, was Edwin Henderson. Born in Washington, DC, in 1883, Henderson studied at Howard University and taught physical education in the district's public schools. After learning the game of basketball while taking supplementary summer courses at Harvard, he began teaching it to his Washington, DC, students in 1904 through the 12th Street Colored YMCA. He soon included the game in the school's curriculum, seeing it as a way to get Black students into predominantly White northern universities by taking advantage of the schools' interest in competitive teams. It was not an easy sell. "Among blacks, basketball was at first considered a 'sissy' game, as was tennis in the rugged days of football," he remembered. But unlike tennis, basketball was a team sport that encouraged cooperation, and unlike tennis or football, it didn't require a substantial investment in equipment that made other games cost prohibitive to a population largely hovering below the poverty line in what was a decidedly segregated city. Basketball, Henderson argued, could be a way out, both physically and mentally. He wasn't able to convince everyone but was able to convince enough.

From there, the Black game developed rapidly in the District of Columbia metro area and in the African American neighborhoods of New York City. Henderson's YMCA team began playing rivals up and down the northeastern corridor. Howard adopted Henderson's group as the official varsity representative of the school, and it won national championships in 1909 and 1910. Henderson was also an advocate for civil rights. He was the founder of the first rural chapter of the NAACP and successfully fought a desegregation battle in Falls Church, Virginia. He was also the "Father of Black Basketball," and significantly introduced the sport through the YMCA. Henderson was a believer in athletics and reform. Sports success was measured by the objective criterion of winning, he reasoned, and that made it a tool for both public health and for civil rights. His wife, Mary Ellen Henderson, was an active leader in Black chapters of the Girl Scouts and League of Women Voters. Theirs was a belief in the Victorian ideal, and early Black basketball fed from that belief, beginning as an amateur agent of human development in the same manner that White basketball developed, then moving quickly to competition.

Two years after introducing the game to his Washington, DC, students, Henderson cofounded in 1906 the Inter-Scholastic Athletic Association of Middle Atlantic States to develop competitive sports among high school and college students in the area. The organization emphasized track and field contests, but also basketball. Churches, athletic clubs, and fraternal organizations soon joined public schools, colleges, and colored YMCA branches in and around the District of Columbia in creating basketball teams.

While Black basketball developed in Washington, DC, from the amateur YMCA tradition of muscular Christianity, in New York teams grew both within and outside those bounds. In 1907, Brooklyn's Smart Set Athletic Club became the first independently organized Black basketball team. Sportswriters for the Black press had already begun naming champions for Black baseball and Black college football, and in 1908 the press named its first Colored Basketball World's Champion, the Smart Set. In December of that year, the Smart Set traveled to Washington, DC, to play the Crescent City Athletic Club, the game's first intercity competition. The teams were amateurs, but the popularity of such contests ensured that professionalization was soon to arrive.

In 1910, the first team of Black professionals, the New York All-Stars, formed. Major Aloysius Hart, who created the team, argued, "That this game has taken a firm hold on our people has been demonstrated beyond a doubt." But league organization and proper play was paramount to build on those gains. "We want to play the game as our white friends play it. That is, in the spirit of fairness and for the benefits that the exercise will give us and the enjoyment we can afford to our friends." It wasn't necessarily the Victorian ideal that drove Hart, as he clearly wanted to turn a profit from his venture, but the shadow of whiteness and White norms clearly hovered over the Black game from its inception.

Inevitably, more teams rose to challenge the dominance of Hart's All-Stars. Pittsburgh's Monticello Athletic Association and Howard University's Big Five featured star players like center George Gilmore, forward Ed Gray, and guard Hudson Oliver. The most dominant player of the era, however, played for Monticello. Cumberland "Cum" Posey grew up in relative wealth in Homestead, Pennsylvania, just outside Pittsburgh. After winning a city title for Homestead High's basketball team, he played for Penn State for two years before moving to the University of Pittsburgh, where he graduated with a pharmacy degree. It was while a student at Pitt that Posey formed his Monticello club, and their success led to the Black press's 1912 Colored Basketball World's Championship. "The mystic wand of Posey ruled basketball with as much éclat as 'Rasputin' dominated the Queen of all the Russias," gushed Harlem's *Interstate Tattler*.

That success led Posey in two decidedly different basketball directions. In the late 1910s, he played for Pittsburgh's Duquesne University under an assumed name, leading the Dukes in scoring for three consecutive seasons. He also formed a new professional team, the Loendi Big Five, which dominated Black basketball in the late 1910s and early 1920s. Loendi earned the title of Colored Basketball World's Champions for four consecutive seasons. "Giants crumpled and quit before the fragile-looking Posey," explained the *Pittsburgh Courier*'s Rollo Wilson. "He was at once a ghost, a buzz saw, and a 'shooting fool.' The word 'quit' has never been translated for him." Eventually, though, he did quit, retiring in the late 1920s to focus on baseball promotion.

It wasn't an unusual move, as Black baseball had provided a model for the burgeoning professional efforts in Black basketball. In the post–Civil

War era, though baseball was dominated by White players, Black players did occasionally play for White teams. Black teams also sometimes played against White teams. But things changed in October 1867 when the African American Pythian Base Ball Club of Philadelphia (originally, like *basket ball*, spelled as two words) was denied admission to the Pennsylvania Association of Base Ball Players. The Pythians' creation led to others, and Black teams began to flourish. That same year, the Philadelphia Excelsiors and the Brooklyn Uniques played a baseball game hailed by the press as the "Colored Championship of the United States."

The shadow of whiteness, however, hovered over baseball, as well, and soon the leagues made gentlemen's agreements to bar Black players from the game. Many of the White players, upon whom professional organizations' popularity rested, were virulent racists, and throughout the 1880s Black participation dwindled to nothing. By 1892, a clear color bar had been established in baseball. And so Black teams developed independently of White teams. The first professional Black baseball team was the Cuban Giants, founded in 1885, calling themselves Cubans so as to be able to book games against White competition. But the lack of league organization was killing the potential success of Black baseball. Thus, in 1920, a former player from Chicago named Andrew "Rube" Foster created the Negro National League. In 1923, a rival Eastern Colored League (ECL) developed, and throughout the mid-1920s the two leagues played an annual World Series. But the ECL folded in 1928, and the Negro National League, though it remained prosperous through the decade, faltered in the early 1930s because of the Depression and the death in 1930 of Rube Foster. Foster was the sole source of strength for the league, and he led with an iron fist and a cult of personality; his death left a power vacuum at the top of the organization.

Cum Posey wanted to be Rube Foster. As early as 1911, he had been playing professional baseball for the local Homestead Grays simultaneously with his basketball career. By the 1920s, he owned the team and would remain a powerhouse in Black baseball until his death in 1946. Posey's talent for basketball and his efforts to become a baseball magnate demonstrated the synergy that existed between the two games in the African American community. It also served as a signpost of Black baseball's ability to function under the structure of league organization and Black basketball's inability to do the same.

Still, whereas Posey attempted to make his fortune in baseball, others were poised to become the Rube Foster of basketball. In an attempt to escape from the game's shadow of whiteness, Robert L. Douglas founded a new professional team in November 1923, the New York Renaissance Big Five, helping to usher in the age of Black professional play known as the Black Fives Era. Douglas was a product of the Great Migration, an immigrant from Saint Kitts in the British West Indies, and his team appeared at the intersection of the migration and the glut of Black cultural production fed by the economy of the Roaring Twenties known as the Harlem Renaissance.

The second wave of the Great Migration was spurred most immediately by the demand for jobs during World War I, a conflict that spurred a vitriolic nativism in the United States that led to a series of immigration restriction laws ensuring that the population of European immigrants would remain near prewar levels, creating a worker shortage in northern factories and other industries. Roughly 1.5 million Black southerners migrated north in the first three decades of the twentieth century, pushed by the overwhelming racism of the Jim Crow South and pulled by new potential employment. As it turned out, however, racism could be overwhelming everywhere. As more Black migrants headed north, Whites in that region began to demonstrate a racial violence often assumed to lie dormant in comparison with its southern counterpart. In 1870, for example, one-third of northern Black workers were skilled. By 1910, only one-tenth were skilled. The Black middle class began a period of decline in the face of a fickle White customer base turning away from Black producers and retailers in response to southern migration and northern racism.

It was a racism of capital that was exacerbated by a racism of culture. The Ku Klux Klan, for example, was revived in 1915. By 1924, membership was estimated at more than four million Americans, north and south, including a half-million members in its women's auxiliary. Along with traditional southern strongholds, the Klan had an influential presence in Oklahoma, Kansas, Indiana, Pennsylvania, Washington, and Oregon. In addition to the danger of physical violence that was part and parcel of KKK ideology, a more subtle form of academic racism gave such organizations the legitimacy they craved. Lothrop Stoddard's *The Rising Tide of Color*, published in 1920, for example, claimed, "Even a general knowledge of historical and scientific facts suffices to show the need for a racial basis to our national life—as it has been, and as we intend that it shall be. We know that our America is a White America."

For Black migrants to northern industrial hubs, the most immediate outgrowth of that thinking was a de facto residential segregation that shunted the African American population into ethnic enclaves within larger cities. And it was a process, despite its racial motivations, that actually strengthened the Black middle class. In those new Black neighborhoods, churches, fraternal societies, and political organizations developed, and a new class of ministers and businesspeople became the core of urban society. Real estate agencies, funeral homes, doctors' offices, newspapers, groceries, and restaurants soon opened for business, selling to a Black customer base with less cumulative capital but a loyalty that didn't exist among the wealthier White customer base. The most successful of those enclaves, and the home base for the Renaissance Five basketball team, was Harlem in New York City.

"Harlem has, in this century, become the most strategically important community of black America," wrote Harold Cruse. "Harlem is still the pivot of the black world's quest for identity and salvation. The way Harlem goes (or does not go) so goes all black America. . . . This community still represents the Negro's strongest bastion in America from which to launch whatever group effort he is able to mobilize for political power, economic rehabilitation and cultural reidentification." Though Harlem was unique, and though most Americans didn't have a specific shared experience of Harlem, Harlem created the cultural identity for Black America, and "without a cultural identity that adequately defines *himself*, the Negro cannot even identify with the American nation as a whole."

There had been a small number of Black residents ever since the first tenement housing went up in Harlem in the 1880s, but it was the Great Migration that fed the first new numbers of Black residents to New York. Initially, however, those migrants could not get into Harlem. The Whites didn't want Black residents in the neighborhood any more than they wanted Jews or immigrants, and remained relatively successful in keeping them out, even through the rough economic times brought by the Panic of 1893. But times remained tight into the first decade of the twentieth century, and it was getting harder and harder to fill houses and apartments in Harlem. As Cruse explained, White residential organizations used "all means—legal, persuasive, and conspiratorial—to stem the negro influx which assumed mass proportions around 1905."

Charles W. Anderson, a Republican politician appointed collector of internal revenue of New York by Teddy Roosevelt, and Philip A. Payton, a real estate salesman, led the way. Together, along with T. Thomas Fortune, editor of the *New York Age*, the oldest Black newspaper in the city, they created the Afro-American Realty Company (AARC), which leased or bought apartments that had either been abandoned by Whites, weren't being rented, or were being leased by Whites who obviously couldn't pay the bills. Then the company rented them to Black residents.

Though the AARC only lasted about five years, the movement it created continued. Payton and a colleague bought two five-story apartment buildings in Harlem. John E. Nail, one of the most influential Black Republicans in New York, took the real estate mantle from Payton, purchasing, then leasing, a series of houses and apartment buildings in the neighborhood. But it wasn't just leading real estate investors who made it their duty to create a place for African Americans in Harlem. The congregation of St. Philips Episcopal Church, for example, bought a row of thirteen apartment buildings for those in need. And though there was bitterness and bickering, and even some lawsuits, that had to be overcome, all of it was done without any major violent incident, and this at a time when clashes between Black migrants and various immigrant groups competing for jobs in other northern urban areas led to massive race riots and violence. "The matter of better and still better housing for colored people in New York became the dominating idea of [Payton's] life, and he worked on it as long as he lived," argued James Weldon Johnson. "When Negro New Yorkers evaluate their benefactors in their own race, they must find that not many have done more than Phil Payton; for much of what has made Harlem the intellectual and artistic capital of the Negro world is in good part due to this fundamental advantage."

So Harlem became "the intellectual and artistic capital of the Negro world," the home of jazz, the soundtrack of the decade. Willie Smith, Count Basie, Fats Waller, and Duke Ellington emerged as household names. Jazz, like basketball, was free of convention; it was improvised; it was new, serving as a precedent document for an age and for a people. Paralleling the rise of jazz was a new Black literary and artistic movement known as the Harlem Renaissance, itself defying convention with new and provocative artistic production. Writers, painters, and sculptors began creating works rooted in Black culture rather than imitating the dominant White styles. "We younger Negro artists who create now intend to express our individual dark-skinned selves without fear or shame," said Langston Hughes, perhaps the most prominent figure of the Harlem Renaissance. "If white people are pleased, we are glad. If they are not, it doesn't matter. We know we are beautiful. And ugly, too."

Basketball could serve as another of those artistic outlets. Though largely defined out of the early White game, Black players could improvise, be free of convention, and express their individual dark-skinned selves without fear or shame. They could be beautiful and ugly too. The first to see that opportunity, the Philip A. Payton of basketball, was Bob Douglas. A Caribbean immigrant like so many influential others in the period—Marcus Garvey, Hubert Harrison, Cyril Briggs, Richard B. Moore, and Otto Huiswoud in politics; Claude McKay and Eulalie Spence in literature; Arthur Schomburg and J. A. Rogers in history—Douglas merged the economic and artistic principles at play in Harlem to create in 1923 the New York Renaissance Big Five.

But his influences did not solely stem from Harlem's Black creative community. The year prior to the Rens' creation, another group of Black professionals, the Commonwealth Big Five, was founded by Jess and Edward McMahon. The McMahon brothers were a pair of White property owners who developed a series of athletic clubs in Harlem, first emphasizing boxing but branching out to baseball. They founded the New York Lincoln Giants, perhaps the most successful Black baseball team of the first half of the 1910s. They also promoted boxing, including the 1915 Jack Johnson–Jess Willard fight in Havana, Cuba, in which the first Black heavyweight champion lost his title. The family's willingness to get involved in businesses in Harlem and in Black sports more broadly carried with it an element of economic colonialism, to be sure, but it also provided necessary outlets for Black fans and athletes. Another of their business ventures was a Harlem casino on East 135th Street known as the Commonwealth. They used the venue for boxing, but in 1922, the McMahons founded a basketball team to play there, the Commonwealth Big Five. The team only played for two seasons, but in those years, they played Black and White teams, including the Rens and the Original

Celtics. Their victories were important, but the team proved unable to
draw large crowds to the McMahons' casino and thus fell away. (The
McMahons would continue to promote sports, however. Jess in particular, simultaneous to his efforts in Black professional basketball, would
begin spending more and more of his time promoting professional wrestling. It would soon become a dominant aspect of the family business, his
second son, Vincent J. McMahon, ultimately founding the World Wide
Wrestling Federation. Vincent's son, Vincent K. McMahon, would take
over the business and shorten its name to the World Wrestling Federation, known today as WWE.)

White economic colonialism would remain a dominant concern in
basketball through the twenty-first century, and it was a concern in the
Harlem of the 1920s. Perhaps the most infamous example was the Cotton Club, opened in 1923, the same year the Rens were founded. It was
created by Owney Madden, a White mobster from Hell's Kitchen, who
built it to attract White patrons to Harlem. Ever since the neighborhood
had begun its renaissance, Whites had begun "slumming" in Harlem,
traveling uptown to experience the swinging nightlife in the area, and
Madden wanted to attract them. He was actually in Sing Sing prison at
the time, serving a sentence for manslaughter, but he supervised the creation of the Cotton Club, decorated in a jungle theme, from his cell in
Ossining, New York. The Cotton Club was a study in contradictions,
as all the performers were Black—and the chorus girls were uniformly
light-skinned Black women under twenty-one years old—but the clientele was all White. The venue imposed a $2.50 cover charge to keep out
the undesirable working class. So restrictive segregation came to Harlem.
Duke Ellington, Cab Calloway, and all the influential Black performers of the era played the Cotton Club, for example, even though Black
patrons weren't allowed in.

The Renaissance Ballroom and Casino at the corner of 138th Street
and 7th Avenue was the antidote to such economic colonialism. Built
and operated by the Sarco Realty and Holding Company, a Black-owned
development firm led by William Roach, another Caribbean immigrant
from Antigua, the Renny, as it was often called, provided a decidedly
Black space for entertainment and organizing. All the same influential
performers who played the Cotton Club played the Renny. It hosted Joe
Louis boxing matches and film screenings. Political organizations and

social clubs also met there. In 1923, when Roach's fellow Caribbean Bob Douglas formed his own Black basketball team to rival that of the Commonwealth, Roach allowed them to use the Renaissance dance floor as a home court. "They set up a basketball post on each end of the floor," remembered Rens star William "Pop" Gates. "The floor was very slippery and they outlined the sidelines and foul lines. It wasn't a big floor. It was far from being a regular basketball floor. Other than high schools or armories, they had very few places to play at, except the Negro college." The Rens competed not only with the opposing team, but with the nightlife going on around them. "It was a well-decorated area—chandeliers, a bandstand," said Gates. "They had the dancing before the ball game. People would pay and [dance] prior to the game, at halftime, and after the game." In order to rival the nightlife around them, the Rens developed an up-tempo, flashy game with overt displays of athleticism considered anathema to White players. There was in the effort less a rejection of the traditional basketball ethos handed down from Naismith and more a desire to woo fans with other available options in the building.

The Rens played against any team they could find, but the Original Celtics were their great white whale. In an era where the Negro National League formed because White baseball teams would not play Black teams, the Rens and the Celtics met often. While team segregation was a decided part of the professional game, segregated teams played against one another commonly and without consequence in a manner impossible for much of the baseball world. The Celtics won the first four contests against the Rens before finally dropping a game to their rivals in December 1925. That year, the Renaissance Big Five were named Colored Basketball World's Champions by the Black press.

Those early teams were led by team captain Clarence Reginald "Fats" Jenkins, a star with Posey's Loendi Big Five before joining the New York squad. He would stay with the team until 1939, all the while playing professional baseball during the summers. It was common for professional athletes like Jenkins to play different sports in different parts of the year, each attempting to earn a living in whatever sports were available to them in a given season. Several of his Rens teammates, like Bill Yancey, did the same. Eyre Saitch, a Rens star from Bermuda, won a 1926 American Tennis Association national championship during his tenure with the basketball team.

In 1928, Douglas sent his team on the road to barnstorm throughout the Midwest, where they would encounter racism like that of the restaurant proprietor in 1934. They became known as the Magnificent Seven in the early 1930s, one of the great attractions in the nation, even touring through the South beginning in 1933. From January to March of that year, the team embarked on an eighty-eight-game winning streak, finally ended by the Original Celtics. From 1932 to 1936, they amassed 497 wins to only 58 defeats. Players like James "Pappy" Ricks and Wee Willie Smith starred for the team. Members of the Original Celtics cited the Rens' Tarzan Cooper as the best center they ever faced. Pop Gates, who would join the team in the late 1930s, was from Alabama, part of that Great Migration, who came to New York and became a star. Finally, there was David "Big Dave" DeJernett, an Indiana phenom who played on integrated high school and college teams and became the first Black player to join a top-tier professional team after attending four years of college.

And their success was taking place during the Great Depression. "The Negro was born in depression," said Clifford Burke, a community volunteer who described his experience for Studs Terkel. "It only became official when it hit the white man." African American urban unemployment rose to 50 percent by 1932, making the maintenance of Black business— basketball or otherwise—a tenuous prospect at best. In the North, where the bulk of Black professional basketball was being played, approximately half of all Black families were receiving some form of relief. It was even worse in the South. For example, 65 percent of Atlanta's Black families needed aid. The surge in unemployment and the lack of disposable income among Black fans made team profitability that much more difficult in the 1930s. The roar of the Roaring Twenties was gone. Only desperation was left.

And yet, despite the difficult economic times, the Rens were a phenomenon, a barnstorming sensation that traveled across the country. In 1939, the World Professional Basketball Tournament began in Chicago, sponsored by the *Chicago Herald American* newspaper. The best teams, Black and White, were invited to compete for the title of World Champion, and in that first season the New York Renaissance Big Five won the tournament, the first recognized world champions of the sport. The following season, however, a new team would take the crown, one formed in a similar Black basketball culture emanating from Chicago itself: the Harlem Globetrotters.

The Globetrotters got their start on the South Side of Chicago, where a team associated with the Eighth Regiment Armory, the first American armory built for a Black regiment, played home games and won the Colored Basketball World's Championship in 1924. From the ashes of that team, a promoter named Dick "Baby Face" Hudson organized the Giles Post Five, playing home games at the armory, which was located on South Giles Street. When it was announced in 1927 that developers were planning to build a new Savoy Ballroom, one that would surpass the splendor of the original Savoy in Harlem, Hudson saw an opportunity. He made a deal with the new venue, changed his team's name to the Savoy Big Five, and moved their home games to the ballroom.

The Savoys were a success and drew crowds to the new venue, but there was dissension in the ranks. Disputes over money led the team to functionally disband, as star players and even Hudson himself abandoned the Savoy. Former Savoy players like Walter "Toots" Wright, Byron "Fat" Long, and Willis "Kid" Oliver joined others like Bill Tupelo and Andy Washington to form a new team, the Chicago Globe Trotters, with Hudson as its manager. One of his first moves was to hire a local promoter named Abraham Saperstein, who booked the team in venues across the country, found transportation, and changed the team's name to the Harlem Globetrotters to signal to audiences the kind of up-tempo, thrilling play associated in American minds with teams like the Rens and to code the team as Black for potential White audiences who might be surprised or offended by the race of the players. Saperstein would ultimately take total control of the Globetrotters, traveling with them around the country and fostering one of its best teams. A consummate promoter, he pushed his team to play more than a thousand games in its first seven seasons, Saperstein driving the players to all their games.

And the game they played was in the free-flowing style made popular by early ballroom teams. At first, they were good. They dominated most of the teams in the Midwest. But in 1929, Inman Jackson joined the team, its first real clown, and the personality of the Globetrotters began to take shape. Clowning in sports was not new. It was, like so many developments in Black Fives basketball, an idea borrowed from the Negro leagues, where teams used various gimmicks to entertain fans and provide the kind of oddity that would fill stadiums. Saperstein was involved in a variety of Black baseball teams and leagues in Chicago and throughout the Midwest and knew that clever antics would bring more people to arenas, even if his team wasn't playing well on a particular night.

On most nights, however, they played well. The Globetrotters of the 1930s and 1940s were not the comic team that they would later become. Saperstein was devoted to the group, but he also profited from them, and his best intentions did not mitigate the economic colonialism of the arrangement. It was a common theme in segregated sports. In later years, critics would express concern that Saperstein paid players from his White athletic ventures more than he did those of his Black teams. Others complained that the clowning that later defined the team made a mockery of legitimate Black talent. Saperstein and the bulk of his players denied such charges, but it demonstrated that even with the best of intentions, White financial interests in Black games inevitably led to ethical problems.

Rarely, however, was Saperstein's sincerity about his devotion to the Globetrotters doubted. Particularly in the days before integrated professional basketball eroded the talent pool for the team, he wanted to win. At the 1940 World Professional Basketball Tournament, the Globetrotters defeated the Rens en route to the championship game, where they bested the Chicago Bruins, George Halas's White American Basketball League team, becoming the second Black organization to win the title. In 1948, the Globetrotters beat George Mikan's Minneapolis Lakers, widely considered to be the best White basketball team in the country. It was one in a long line of demonstrations, along with the thicket of potential problems related to White ownership of Black teams, that segregated professional basketball in the post–World War II era was no longer useful. Unlike segregated baseball, professional basketball had always included play between Black and White teams, but the year prior to the Globetrotters' stunning victory over Mikan's Lakers, Jackie Robinson had desegregated baseball, the most segregated of segregated team sports.

Times were changing, and professional basketball was going to have to change with them. But Robinson's Brooklyn Dodgers weren't the only model of how to make such changes. Because of its Victorian beginnings, and unlike baseball, basketball's popularity also developed along a different track, an amateur track that fed from those original ideals of muscular Christianity and took hold in America's universities. While less progressive than the pros when it came to style of play, the college game would prove far more advanced when it came to desegregation and racial inclusivity.

4

Early Collegiate Basketball

BASKETBALL WAS CREATED as an educational tool, a way to instill a proscribed set of values into those who played it. The students at Springfield were training to be physical education directors at high schools and colleges. And so while professional play developed with alacrity after the game's invention, it also took hold early in the country's institutions of higher learning. Education was the backbone of the Victorian ideal, and muscular Christianity was built into its foundations. "The object of education," argued the *Spirit of the Times* in 1857, "is to make men out of boys. Real live men, not bookworms, not smart fellows, but manly fellows." In 1852, Harvard faced Yale in a crew race. It was an informal contest, but it was the first American intercollegiate game. Other northeastern schools would follow, usually competing in crew. And the competitions were soaked through with Victorian idealism. "Will a kind fortune ever bring the day when the first scholar of his class can also claim the high honor of being the stoutest oarsman of the college?" asked *Harvard Magazine* in 1858. "If he attain a seat in a university boat, must he rigidly practice austere virtues; and drill himself into such self-denials as tell on the moral character not less than on the muscular system?" Soon, the contests would expand to other sports. In June 1859, for example, Amherst College and Williams College played the first intercollegiate baseball game.

Football, however, would become the signature sport of American colleges in the late nineteenth century. Rugby began in 1823 at the famous Rugby Boys' School in England. At the same time, a group of students at Princeton began playing what was then known as "ballown." First using their fists to advance the ball, and then their feet, the game's one goal was to move the ball past the opposing team. Meanwhile, at Harvard, the freshman and sophomore classes competed in a football-type game, played on the first Monday of each school year, an event that came to be known as "Bloody Monday" because of the roughness of the game. Soon after the conclusion of the Civil War, around 1865, colleges began organizing football games. In 1867, Princeton led the way in establishing some rudimentary rules of the game. Rutgers College established a different set of rules that year, and with the relatively short distance between it and Princeton, a game was decided upon by both universities, and on November 6, 1869, Rutgers defeated Princeton by a score of six goals to four in what has become known as the first intercollegiate football game. It only grew from there, spreading across the nation and becoming the most popular sport at American universities.

Amos Alonzo Stagg became a coach decidedly associated with college football, but he had also been part of Naismith's basketball experiment in Springfield when he founded the game in 1891. The following year, in 1892, the University of Chicago opened, and Stagg was hired to be the school's athletic director. He led a powerhouse football team at Chicago, but he also created a basketball movement at the school. In March 1893, during the institution's second semester, Stagg staged a game in the gymnasium for the students, and in 1894 he established and coached a varsity team, playing locals in and around the city. Two years after that, in 1896, the Maroons began intercollegiate play with a series of contests against the University of Iowa.

Stagg's Chicago teams became collegiate powerhouses, winning seven Big Ten championships during his tenure, but his program was not the first. By the time he had organized the Chicago varsity, another Springfield alum, Charles O. Bemies, had introduced basketball in early 1892 to the students of Geneva College in Pennsylvania. Meanwhile, Stagg's Chicago team had midwestern opponents to play because other universities were developing programs, as well. Henry F. Kallenberg, who would replace Luther Halsey Gulick at Springfield, introduced basketball to Iowa in 1893, at both the university and Iowa City's branch of the YMCA. Then there was Ray Kaighn, another member of Naismith's Springfield cohort, who that same year led the athletics program at Hamline University in Minnesota, scheduling basketball games between the students and members of the local YMCA. In February 1895, Hamline faced the Minnesota State School of Agriculture, losing 9 to 3 in the first intercollegiate game. Charles M. Williams, another student of Naismith, brought the game to Temple University in 1894, and a month after Hamline's first intercollegiate contest lost a game to Haverford College 6 to 4.

The games at Hamline, Geneva, Temple, and others were played with different numbers of players on the court at any given time. Original YMCA games had been played with nine per side, and early collegiate efforts based play on the number of available players instead of any hard-and-fast rule. It was in 1896, when Stagg's Maroons traveled to Iowa City to face Kallenberg's Hawkeyes, that an intercollegiate contest included five players on each side, setting a standard that would become a norm before becoming an official part of the rules.

The games were competitive ventures, but they were part and parcel of the muscular Christian ideal, coming as the founders did from Springfield, and would play against and associate with the local YMCAs in their communities. And while Naismith's students and colleagues spread out and brought basketball with them to universities across the country, so, too, did Naismith himself. After he and his new game arrived at the University of Kansas in 1898, the school almost immediately became obsessed with the sport. "It appears that the basketball mania would carry all before it," the student newspaper reported at the end of 1898.

Like other programs newly developed in the decade, Kansas played most of its games against local YMCAs, along with schools like Missouri's William Jewell College and the nearby Haskell Institute. Haskell's team began in the early twentieth century, and, along with the basketball play of Pennsylvania's Carlisle Indian Industrial School, demonstrated the game's reach to the Native community. It was football that made the schools' names, both of them competing against the dominant college teams of the day and Carlisle producing Jim Thorpe, one of the most successful and accomplished athletes in American history. But Thorpe also played basketball for Carlisle, and the colonial Americanizing missions of such schools ensured that the Victorian sensibilities associated with Naismith's game would redound to them, as well.

The programs at Carlisle and Haskell would be short-lived, while the University of Kansas team would expand to dominance in the coming decades, but basketball had proven for the professionals to be most viable in the northeastern corridor, and the schools that would later become known as the Ivy League, which were so influential in generating the popularity of college football, would also take the mantle for basketball. Yale formed its first competitive team in 1895 and the following year joined with Trinity and Wesleyan to form the Triangular League, the first college basketball conference. It didn't last long, as Wesleyan did not survive that first campaign. Penn tried to form a team as well, but, like Wesleyan, sputtered in fits and starts until the early twentieth century. But Yale proved strong, as it had in football, and soon began touring the Midwest like its professional counterparts, engaging in the first intersectional collegiate games.

Yale's captain and star player was John Kirkland Clark. After graduation in 1900, he began attending Harvard Law School, where he formed a team for the Crimson, played for it, and coached it, though he did abstain from participating when Harvard played Yale. The following year, Harvard and Yale joined with Princeton, Columbia, and Cornell to create the Eastern League, forerunner of the modern Ivy League. Cornell's efforts had recovered from its original ban prompted by the twenty-five-man disaster of its early basketball attempts, but neither the team nor its fellow league competitors were able to stop Yale from winning the first title. Also in 1901, another group of northeastern teams, including Trinity, Dartmouth, Amherst, Holy Cross, and Williams, formed the New England League. The next season, the United States Military Academy at West Point formed its first team. The sport was spreading quickly, but so too was the organizational infrastructure that surrounded it.

As the professionals and the early collegiate team formations had demonstrated, however, basketball was also exceedingly popular in the Midwest and its leaders knew how to organize. The University of Minnesota began its own program in 1895, playing in a league that included the Minnesota State School of Agriculture, Macalester College, and local YMCA and National Guard teams. In 1900, the school destroyed a respected Iowa team 30–4. From 1902 to 1904, it won thirty-four games in a row. That success, and the success of others like Chicago, led in 1905 to the creation of the Western Conference, forerunner of the modern Big Ten, with Minnesota and Chicago joining Purdue, Indiana, Wisconsin, and Illinois. Minnesota won the first Western Conference title, but Chicago dominated the group through the rest of the decade.

Of course, conference organization led to championships, and championships led to discussions about which champion was best. The lust for accolades begat lust for more accolades. It was a cycle at the core of Naismith's original concerns. In collegiate conference basketball's infancy, there was no recognized annual tournament or judging rubric to determine a national champion, leaving colleges to claim mythical titles against one another. In 1904, Ohio's Hiram College won an outdoor basketball tournament in St. Louis, allowing it to claim a national championship. In 1905, Columbia's twenty-six game winning streak, including wins over Western Conference opponents like Minnesota and Wisconsin, gave it a claim to champion status. The dominant University of Chicago made a similar claim in 1908.

By the time that Hiram won the St. Louis tournament, another program was beginning three hundred miles to the southeast. In 1900, Vanderbilt University in Nashville, Tennessee, first fielded a sanctioned team, bringing basketball to the South. The team's four games that season were against the Nashville YMCA and the Nashville Athletic Club, but Vanderbilt's southern collegiate cohort would soon catch up. The school was part of the region's first athletic conference, the Southern Intercollegiate Athletic Association (SIAA), founded in 1894, which included Alabama, Auburn, Sewanee, Clemson, Tulane, Louisiana State University, and others. The schools originally organized contests in football, baseball, and track, but Vanderbilt's development of a basketball program would soon encourage other member schools to participate in the sport.

In 1903, a group of students at the University of Kentucky, another SIAA school, combined their scarce resources to buy a basketball. "If something happened to that ball," explained Thomas G. Bryant, a member of the first Kentucky team, "we couldn't have played." But nothing happened to the ball, and the program at Kentucky would mark the continued spread of basketball into the South. The team wasn't successful in its early seasons, amassing a 15–29 record in its first five campaigns, leading the faculty athletic senate to propose abolishing the school's basketball program. But the university hired a new football coach in 1909, Edwin Sweetland, and a group of students desperate to see basketball continue presented a plan to the faculty senate for installing a wooden floor and new lighting in the university armory and tasking Sweetland to coach the basketball team. The squad had never had a paid coach, and the students saw Sweetland's influence as providing a real avenue to become better. Under his leadership, the team would post its first undefeated record three years later. Sweetland wouldn't stay long, leaving the school in early 1913 after being implicated in the arson of the office of a faculty critic of the school's program. Sweetland was cleared of involvement but was scarred by the charge and decided to leave, despite his success in both basketball and football. The incident demonstrated the mania for basketball at Kentucky and the stakes that many saw in its success. Kentucky was a poor state in a poor region, and a winning basketball team at the state's flagship university drove an aspirational identity to which many on the campus and in the region gravitated. Sweetland left the school, but he left it with the athletic achievement that the students and many others craved.

Farther east, university teams were developing in the southern states of the Atlantic seaboard, as well. In 1905, the University of Virginia, which had originally flirted with participation in the SIAA, organized its own basketball team, led by Welsh immigrant Henry "Pop" Lannigan. At the end of the program's first decade, Virginia posted an undefeated record and proved one of the top early national teams. A year after Virginia started its basketball team, North Carolina's Trinity College started its own. The school that would later change its name to Duke University started its program slowly, but the team developed over the years until the school's first state championship in 1920, playing its first contest that season with the institution that would become its fiercest rival, the University of North Carolina. Carolina started its program in 1911 under the leadership of track-and-field coach Nathaniel Cartmell, who had medaled in the 1904 Olympics, where basketball made its first appearance.

Meanwhile, though it was slower in developing, basketball was also moving west. Stanford University students began playing the game in 1896, as did those at the University of California, Berkeley, though it would take longer for the schools to develop full intercollegiate programs. The University of Oregon began its first season in 1902, playing only two games in its first campaign. The University of Arizona began its team in 1904, the University of Southern California in 1906, and the University of Utah in 1908. St. Ignatius College, later to become known as the University of San Francisco, began its program in 1910. Like dominoes that stretched across the nation, universities began falling to the new passion that had been developed as a staple of amateurism and education.

But as the professionals had demonstrated, amateurism was a difficult model to maintain. Administration of the collegiate game fell to the Amateur Athletic Union (AAU), the only real governing body that existed for the collegiate game at the turn of the century. Yale, which would run afoul of football administrators, as well, would suffer AAU suspensions during its 1897–1898 season and its 1904–1905 season for using disqualified players. During its second suspension, AAU officials warned Penn that playing its game against Yale would be a breach of union policy and result in a suspension for the Quakers themselves. Penn's athletic director was enraged, responding by sending letters to 365 schools calling for an April meeting at the Penn Relays to discuss taking control of basketball from the AAU.

The Penn Relays were one of the premier interscholastic and collegiate track-and-field spectacles in the country, founded in 1895, with tens of thousands of spectators watching hundreds, even thousands of athletes. Despite the popularity of the relays, however, only fifteen representatives from invited schools appeared for the meeting. That group organized seven of those university representatives into a committee to draft an agreed-upon set of rules. Ultimately reduced to four, in July 1895, a group from Yale, Princeton, Penn, and Columbia met, created, and formalized rules for the college game and built the rudiments of what would become the Intercollegiate Athletic Association the following year, and which in 1911, as North Carolina was forming its own basketball program, would change its name to the National Collegiate Athletic Association (NCAA).

Along with creating a formal structure for basketball, the new association concerned itself with making college football safer, banning rough mass plays that caused many serious injuries, and even deaths. Football bred controversy over whether the game was beneficial for university students. Basketball, though, bred its own violence. Harvard president Charles Eliot temporarily ended the school's program in 1909 because it was "even more brutal than football." The school's athletic committee argued that "the games more closely resembled free fights than friendly athletic contests between amateur teams." Harvard officials weren't alone in their concerns, but other schools didn't follow their lead because they saw prospects for success. Of course, Harvard's ancillary motivation for eliminating basketball was more calculating. "We are being defeated all the time at basketball," explained the team's manager. "It is a poor sport. Therefore we had better abolish it." Winning, rather than safety, was driving such decisions, foreshadowing the broader development of the game in the decades to come.

And winning could provide a real windfall to schools playing basketball. The University of Texas introduced the sport in the southwest in 1906 and between 1913 and 1917 embarked on a forty-four-game winning streak. The game the team played in those early years was an outdoor game, but its success convinced the university to build an indoor gymnasium. "Basketball can no longer be said to be one of the minor sports, both from the spectators' point of view and that of the players," the student newspaper reasoned. "Never before in the history of the institution has basketball been so popular." In one sense, it wasn't basketball that was popular at Texas; it was winning basketball, and it was a phenomenon mimicked at schools across the country. The University of Wisconsin had its own undefeated season in 1914 and Illinois and Virginia performed the feat in 1915. Oregon State went undefeated in 1918, Navy in 1919, and Texas A&M in 1920. In 1923, Army managed to go without a loss; in 1924, North Carolina finally managed the feat.

Meanwhile there were other teams that dominated in the 1920s without necessarily amassing undefeated records. Montana State teams of the 1920s under the leadership of Ott Romney became a powerhouse, as did much of the state of Indiana, which underwent what became known as Hoosier Hysteria in the decade. Indiana University fielded its first team in 1900, playing its first game against Indianapolis's Butler University. The school's first real success, however, came in the 1920s under the leadership of Everett Dean, its first All-American who stayed on to coach his alma mater in 1924.

The Hoosiers, however, would be overshadowed in the state by the unlikely Franklin Wonder Five, a group of players from tiny Franklin, Indiana, who managed to win three consecutive state high school championships in the first years of the decade, before moving on to Franklin College, dominating basketball in the Midwest and posting an undefeated record in their first collegiate season. "Not only has this team been the best Franklin College ever had," gushed the *Detroit Free Press*, "but it is considered as the best collegiate team ever seen in Hoosierdom, the basketball center of the world." It was a demonstration that the small number of players on the court and the uneven level of competition across the country could create incredibly dominant teams, leaving a system of "haves" and "have-nots" in collegiate basketball that the game has never been able to completely shed.

And perhaps it didn't need to. People loved winners, and basketball dynasties grew the popularity of the game. That growth took place during the period of sports heroes, the roar of the Roaring Twenties, that had proven so successful for professional basketball; universities with winning teams began moving those teams from school armories and gymnasia into new palatial stadiums. Stanford, Butler, Indiana, Minnesota, Iowa, and others constructed arenas that held anywhere from five thousand to sixteen thousand paying customers. Even under an amateur rubric, a subsection of America's colleges began to see basketball as a profitable commodity.

It wasn't the direct inversion of Naismith's original idea, as was professionalization, but it was, to be sure, a modification of his thinking. The players were amateur, but that amateurism was creating substantial profit for those who didn't actually play based on significantly competitive contests that regulated how much money would be made. For many critics, the new model was a grift, and many collegiate players who drew crowds without compensation were also beginning to see it that way too. It was a situation that would lead to substantial problems down the road, but back in the Roaring Twenties, universities rushed to take advantage of the trend while Naismith lamented the state of a game that had grown beyond the boundaries of his original intent.

By that time, however, Naismith had moved on from his coaching duties at Kansas. Naismith was only a reluctant coach even while there, his conflicted thinking about the job leading to a losing record during his tenure at the school. He advised one of his star players, Forrest "Phog" Allen, when he was considering becoming a basketball coach, "You can't coach basketball; you just play it." By the time of the college game's great boom of the 1920s, however, Kansas's leader was the former player who had ignored Naismith's advice and returned to coach his alma mater.

After his playing days in Lawrence, Allen began his coaching career at Baker University in Baldwin City, Kansas, before spending two early seasons back in his state's flagship in Lawrence. Then it was on to Haskell, then Warrensburg Teachers College in Missouri. But after World War I, in 1919, Allen returned to Kansas to take over a program that had some regional success and Naismith's legacy, but little else. Under his leadership, Kansas thrived, winning conference championships consecutively from 1922 to 1927. Allen would continue coaching his alma mater until 1956, but back in the halcyon days of the 1920s, one of his star players was Adolph Rupp, the son of German immigrants raised in Halstead, Kansas. In 1930, Rupp would begin coaching his own collegiate program at the University of Kentucky, where he would stay until 1972.

The spread of college basketball was dependent upon the existence of colleges across the country, making the game more ubiquitous than its professional counterpart, and the coaching trees that grew from successful programs ensured that there could be tangible national success for even small and rural schools in far-flung parts of the United States. It was also during this period, for example, that historically Black colleges and universities (HBCUs) began to develop powerful teams, like their White counterparts moving from points north to points south in their evolution. Howard University, Lincoln (Pennsylvania), Wilberforce, and Hampton Institute all developed teams in the early twentieth century. By the 1920s, Morris Brown, Tuskegee, Atlanta University, and Morehouse had developed dominant programs. The number of potential opponents for them was limited by a lack of Black institutions of higher education, and so many of the schools chose to barnstorm like their professional counterparts. In 1922, Morehouse carried a forty-two-game winning streak to New York to take on the St. Christopher Club, a group founded by New York's St. Philip's Protestant Episcopal Church to stave off moral decay. The church was located in the notorious Tenderloin vice district in the city, and the club sought to provide a bulwark against such temptations. In 1905, hewing to the dictates of muscular Christianity, they created a basketball team that eventually centered itself in Harlem. St. Christopher defeated Morehouse in February 1922, but the Atlanta school's travel for the game demonstrated both the need for Black colleges to play noncollege opponents and the desire of all collegiate basketball teams, Black or White, to make it to New York, which was soon to become the mecca of the sport.

New York University, City College of New York, and Brooklyn's St. John's College, for example, all launched incredibly strong programs during the same period as the nascent development of HBCU basketball.

NYU won the AAU national championship tournament in 1920, one reporter watching the contests calling the Violets' star player, Howard Cann, "the greatest basketball player in the world." Toward the end of the decade, it was the Redmen of St. John's who dominated, losing only three games from 1929 to 1931 and earning from the media the nickname Wonder Five, taken from Indiana's Franklin teams. St. John's didn't build one of the massive new arenas that universities were dedicating to the game. Instead, the team played its home games in a local dance hall. There were, however, other venues in the city.

On January 21, 1931, New York mayor James J. Walker decided to host three collegiate basketball games in Madison Square Garden to raise money for unemployment relief. It was the second full year of the Great Depression; unemployment was skyrocketing; individual need was outpacing the government's ability to meet it. Walker had already sponsored a charity college football game at the venue and now turned to the city's other popular collegiate sport for help. All of New York's major programs would participate. Columbia defeated Fordham, Manhattan College beat NYU, and St. John's took the finale against The City College of New York (CCNY).

The Madison Square Garden in which they played was the third of four incarnations of the venue. The first was built in 1879 and leased to showman P. T. Barnum. That original structure did not have a roof and proved vulnerable to weather, so in 1890, Barnum teamed with robber barons like J. P. Morgan, Andrew Carnegie, and others to hire architect Stanford White to design a new Garden. It was a large, expansive venue, but proved, like the first version, to be a financial failure. In 1925, a third Madison Square Garden opened at 8th Avenue and 50th Street, designed by Thomas Lamb and financed almost in its entirety by Tex Rickard.

Rickard was one of the most prominent sports promoters in the country, focusing most of his attention on boxing. He "first recognized the potential of the star system," according to Frank Deford, and through much of the 1920s Rickard spent his time promoting one of the biggest stars of the age, Jack Dempsey. Born to a poor Colorado family, Dempsey originally fought in bars for small wages. His name was made by his fierce fighting and his popular persona, but more than anything, his name was made because of Rickard, who created a public image of Dempsey as "Jack the Giant Killer." Dempsey was just over six feet tall and 190 pounds. When he fought Jess Willard, six inches taller and more than fifty pounds heavier, in 1919, Rickard played up the name after Dempsey's third-round knockout. In 1926, the year after opening his Madison Square Garden, Rickard staged the "Battle of the Century" between Dempsey and Gene Tunney in Philadelphia. There were 120,757 fans in attendance; several million others listened on the radio. It was the largest civic gathering in American history up to that point. But the pinnacle of Rickard's promotional career came with the rematch, the second "Battle of the Century" in 1927. This time, more than 140,000 showed up at Soldier Field in Chicago. An estimated fifty million Americans heard the radio broadcast. Before the second Dempsey-Tunney fight, no boxing match had ever exceeded more than $300,000 in gate receipts. The 1927 receipts exceeded $2 million.

That year, back in Philadelphia, a new cathedral of college basketball was completed, pushed by the growth of the college game and the success of sports spectacles more broadly. The Palestra was constructed on the campus of the University of Pennsylvania, a showcase facility seating almost ten thousand fans in 1927 and designed specifically for the new game. Penn would open the facility to professional and collegiate contests, and eventually the Palestra would host all the contests between the Big Five schools in the city—Saint Joseph's, Temple, La Salle, and Villanova—joining Penn in games against one another hosted in the facility. Then there would be NCAA tournament games, professional contests, exhibitions. College basketball had its own showcase venue.

It was that kind of success, playing on the potential provided by the economic windfall of the 1920s, that drove Rickard's efforts with the new Madison Square Garden, though unlike the Palestra, the Garden featured more than just basketball. The venue also hosted hockey. Rickard would go on to organize the New York Rangers hockey club to fill dates. But boxing and hockey still left many available times for other sports to use the new space, and on January 21, 1931, college basketball became one of them. The mayor's charity triple-header was a financial success. Sixteen thousand spectators attended, bringing in more than $20,000 in net revenue. But the fans left frustrated, as St. John's defeat of CCNY was facilitated by slowing down the pace of the game, holding the ball over the entire court, and keeping it out of the hands of the defenders. It was a decidedly different style compared to the up-tempo play of the pros, and one that dissatisfied many New Yorkers emerging from a decade that celebrated the improvisational style of jazz and teams like the Rens.

It was a seminal moment, a point of no return for the college game. To fix the problem, rule changes created a center line and gave offenses ten seconds to bring the ball up the court. In 1935, offensive players were only given three seconds to remain in the foul lane. Winning was no longer enough. Games couldn't just be competitive; they had to be entertaining.

One of those assisting in the promotion of the Garden triple-header was a New York *World-Telegram* sports reporter and part-time promoter, Ned Irish, who saw in the event new possibilities for college basketball. He made several stunted attempts at promotion in the New York area in the coming years, but finally found success in 1934, when he reserved the Garden for six dates during the 1934–1935 season. He had to guarantee the rental fee and provide the finances for a portable floor, but it was an investment that would pay. In the run-up to his first late December date, the work he was putting in took a toll on his job at the *World-Telegram*. "You'd better decide whether you want to be a promoter or a sportswriter," his editor told him. It was not a difficult decision for the aspirational Irish.

"Metropolitan college basketball will step out of its cramped gymnasiums and gloomy armories tonight into the bright lights and spaciousness of Madison Square Garden," announced the New York *Herald-Tribune*, "for the first of a series of six doubleheaders arranged in the hope of proving this winter that the sport deserves and will thrive in a major league setting." Irish hoped that games between St. John's and Pennsylvania's Westminster College and NYU and Notre Dame would bring in ten thousand paying customers, but they brought more than sixteen thousand. "College basketball made its big-time debut in Madison Square Garden last night," wrote the New York *Daily News*, "and scored a smashing success."

Irish's second Garden doubleheader occurred one week later, and this time included Adolph Rupp's team from the University of Kentucky. The 1931–1932 Kentucky squad would go on to win the first of what would become myriad conference championships under Rupp, and they did so with a more up-tempo style than plodding St. John's. The popularity that accrued to them as a result ensured that even though Kentucky lost that first Garden contest to NYU on a controversial late foul call, the team would continue to return when invited to what was quickly becoming the showcase of college basketball.

And they would in the coming seasons have a new local challenger, Long Island University (LIU). Not a traditional power in the city, LIU didn't even have its own gymnasium, playing home games at the facility of the Brooklyn College of Pharmacy. But the team known as the Blackbirds began to change its reputation in 1932 after hiring an ambitious and innovative new coach from West Virginia, Clair Bee. From early 1935 to late 1936, spanning three separate seasons, Bee's LIU teams amassed a forty-three-game winning streak, one that only ended at another of Irish's Madison Square Garden epics. In late December 1936, LIU faced Stanford, which featured one of the most celebrated collegiate players of the decade, Hank Luisetti, who wowed audiences by dribbling behind his back and shooting with only one hand. Luisetti dominated LIU from his forward position on both offense and defense. When he left the game with thirty seconds left in the contest, a comfortable victory assured, the Garden's overflow crowd gave the visitor a standing ovation.

Luisetti's performances helped change the college game, playing into the desire of promoters to speed up the often plodding contests. One of the principal barriers to faster play was a rule that required a jump ball at center court after every made basket. After that 1936–1937 season and Luisetti's dominance of it, basketball officials eliminated the rule. It meant more actual game action, but it also meant more points. The college basketball clock was kept running after made baskets, meaning that a disproportionate amount of game time was wasted in setting up new center jumps after scores. By allowing the defending team to take the ball immediately after their opponents scored, more actual playing time meant more opportunities for points and more action for the paying customers.

Scores began rising, and with them attendance at college games. Ned Irish realized that the growing popularity presented a real opportunity to leverage the prestige of Madison Square Garden to create a tournament that would decide an undisputed national champion. In the winter of 1938, he convinced the Metropolitan Basketball Writers Association to sponsor a tournament that they described as the "Rose Bowl" of basketball. Six teams would play in the first National Invitation Tournament (NIT), with Temple winning its first title. Perhaps even more importantly, the tournament was a financial success. The health of amateur basketball was now unquestionably determined by money. Perhaps fittingly, James Naismith died the following year.

But as he died, the organization born to regulate his amateur game, the NCAA, decided that it could replicate Irish's NIT and cash in on the collegiate game's new popularity. The association staged its first national tournament in 1939 at Northwestern University. The University of Oregon took the title.

The following season witnessed yet another milestone in the college game's growth, as one of Irish's Madison Square Garden doubleheaders on February 28, 1940, was televised on W2XBS. The first television sports broadcast had taken place two years earlier, but it was still a technology in its infancy. The picture failed several times during the broadcast, and most families didn't have television sets anyway, but it would set a precedent for the next major avenue for profitability and popularity. The only real threat to the seemingly limitless possibilities for the game would be some kind of calamity from outside the bounds of its established structure.

And then calamity came. On December 7, 1941, Japan bombed Pearl Harbor, destroying much of the Pacific fleet, killing more than 2,200 Americans, and taking the United States and many of its college-age athletes to war. Still, the game survived, schedules were played, and both NIT and NCAA tournaments continued, the game dominated in the war years by teams like the Whiz Kids of the University of Illinois and the Blitz Kids of the University of Utah. And then there were the big men, as height and size became the standard during the war years. Those players outside of the military draft's height and weight requirements were left to dominate a different field of battle.

George Mikan, who would be so instrumental in the evolution of the professional game, would have a similar influence for the college game. He entered DePaul University for the 1942–1943 season, an awkward, nearsighted, six-foot, ten-inch freshman who would grow into the most dominant player of the era. His only real rival was another big man, seven-foot Bob Kurland, who enrolled at Oklahoma A&M the same year Mikan joined DePaul. Both Mikan and Kurland would rule over a limited talent pool during the years of World War II, helping to springboard the careers of their coaches, DePaul's Ray Meyer and Oklahoma A&M's

Henry "Hank" Iba. Their dominance would not only drive the success of their programs and coaches, it would fundamentally alter the rules of the game. Their ability to block the shots of shorter players near the rim led to the creation of a goaltending rule. Kansas's Phog Allen was so worried about the rise of towering centers that he suggested raising the goals to twelve feet and even tried it in a game against New Mexico State, a team that featured its own big man, seven-foot, one-inch Elmore Merganthaler, who destroyed the Jayhawks with forty-one points. The tallest players would remain the tallest players no matter how high the baskets were.

And so Mikan and Kurland would tower over the sport. In their junior seasons during the final year of World War II, Kurland's Oklahoma A&M Aggies won the NCAA tournament and Mikan's DePaul Blue Demons won the NIT tournament. During the war years, the winners of the two tournaments played a charity game in Madison Square Garden to benefit the Red Cross's war effort. In the last of those Red Cross championships, Mikan's team defeated Kurland's in a showcase of what a game dominated by height had become. The following year, with all the veterans back on campus and college teams at full strength, Mikan led the nation by averaging 23 points per game and Kurland scored 643 points, more than any college player had ever scored in one season, leading his team to a second consecutive NCAA Championship.

The game had forever changed, traveling far from Stagg's University of Chicago dynasties of the 1890s. The big men now dominated, but so, too, did spectacle and profit, and the money that the muscular Christians always feared would corrupt the game would soon bring the edifice of men's college basketball to its knees.

Men, however, weren't the only ones playing.

5

The Growth of the Women's Game

Less than a year after Naismith invented his new game in Springfield in 1891, the director of physical culture at Smith College just twenty miles north led her students in one of the first women's basketball games. Berenson was a Jewish immigrant from Lithuania who came to the country as a child. Constantly ill in her youth, Berenson turned to physical education as a remedy and would dedicate her life to the field. After reading an article by Naismith, she was convinced that basketball could be adapted for women's physical fitness, despite early worries that her charges could suffer "nervous fatigue" from hard play. Hers was a similar evangelism to that of the muscular Christians, but her version of the evolutionary theory of play was one that included reforms to include women in such Victorian betterment projects.

At the same time, Clara Baer took on a similar role at Newcomb College in New Orleans, and, though it took several years to impress upon students and parents the value of such athletic endeavors, the women began playing in 1895. Baer, a New Orleans native, was also a sickly child who believed in active play to remedy the body. In her version of the game, women remained in predetermined zones on the court and didn't dribble or guard. The early contests at women's colleges were intramural and emphasized the exercise value of the game over and against its overt competitiveness. At other coeducational schools, however, some real attempts at competition did make an appearance.

On April 4, 1896, women's teams from Stanford and the University of California, Berkeley, played the first intercollegiate game in a San Francisco armory before an audience of more than seven hundred. The *San Francisco Chronicle* was less charitable, claiming that "the girls [Berkeley] depended upon to score for them missed the basket repeatedly." But even the skeptical paper was impressed with the contest: "There is not an instant of ennui in basket ball. All is motion, change, excitement." After Agnes Morley made a "long, fine straight throw clean from the shoulder," Stanford won the contest 2–1, returning to campus to throngs of exultant male students. As reporter Mabel Craft explained in her story on the game, basketball "wasn't invented for girls, and there isn't anything effeminate about it. It was made for men to play indoors and it is a game that would send the physician who thinks the feminine organization 'so delicate,' into the hysterics he tries so hard to perpetuate."

Inherent in Craft's description was a broader critique of the patriarchal system that made such contests so rare. For most of the nineteenth century, relations between the sexes were dominated by "separate spheres." The male sphere was work, politics, and public events; the female sphere was domesticity, moral education, and child rearing. Women in politics, women working outside of the home, or women having pleasurable sex were all considered unnatural. This doctrine of separate spheres increasingly frustrated women who were more educated and wanted to work and experience more of the wider world. After the Civil War, some women adopted the new consumerism to make their lives better. New books and magazines taught women how to properly furnish the middle-class home. Women ventured outside the house and began shopping at downtown department stores, which provided a place to meet outside the confines of the home.

Women also began spending less time with childcare. School enrollment began to rise. The kindergarten movement brought children to school at an earlier age than ever before, and a growing number of high schools kept teenagers out of the house for more years than before. And these new education initiatives dramatically affected the girls as well. Between 1870 and 1900, the number of female high school graduates went from 9,000 to 57,000. In the 1870s and 1880s, the nation's premier women's colleges—Barnard, Wellesley, Smith, Bryn Mawr, and Radcliffe—were founded to take advantage of that rise. The number of female college graduates from 1870 to 1900 rose from 1,378 to 5,237.

And physical education was a decidedly important part of the educational regime at the new schools. The calisthenics of the antebellum era gave way to actual competitive games for women who chose to attend the new and growing women's colleges. Swimming, tennis, and basketball all gave the students new outlets for their competitiveness and creativity. Of course, male commentary was split. Some thought that strenuous female activity damaged a woman's internal organs, making them barren through continued exercise and play. Others, usually women pushing back against such assumptions, argued that the strength gained from sports gave women a leg up in the new job markets that were opening for them. They also trumpeted athletic endeavor as a way for women to escape the domestic sphere.

The 1890s were the age of the New Woman. In the immediate wake of the Civil War, the ideal woman as presented in magazines—all published by men—was a plump, round-faced woman with rich, gaudy dresses. The New Woman, made famous by the magazine illustrations of Charles Dana Gibson, was tall, slender, and athletic. She dressed practically, not ornately. Women in the last decade of the nineteenth century were working, playing in public, and dressing less and less like ladies. They would play sports, too, as intercollegiate games like that between Stanford and Berkeley attested.

The coach of that Stanford team was Clelia Mosher, a Stanford graduate from New York who, like Berenson and Baer, grew up with a variety of ailments and overcame them through calisthenics and sports. In that first intercollegiate game and in the bulk of her life, Mosher advocated for women's athletic ability and against the dominant male assumptions of frailty and hysterics described by Craft. Corsets and other social standards for women created many of the outward examples of that assumed frailty, she argued in her master's thesis at Johns Hopkins, demonstrating that without such clothing, women's assumed physical inferiority to men dissipated. Her later work on menstruation argued that physical exercise could reduce the pain of menstrual cramping. "Born into a world of unlimited opportunity, the woman of the rising generation will answer the question of what woman's real capacities are," she wrote in 1923. "She will have physical, economic, racial and civic freedom. What will she do with it?"

Mosher was not alone in her efforts to create sustained programs of physical education for women, nor in encouraging intercollegiate competition. Later in April, two weeks after the Stanford–Berkeley contest, the University of Washington played Ellensburg State Normal College in

another contest. In 1898, the University of Nevada played Oakland, California's Mills College. Unlike the men's intercollegiate game, which largely
developed in the northeast before spreading south and west, the women's
intercollegiate game began in the west before migrating across the country.

It was a phenomenon fed by cultural movements outside of sports.
In 1890, suffragists formed a new organization, the National American
Woman Suffrage Association (NAWSA), led by Elizabeth Cady Stan-
ton and Susan B. Anthony, reinvigorating the fight for women's right to
vote. That same year, Wyoming became a state and became the first state
to grant women the franchise. Colorado did the same in 1893. Idaho and
Utah followed in 1896. The impetus for women's voting was emanating from western states simultaneous to basketball's expansion. Significantly, however, the female franchise was not borne of an implicit western belief in the inherent equality of women. Instead, the men making
such decisions reasoned that women were gentler and more nurturing
than their male counterparts, which would tame and civilize the votes of
rugged and often lawless frontier men. NAWSA followed suit, making a
case for women's suffrage based on unique female attributes rather than
inherent gender equality.

Basketball seemed to give lie to such claims, as the game those women
played proved every bit as rugged and competitive as that of their male
counterparts. In describing a Berkeley defeat of Nevada, Craft explained
that "the athletic girls from the Berkeley hills proved that if the young
men can seldom win at anything, the girls at least are capable of uphold-
ing the college honor." It was a pointed statement for a reason, foreshadowing the gendered problems in the game to come. The male athletes at
Berkeley had voted not to allow female athletes to receive varsity letters,
despite the fact that the women's team was so much more successful than
their own.

Some women, however, also worried over female play. "There is
an irresistible temptation when a ball is rolling along the floor for the
players in the vicinity to go sliding after it," complained another physical educator, Agnes Childs, "and nothing makes a game more rowdyish
in appearance and causes more adverse criticism than this most natural
temptation to go after the ball by the quickest means." Berenson herself
worried about women gaining "dangerous nervous tendencies and losing
the grace and dignity and self respect we would all have her foster."

The University of Illinois actually developed its women's team before it created one for the men. It was female students who first played on campus in the late 1890s, drawing male spectators and turning the games into makeshift parties that worried the administration. The resulting ban was only lifted in 1903, when women's basketball returned more formally. A men's team was formed two years later to compete in the new Western Conference.

In 1899, Stanford was witness to a similar gendered retrenchment, as its faculty athletic committee disbanded women's athletic competition "for the purpose of guarding the health of the individual player." The team, however, kept playing, forming a club technically independent of the university, and taking on its schedule. Stanford reinstated its women's basketball program five years later.

All of the women in those early western collegiate contests were White, but the impetus to play basketball was not confined to one race. Just as Carlisle and Haskell served to create Native teams that thrived despite the colonizing mission of such schools, Montana's Fort Shaw Government Indian Boarding School did much the same for its women's team, which even competed in a series of exhibitions at the St. Louis Olympic Games in 1904. Native American play demonstrated the seeming solidity of the game's popularity in the west.

These early successes, however, did not produce the kind of rapid growth witnessed by men's basketball. Berenson, Mosher, and other women's physical educators still hewed to the arguments of groups like the NAWSA, the arguments that won women the right to vote in western states. Agnes Wayman proposed "neatly combed hair" for all players, along with "no gum chewing or slang, never calling each other by last names and never laying or sitting down on the floor." Living up to Wayman's standard, Berenson responded by creating a set of rules for the women's game decidedly different than those of the men.

Under Berenson's rubric, the court was divided into three sections, with forwards nearest the opponent's basket, centers patrolling the middle section, and guards defending their own basket. When five players participated, there were two forwards, one center, and two guards, but up to ten players per team could play at any one time. None of them, however, were allowed to leave their particular section of the court. There was no physical contact, and players could only dribble three times during a given possession, creating a game that one observer described as "a slow almost stately game with careful passing and deliberate shot selection from an almost statuelike pose." Berenson's rules would dominate after she published them in *Spalding's Athletic Library*, and women's basketball would take the three-zone format until the 1930s.

Most importantly, physical educators like Berenson, Childs, and others argued against female competition. Sports were identified with men and manliness. So, when women played sports, they were going to call attention to the physical differences between the sexes, but also to the cultural constructions of femininity and masculinity. It was an NAWSA mindset, one that proposed female difference not as a sign of inferiority but as one that could ultimately generate equal treatment. Women, Berenson argued, "need, therefore, all the more to develop health and endurance if they desire to become candidates for equal wages."

The real conduits that allowed female sports to develop were schools such as the Sargent School, founded in 1881, and the Boston Normal School of Gymnastics, founded in 1889, which groomed female physical education teachers in much the same way that Springfield did for men. As Boston Normal's Nils Posse explained in 1903, women's athletics served to "develop the body into a harmonious whole under the perfect control of the will. It is not to produce great bulk of muscle, but to cause that already present to respond readily to volition." School founder Dudley Sargent, echoing the social Darwinism and eugenic thinking of the age, argued that such developed bodies "tend to inspire admiration in the opposite sex and therefore play an important part in what is termed 'sexual selection.'" There was, in other words, a specifically gendered determinist role for sports to play in the development of the human race. Graduates from schools like Sargent and Boston Normal, then, took such thinking into physical education departments at colleges and high schools across the country.

Upper class women's games like archery, croquet, tennis, and golf were all individual sports that fit within that rigid rubric by not requiring much brute masculinity. They could be played behind the walls of a private club. They were, therefore, perfect entrees into sports for women. As early as 1875, the Ladies' Club of Staten Island was founded, with women's tennis as its bedrock activity. The club sponsored tournaments and other events. Within a decade, it had more than two hundred members.

Fitting the evolutionary ideal, however, the games reinforced gender differences rather than breaking them down. Women generally played in full-length dresses, wore corsets, and played with discretion. A woman would never, for example, place a croquet mallet between her legs to get a more effective shot. She wouldn't smash overhand winners in tennis. And she wouldn't push against her opponent in basketball.

The apotheosis of this gendered sporting ideal was bicycling, which, along with basketball, served to break women's sports out of the cloister of the upper-class clubs. Bicycling got middle-class women not associated with colleges or women's clubs out of the house; it gave them an acceptable form of physical expression and promoted the wearing of more comfortable, functional skirts. Just as with basketball, however, there were critics. Cycling might lure young women away from the home and its duties; it might lead them to remote spots alone with men where they might succumb to seduction. It might stimulate the genitals, resulting in equally unimaginable horrors.

The first woman to really take advantage of the new opportunity provided by sports in a decidedly public way was Eleanora Sears, who won four national women's doubles tennis championships, a mixed doubles championship, and a national women's squash championship. She swam, raced cars, and flew planes. But when she tried to play polo with men, she was rebuffed by both men's and women's groups. People who had been conditioned by basketball debates simply weren't ready for that. In 1898, reformer Charlotte Perkins Gilman said, "Even today, when athletics are fast opening to women, when tennis and golf and the rest are possible to them, the two sexes are far from even in chances to play."

Butting up against that lack of chances, the new physical education teachers began realizing that girls in their charge often preferred competitive sports to exercising, and the sport they played most was basketball. Class teams, physical education class participation, and even varsity basketball dominated women's college athletics in the late nineteenth and early twentieth centuries. It dominated even more at the high school level. Prior to 1925, more than half of the states scheduled high school championships for girls. But the game's popularity would leave it open for criticism. Basketball grew women's muscles, and thereby reduced the differences in body shapes between men and women. It could, in a familiar refrain, damage the reproductive organs. Most importantly, it could unleash uncontrollable passions that women would be unable to process. Players were bouncing and jumping and rubbing up against one another. There was inherent in the critique a charge that basketball would turn women into lesbians. As such critiques grew louder, reports across the country told of young men being caught peeking into gymnasium windows, even using binoculars, all to see women playing basketball. Whether it was hetero or homo, basketball was a danger because it was a conduit of lust.

And so, Berenson's modified rules system for women would answer for such potential dangers. Men's rules, she argued, encouraged too much roughness, too much physical and emotional exertion. The physical exertion could be mitigated by divided courts, the emotional exertion by discouraging the kinds of rivalries that drove the game's early development. It made intercollegiate competition exceedingly rare in the first decades of the twentieth century. Men were banned from attending games and female physical educators cordoned off spaces in coeducational schools for women's sports. Anna Hiss at the University of Texas, for example, built a basketball court shorter than the standard men's court specifically to ensure that the men's team would not co-opt a space reserved for women.

Cordoning off a space specifically for women's sports only helped it grow, particularly in the 1920s, when the acquisitive culture of marketing and celebrities exacerbated interest in all sports. The decade began with the payoff on the work of almost a century, but reignited by the creation of NAWSA in 1890, as women first earned the right to vote. That new empowerment was represented in sports, as well. Suzanne Lenglen of France, for example, dominated women's tennis from 1919 to 1927. She was followed by American Helen Wills, who dominated from the mid-1920s to the mid-1930s. They were both beloved. Both incredibly successful. But they were undeniably different.

Lenglen was tennis's version of the flapper. She exposed more of her body than any women's tennis star to date. She was athletic and graceful. She was uninhibited. She was sexy and flaunted her sexuality. "I just throw dignity to the winds," she said, "and think of nothing but the game." By contrast, Helen Wills was far less daring. She wore pigtails and was very mild and placid. She was a reassuring, all-American, wholesome girl. While she clearly worked hard on the court, off of it she was the picture of feminine grace. The American conception of women's sports in this era had room for both of these depictions of athletic womanhood, and basketball would merge them in a more physical team game.

But it was not the only game. Swimming, too, produced females in the hero-culture mold. In 1924, Sybil Bauer broke the men's world record in the backstroke. In 1926, Gertrude Ederle became the sixth person to swim the English Channel. Ederle was from a working-class, ethnic background. When she rose from nothing to become the first female to swim the Channel, she became a celebrity. She was given a massive ticker-tape parade in New York. People wrote songs about her. She was lauded in every media outlet in the country.

What made Ederle so famous, though, was her perfect blend of everything people, and men in particular, were looking for in their women, in their athletes, and in their heroes. Ederle's mother always said that she got her athletic prowess from doing household chores. She preferred sewing and cooking to drinking and partying. She was also defending American honor overseas. "It was for my flag that I swam," she said. Not only did she swim the Channel, she beat the best men's time by two hours, helping dispel the idea of women being the "weaker sex." She was, in a way, a mix of Lenglen and Wills.

And then, following Ederle, came the most dominant and successful woman athlete of the twentieth century: Mildred Ella "Babe" Didrikson. Didrikson grew up in Beaumont, Texas, the child of immigrants. Texas working-class culture had far fewer strictures on what girls could and couldn't do than did other parts of the country, and Babe always participated with the boys in local games. She also played all the high school sports available to girls. In 1930, she was hired by the Employers Casualty Company as a ringer for its semipro basketball team. It also sponsored her at the women's Amateur Athletic Union (AAU) track and field championships in 1932. In three hours at that meet, she won six gold medals and broke four world records. She broke three more in the Olympics later that summer. Like the sports heroes who came before her, Didrikson tried to capitalize on her stardom, but those avenues weren't as available to women as they were to men. She traveled around the country putting on athletic exhibitions and making personal appearances. She played in inter-sex basketball games. In 1935, she pitched in spring training games for several Major League Baseball teams before touring with the House of David. In the late 1930s she became a professional golfer, where she had no equal. She won thirty-four of the eighty-eight tournaments she entered.

Babe was incredibly popular, but she was also predictably criticized for blurring gender lines. One of her critics, Paul Gallico, called her a "muscle moll" and argued that she "never wore make-up," she "shingled her hair until it was as short as a boy's," and she "despised silk underthings as being sissy." Didrikson responded. In 1938, she married professional wrestler George Zaharias and cultivated a more feminine image in her later years, less because of an innate desire to do so and more because public pressure left her little choice.

As Didrikson's career illustrated, much of the opportunity for women in sports came from commercial and industrial concerns. From the 1920s to the 1940s, assorted industries offered sports to all interested female employees, contests organized under the auspices of the AAU, which began sanctioning women's swimming in 1916, track in 1924, and basketball in 1926. Corporate teams like that of Employers Casualty began in the early twentieth century for both men and women as a way to make better and more loyal employees. "Players have come to realize that it is teamwork that counts in the end, and they have coordinated their effort on the basketball court and in their daily tasks," said the president of the Southern Textile Athletic Association in 1929. "They realize to become efficient they must know their job, and must be able to get along with their associates and know how to accomplish the best results by working with them." There were, however, other motivations behind the trend. For the most talented female athletes, company teams traveled around playing semiprofessional basketball games as a way of advertising the company. They were not technically paid for basketball but instead for other jobs they did for their firms. Employers Casualty, for example, fielded a successful team that featured its athletes in skimpy outfits. Their average game attendance was 5,000.

That success, built in some measure on more revealing outfits than previous generations were able to wear, would lead critics like Gallico to again judge women on their appearance rather than their skill. Demonstrating the hypocrisy of the male gaze, when women wore restrictive clothing, men worried that their play would turn them into lesbians; when their clothing expanded their motion and made them better players, men judged those not within the bounds of the male conception of feminine beauty to be potential lesbians. It was a double standard that would dog the women's game for decades.

Still, all of the success bred by the new competition was opening doors for women. The Olympics, for example, based largely on international pressure, featured a separate Women's Olympic Games in Paris in 1922, then developed a five-event track program for women at the 1928 Olympics. But not all women were pleased by the turn.

Physical education teachers like Berenson and Baer resented what they saw as a takeover by the AAU. They were professionals; they had been trained specifically to help women with athletic concerns, and they knew what was best for those they trained. Women's physical educators launched an all-out assault on the AAU, Olympic officials, and others. They founded the Committee on Women's Athletics in 1917. They founded the National Amateur Athletic Foundation in 1922, whose Women's Division comprised leaders in women's education, the Girl Scouts, the YWCA, and other women's clubs. Women's athletics, the Women's Division argued, "should be protected from exploitation of the enjoyment of the spectator, the athletic reputation, or the commercial advantage of any school or organization." The group explained that "individual accomplishment and the winning of championships" should be subordinated to universal participation. Women's sports, they claimed, in the tradition of NAWSA, were fundamentally different than men's sports and therefore should have different goals. Highly competitive sports like those played by men were missing the point of women's athletics. It was an argument typical of those under the broader scope of the YWCA, the women's version of the YMCA, defending an amateurism that emphasized the making of muscular Christians over and against active competition.

Of course, though the battle would continue through the 1920s, 1930s, and 1940s, physical educators would never be able to conquer the AAU. Women's competitive sports were becoming a business. And when they did, competition would always win out.

Competition, however, was not a Whites-only endeavor. African American high schools and universities joined local community teams in fostering the women's game, and while there was always a social, moral, and athletic benefit to such play, Black women, who had been left out of so many White conceptions of Victorian morality, were free to engage in competition without a consistent refrain of social Darwinian inappropriateness. Club teams like the Germantown YMCA Hornets and the Tribunes, sponsored by the Black newspaper the *Philadelphia Tribune*, not only dominated in their Philadelphia hometown but also drew crowds up and down the Atlantic seaboard, sometimes even outdrawing professional male counterparts like the Rens. Without an established network of such club teams, teams like the Hornets and the Tribunes played local high school and college squads, and they too would have a dramatic impact.

Private colleges like North Carolina's Bennett and public institutions like Alabama's Tuskegee Institute fielded powerful teams in the 1930s and 1940s, but had their own appropriateness standards that would shape the politics of the women who played for them. The administrators of historically Black colleges and universities were notoriously authoritarian, instilling a middle-class ethic in their students and projecting that image to White sources of funding, be they private or public. Their goal was not to rock too many racial boats, and that imperative included the behavior of its female athletes. "If you in any way showed any sign of not following instructions, and so forth, he would bench you," one Bennett player said of her coach. "He would call you off that team and sit you down for a while. Until you would straighten yourself out." It was the same in Alabama. "Tuskegee kind of came up under the old tradition of 'ladies had to sit a certain way,'" remembered one player. "I had to sit straight up, head up, hair had to be groomed at all times. Your body had to be groomed. . . . You had to have on stockings and shoes at all times."

The teams produced a variety of stars. Ora Washington was one of the most successful basketball players of the 1930s, as was Tuskegee's Alice Coachman and Bennett's Ruth Glover. But there would always be an artificial ceiling to their wider popularity. Washington, for example, was also one of the leading Black tennis players in the American Tennis Association (ATA), along with players like Lulu Ballard and Isadora Channels. But players from the Black ATA were barred from playing in the White United States Lawn Tennis Association, so Washington never had the opportunity to play against stars like Suzanne Lengelen or Helen Wills. Similarly, championship basketball sponsored by the AAU was dominated by White southern teams, and thus discouraged Black women's teams from participating. Despite the fact that the AAU's track and field tournaments were integrated, and despite the success of teams like the Rens and the Globetrotters in world championship tournaments that included both White and Black teams, African American women did not have the same opportunities.

Those tournaments, however, despite their racial exclusivity, did have an enormous impact on the women's game writ large. The AAU's national women's tournament only grew from its original incarnation in 1926. The gendered double standard was still part of the event, and a beauty pageant even accompanied the festivities, but the teams who played vied for what was roundly considered to be the national championship; its all-tournament selections were the equivalent of the men's All-Americans.

In the early 1940s, the AAU ranks swelled with teams from wartime production industries who employed women at record rates. As the demand for industrial supply rose, so did hiring. Initially, those jobs were almost uniformly filled by White males. But as the White males continued to be sent to Europe, the labor force began to change dramatically. Women became welders, shipbuilders, lumberjacks, and miners. Married women, barred by many states during the Great Depression from taking jobs, were allowed back into the workforce. Women's work caused more and more people to begin discussing gender equality in the United States. More than 350,000 women volunteered for military service during World War II, leading the government to establish a women's corps for each branch of the military. That work and the service of women, in turn, led to new discussions of the Equal Rights Amendment, originally proposed in 1923. Though it wasn't passed, it demonstrated a changing status for women in society, one that would bleed over into sports.

Just prior to the war, for example, working-class women began playing the new sport of softball, a game that, like working women more broadly, took on a more masculine image as the war years continued. "Give 'em a cud of tobacco," wrote Robert Yoder in the *Saturday Evening Post* in 1943, "and these softball players would look just like their big-league brothers." That made the transition easy for Philip K. Wrigley, chewing gum magnate and owner of the Chicago Cubs, when he responded to fears that Major League Baseball might shut down during World War II by organizing the All-American Girls Softball League in 1943. Two years later, the organization changed its name to the All-American Girls Baseball League. Its 108-game schedule attracted 176,000 spectators in its first season. At the peak of its popularity, it attracted nearly one million fans per year. Like its basketball counterpart, the league clearly played up the femininity of its players. "The more feminine the appearance of the performer, the more dramatic the performance," said Arthur Meyerhoff, the league's operator. Short skirts were mandatory. Players had to attend charm school. Playing predominantly in medium-sized Midwestern cities, the league lasted until 1954.

It was a phenomenon that demonstrated the full possibility of the drawing power of women's sports, and as Wrigley was forming his league, the AAU was also taking advantage of women's work and the basketball teams attached to those industries. The AAU championships during the war years were dominated by the Vultee Bomberettes, playing for the Vultee Aircraft Corporation in Nashville. Many of the leading players joined the firm, drilling, cutting, and riveting parts for military aircraft. Alline Banks, Margaret Sexton, Doris Weems, and other players won the championship in 1944 and again in 1945. Banks was the consensus best player of her generation. In three consecutive AAU championship tournaments, Banks outscored the combined total of her team's opponents. She was the tournament's most valuable player seven times. She won championships with three different teams. "On the basketball court she follows no set plan, has no particular style of shooting," chronicled one amazed reporter. Banks "just gets the ball into the basket with whatever type shot comes into her mind as she gets ready to make it."

After the conclusion of World War II, Banks's Bomberettes were replaced as the dominant team by another southern outfit, Hanes Hosiery, part of a glut of teams from regional textile mills that had

been playing competitive basketball since the creation of the Southern Textile Association Basketball Tournament in 1920. Led by players like Jimmie Vaughn, Lurlyne Greer, Eunies "Eunie" Futch, and
Eckie Jordan, the Hanes Hosiery Girls set the pace for women's basketball through the 1940s and into the early 1950s, the team finally
disbanding in 1954.

That year was steeped in the long shadow of *Brown v. Board of Education*. The following year would not only witness *Brown II*, but also
the murder of Emmett Till and the onset of the Montgomery bus boycott. Times were changing, and they were changing in women's basketball, as well. In 1955, during all of the racial tumult surrounding
them, the AAU invited a team from Little Rock, Arkansas's Philan-
der Smith College to participate in its annual tournament. The first
historically Black college to play in the event earned its place by winning the South Central Athletic Conference title. The team advanced
to the quarterfinals before being eliminated, but its presence and its
competitiveness gave lie to the myth of White superiority, even if it
didn't usher in a broader integrationist movement among the tournament organizers.

The team that won that 1955 tournament came from Wayland
Baptist College in Plainview, Texas. Wayland's team was the first
collegiate winner of the tournament and would signal a shift from
company teams to full collegiate dominance. The rest of the 1950s
and most of the 1960s were dominated by Wayland and another collegiate squad from the Nashville Business College, led by Nera White.
"I coached two Olympic teams and I've seen the best players in the
world," remembered legendary Sue Gunter. "Nera White is the best
of them all. She is the greatest of all time." Still, White suffered the
same kinds of criticisms launched at earlier stars like Babe Didrikson,
the gendered double standard not changing with other modifications
and progressions in the women's game.

There were, however, real and consequential progressions. Just
prior to World War II, many players decided, like their male counterparts, to leave amateur basketball for the ranks of the professionals.
Because it was a relatively small group without league organization,
the players barnstormed throughout the country, taking on a variety
of amateur women's teams and other professional men's teams to earn

their living. The two who dominated in those early days of professional play were the All-American Redheads and Hazel Walker's
Arkansas Travelers. The Redheads, unsurprisingly, dyed their hair
red as an organizing gimmick and often engaged in comic routines
to draw fans to the arena. The Travelers were led by Walker, one of
the most accomplished players of the period. Like their compatriots
playing women's professional baseball, professional basketball players
constantly came into conflict with a series of gendered double standards. One argued that women should not be professional athletes,
another that they shouldn't be spending their time traveling around
the country without husbands in tow. Any women who chose that
life, so the reasoning went, must be mannish, "muscle-molls" like
Didrikson or White. In addition to those biases, basketball professionals had to deal with the assumption of many that basketball was not
a professional sport, the ghost of Naismith looming large over beliefs
about the game.

The only way to convince fans that basketball was a legitimate
professional endeavor was to demonstrate the skills of the team. And
to demonstrate feminine comportment when traveling. Teams like
the Redheads and the Travelers had to play rugged basketball on
the court and observe the politics of gendered respectability off of it.
"We had to act like ladies, and when we came out of the motel room,
we had to be fully dressed," said professional player Doris Coleman.
"Everything had to be perfect."

Professional development in the 1950s and 1960s did not prove emi-
nently stable; the women's game was still dominated by amateur play,
but it had grown substantially from the first contests of the 1890s and
from physical education instructors manning the barricades against
competitive play. More and more colleges were fielding women's
teams, leaving the sport to grow in new directions in the decades to
come. By that point, however, their men's collegiate counterparts had
come out on the other side of a scandal that threatened to destroy all
future university basketball.

6

Midcentury Scandal

IN MARCH 1944, gamblers approached University of Utah coach Vadal Peterson, whose team, the Utes, was scheduled to play in the National Collegiate Athletic Association (NCAA) championship game that season against Dartmouth. They asked Peterson how much it would cost them to convince the Utes to lose the game. An incredulous Peterson didn't respond, and his team would go on to win the championship by 2 points in overtime. But the brashness of the gamblers, the ease of their assumptions about the possibility of throwing games, signaled that the effort was by no means a first. Kansas coach Phog Allen responded to news of the attempt by warning of a coming scandal in a sport that had become associated by many with gambling and its attendant corruption. It would, he predicted, "stink to high heaven."

It was, perhaps, the inevitable consequence of the swift flight from Naismith's original ideal. Competition drove the possibility for profit. In collegiate contests, that profit chiefly redounded to the coaches and universities. In professional games, the players shared in some of the wealth. But there was profit to go around, and fans realized that they, too, could make money on the game so many loved to watch. Meanwhile, college players, who, like the fans, found themselves on the outside looking in on the game's profitability, also sought ways to monetize their relationship to the game. In March 1931, a member of the St. John's Wonder Five was offered $3,000 by a gambler to throw a game against Manhattan College. In one particularly heated contest between New York University (NYU) and The City College of New York (CCNY) in 1934, tickets in the New York market were in such demand that one of the NYU players had to be bailed out of jail so that he could play in the game, as police had arrested him for scalping tickets outside the armory where the teams were playing.

Competitive basketball was early associated with scalping, gambling, and vice, a reality that hurt the game outside of major metropolitan markets and the college towns that dotted the American countryside. New York, in particular, home to schools like NYU and CCNY, became the center of early financial problems in college basketball. Ned Irish's Madison Square Garden doubleheaders, for example, pushed the possibility of corruption. When scheduling his big-ticket events, noted the *New York Herald Tribune*, "he inadvertently also filled in open dates in the business schedule of the betting gentry." One early 1930s contest between NYU and Temple University generated more than $50,000 in bets, the line moving suddenly from 13–5 in favor of Temple to 9–5 against them. "Basketball has been adopted by those unerring feelers of the public pulse, the betting commissioners," worried the *Herald Tribune*. One of Temple's players had fallen ill, but only those in privileged betting positions realized it. It was the kind of potential corruption that would spell problems for the sport in the future, but in the depths of the Great Depression, "there was a new sporting wheel in town," explained historian Larry Fox, "and the world of college basketball was only worried about getting on for the ride."

Originally, gambling on basketball followed a straight betting line, but in the early 1940s bookies realized that providing point spreads gave a greater illusion of potential success and thus increased business. It also meant that manipulating scores to rise and fall around a given spread could guarantee profit for gamblers. And if the players chose to gamble themselves, they could manipulate the total score, guarantee their winnings, and still not sacrifice winning the actual contest. Known as point shaving, the process was in most cases functionally undetectable. To open the players to a willingness to participate in such schemes, high-level gambling operators employed hundreds of members of collegiate varsity teams at summer resorts in the Catskill Mountains. The summer jobs gave the players an income, allowed them to play basketball games against top-level competition in the off season, and solidified their relationships with the gamblers. And they feted players from all over the country, not just from New York. Gambling magnates like Salvatore Sallazzo recruited top players from a variety of different regions whenever they arrived in the city to play games in Madison Square Garden.

The prevalence of such incidents created a bad reputation for the game, and the lack of consequences for the abusers ensured that the behavior would only continue. In 1944, for example, Lenny Hassman, a point-shaving player for CCNY, offered the team's star, Paul Schmones, a bribe to participate in the scheme. Schmones reported the offer to coach Nat Holman, who likewise reported it farther up the university chain. Holman had been one of the early stars of the Original Celtics, and while he dismissed Hassman from the team, the offer wasn't publicized. As historian Albert J. Figone explains, "Exposing a disease that had grown virtually unchecked was outweighed by the unparalleled gate receipts the game was now generating." The unwillingness of university administrators to take more systematic action to curb the problem would continue in the proceeding years. Hassman's dismissal was a Band-Aid on an open wound, both demonstrating the rot that had infected college basketball and ensuring that it would continue.

It was the kind of activity that created a snowball effect, the uncovering of one scandal leading to further discoveries, building upon themselves, revealing themselves to be part of the fabric of the institution itself. In early 1945, later in the same season of Holman's dilemma, two Brooklyn College players were caught during a sting of a fencing operation. Though the officers were not there to investigate basketball fixing, the two players readily admitted to taking $1,000 to divide between themselves and three of their teammates to shave points in a game against Akron scheduled for the Boston Garden. Though the players weren't indicted, three others were convicted and sentenced to one year in prison each.

But then there was the snowball effect. One player who was part of the scandal was discovered to have not actually been enrolled in school while playing for the team. That disclosure led to the realization that a player on CCNY's team had similarly participated without attending classes at the college. The "laxity, indifference and negligence by the faculty," remarked a frustrated Mayor Fiorello LaGuardia, "borders on the unpardonable." Then there was also the seeming indifference and negligence of the organization supposed to police the game.

Prior to 1941, the NCAA's authority had been so limited by its member universities as to make it virtually powerless. The association did make and regulate the playing rules for various sports. It supervised many of the national tournaments, and it served an important titular, figurehead role for the symbolic governing of collegiate athletics. But it did little else. With collegiate athletic recruiting, and the corrupt practices that often attended it, spiraling out of control near midcentury, the NCAA responded by frequently issuing statements condemning financial subsidies to players and unethical recruiting practices. Though such statements were public, however, they weren't binding. They had no force of law. The NCAA was essentially relying on moral suasion to make a legal case.

The colleges, for their part, believed that since they were supposed to be honorable institutions of higher learning, they could police themselves without an overarching regulatory body. But as the scandal at Brooklyn College demonstrated, self-policing left much to be desired. Gamblers were a problem, but the enrollment scandal demonstrated that the universities had just as much for which to answer. Many southern schools, for example, were unapologetically offering athletic scholarships despite the association's prohibition against it. Many northern schools, meanwhile, refused to do so. There were 120 colleges under the umbrella of the NCAA at midcentury, and without a draft, without a systematized way of distributing available high school players, they were all competing for the same recruits. Eventually, the schools would turn to the NCAA for help, finally vesting it with the authority it lacked to regulate the conditions of competition.

The first step in the regulatory process came in 1940 when the NCAA convention ruled that schools that violated NCAA statutes could be expelled from the organization by a two-thirds vote of member schools. It sounded good; a peer pressure system that could instigate real accountability, but though many (if not most) schools were breaking the rules, none were expelled under the 1940 provision.

And so the colleges came up with a new strategy: if you can't beat them, join them. Prior to 1948, providing athletic scholarships to students was technically against the association's bylaws. Athletic scholarships were a form of payment to an athlete specifically for engaging in athletic competition, and collegiate athletes were supposed to be amateurs. Universities, in the association's original understanding, were intended to field teams from their student body, not to recruit athletes to supplement that student body. In 1948, however, member schools, under the auspices of the NCAA, passed what became known as the Sanity Code, which permitted the extension of scholarships and jobs to athletes, as long as those scholarships were awarded solely on the basis of financial need.

The Sanity Code was a half-measure, a compromise position, and it would be untenable. Financial need was difficult to prove, allowing universities to run roughshod over the code's original intent. In addition, providing scholarships to students only funded their tuition; it didn't pay for the other necessities and desires of typical collegians, keeping them, in any pragmatic sense, unpaid workers who could easily be seduced by the prospect of monetary reward for a set of actions that were already making so many others so much money. Ultimately, the demise of the Sanity Code would come from continued scandal that demonstrated its obvious inefficacy and the necessity of stronger, more substantial NCAA regulation.

So much of that scandal in collegiate basketball came from New York, partly because of the influence of the city's bookmakers and organized crime, but also because Madison Square Garden was the venue that drew so many of the country's top teams, housing the National Invitation Tournament (NIT) and other games of national interest that drew the most betting money. The Big Ten Conference barred its teams from playing in the Garden to avoid potential corruption, but other leagues welcomed the exposure and the financial windfall that came with such contests. New York teams, of course, were particularly susceptible because they played many games every season at the venue. Gamblers were seen berating coaches on the bench during games at the Garden. Missed shots led crowds to chant that the player was shaving points. Fans often cheered for losing teams to cover point spreads.

It led many to argue that play at Madison Square Garden might need to stop for the benefit of the reputation of the game. In 1947, even CCNY's Holman predicted that more scandal was to come without some kind of reform. At the 1948 NCAA meetings, however, the group who enacted the Sanity Code also decided against moving any play away from the game's premier venue. "We owe a big debt to the Garden for saving basketball during the war years," explained NCAA president Karl Leib, "when we had to take the game to the public because transportation difficulties kept the public from seeing the game." It was an argument for loyalty to the Garden for its years of service, but the real reason for that loyalty was the money that the championship games at the venue brought to the coffers of the NCAA, which in 1947 totaled almost $60,000.

And so the games at Madison Square Garden continued, as did the gambling and corruption. In 1948, a group of New York gamblers approached the co-captain of George Washington University's team about fixing a game against Manhattan College. The player, David Shapiro, reported the offer and agreed to bait the gamblers by accepting the bribe. When Shapiro took the money, giving gamblers the assumption that the fix was in, but played up to his normal standard, gamblers lost as much as $5 million. More pertinently, New York City's district attorney, Frank Hogan, charged and convicted four of the gamblers. Perhaps the most foreboding element of the case was that the New York gamblers made trips to Washington, DC, to coordinate the fix, demonstrating that while the conspiracy was born in New York, it wasn't simply a localized endeavor.

And corruption wasn't localized to college basketball either. Football was the most popular collegiate sport and stood for many as a representation of what was going on with university athletics. While many outside New York or college towns may have looked past gambling concerns with college basketball at Madison Square Garden, for example, everyone, by the very nature of its existence, had a vested interest in the United States Military Academy.

In the 1940s, the United States Military Academy was one of the top football programs in the nation. In 1941, the school hired coach Earl "Red" Blaik, and under his leadership the team would win back-to-back national championships in 1944 and 1945 and came in second in 1946 after a scoreless tie against Notre Dame. The team maintained a thirty-two-game unbeaten streak from 1944 to 1947. Army had a similar streak between 1948 and 1950, winning twenty-five games with one loss and one tie. In 1951, however, Army would only win two games, one of its worst seasons ever, and its only such season under Blaik. That's because it lost all its players.

West Point had an honor code whereby cadets pledged to obey the rules. "A cadet will not lie, cheat, steal, or tolerate those who do." The development of a winning program, however, meant more expectations, which meant more pressure, more practice time, more demands on players from the football program. Combined with the rigorous coursework at the Military Academy, the task became too much for many of the students, and in the late 1940s and in 1950, several developed a system to facilitate cheating on class exams.

Upon discovery of the scheme, Blaik self-reported the violation and kicked the offenders off his team. Every varsity football player but two were dismissed. It was earth-shattering news to the general public. Army wasn't just another football team; it was a representation of the military. And the scandal took place in the early years of Cold War containment and the onset of the Korean War. The debacle at West Point was not conditioned by gambling; the cadets never intentionally lost games for a financial benefit. But the scandal increased the national sensitivity to problematic corruption, enhanced the public recognition and fear of the real pitfalls that accompanied amateur athletics. That heightened awareness, then, would turn on college basketball when an even more devastating and wide-ranging scandal engulfed the other major amateur sport.

During the 1950–1951 basketball season, as Army was playing its last great season before collapsing in scandal, gambling concerns portended a similar collapse for college basketball. In January 1951, an exposé in the *New York Journal American* reported that Long Island University (LIU) often fixed games and shaved points, prompting the anger of the team's coach, Clair Bee. He wasn't mad at the game fixing; he was mad at the reporting, claiming that the coverage was bad for the game's image.

That tarnished image, however, was not the fault of reporters. In the same month, for example, former Manhattan player Hanke Poppe offered one of the team's star players, Junius Kellogg, $1,000 to fix a game between Manhattan and DePaul. "It's easy!" Poppe told him. "You can miss a rebound once in a while. After you get a rebound don't look to pass it down court. Hang on to it and give the defense a chance to set up. Then you can try shooting your hook shot a little hard. And don't try to block the other guy's shot. Throw the ball away when you get the chance." He reminded Kellogg that "Manhattan doesn't actually have to lose the game. All you have to do is control the margin of victory." The most important element of point-shaving, however, was "don't stink up the joint. Make it look like you're trying."

Kellogg only had intentions of trying and reported the attempted bribe. The resulting arrest of Poppe and a co-conspirator led to the discovery of a wider scheme and more arrests. Gamblers paid Manhattan players to lose three different Madison Square Garden games, and to shave points in two others. The Manhattan scandal shocked many, despite being jaded by the perfidy of the darker corners of the collegiate game, but Manhattan was just the tip of an insidious iceberg.

The 1949–1950 college basketball season had been dominated by City College. Nat Holman's group became the only team to win both the NIT and NCAA tournaments in the same season, and the 1950–1951 campaign promised more success. But just as it had for the cadets of West Point, trouble loomed on the horizon. In February 1951, just weeks after the Manhattan College arrests, New York County district attorney Frank Hogan arrested three players from CCNY, one from NYU, and a former player from LIU. It was an escalation in the fight against corruption. Previously, the gamblers who attempted to influence the players were the ones facing charges. In Hogan's conception of the problem, however, the players weren't victims of a gambling scheme; they were co-conspirators.

Of course, the middlemen and the principal fixer, Salvatore Sallazzo, were also arrested and charged. But the player arrests signaled something new. The CCNY players admitted to deliberately losing four games that season and even to receiving payments for winning games that pleased the gamblers. Two days after the arrests, three LIU players also admitted to shaving points and throwing games in exchange for thousands of dollars from gamblers. It was an LIU team that only lost four games during the 1950–1951 season, a legitimate collegiate power. The team's star was Sherman White, who came close to breaking the all-time college scoring record and was named Player of the Year by the *Sporting News*. He was also one of the fixers. White explained that game fixing was so common at LIU, the culture so entrenched in the program, that players were left to either sit quietly by and watch or participate in the scheme and make money in the process.

Following the LIU arrests, another CCNY player admitted complicity and three more were arrested. Then it was another three LIU players, as Hogan and New York authorities peeled back the layers of the conspiracy like an onion. Jackie Goldsmith, a former LIU player, was another victim of arrest. Goldsmith had profited from the fixing scheme while a player but left college before his senior season because the money involved in promoting fixed games was more than he could ever hope to make with his degree. Goldsmith, as reported in the *New York*

Journal-American, was "responsible for the corruption of more college basketball players than any other single person."

Goldsmith's actions were a symptom, however, not the disease itself. In the months that followed the first arrests, as the sports media spread the story of the scandal across the nation, into the college towns of the Midwest, South, and West, basketball fans looked with disdain on the cesspool that was New York. The city and its seminal arena were gifts that both gave and took away. *Sport* magazine's Stanley Woodward explained to readers that "most of the finagling has been centered in New York City where gambling on college basketball games is far more common than anywhere else in the country." Critics, however, would soon be forced to cede the moral high ground. In July, Hogan's office questioned three players from the University of Toledo about fixing a game against Niagara. Two of the team's players had worked in the Catskills and there had made contacts with the gambling set that governed crooked play. They offered the players money for each teammate they were able to recruit to participate in point shaving and game fixing. Only three had participated in fixing the game against Niagara, the only one potentially under the jurisdiction of New York officials, but others participated in fixing other games. Toledo was a powerhouse that 1950–1951 season, winning twenty-two games and making the national rankings, and that success had drawn the attention of a variety of gambling concerns, who often frequented the team's home games and tried to influence players from the stands. Concerns from university officials led to a series of raids on local gambling operations in the city.

The virus was spreading outside the bounds of the northeast, and it next appeared in Illinois, when New York detectives arrested three players from Peoria's Bradley University. Gene Melchiorre, Bill Mann, and Mike Chianakas stood accused of fixing the 1949 NIT consolation game between Bradley and Bowling Green played in Madison Square Garden. After the jolt of the arrests, four additional Bradley players admitted to a Peoria grand jury that they, too, had fixed games during the following 1949–1950 season. Melchiorre in particular, indicted in New York as the orchestrator of Bradley's scheme, had been the first pick in the professional draft in 1951. It was a long fall from that lofty position to prison on Rikers Island, Melchiorre and his teammates indicted along with four gamblers who helped perpetrate the scheme.

Not only did Bradley's involvement indicate that the scandal was very much present in the heartland, but it also provided a new element of perfidy, as the Bradley players themselves initiated contact with gamblers, sought out the possibility of profit for tainted play. One of the players, Aaron Preese, called notorious New York gambler Eli Kaye and professed a desire to do business. One of Kaye's henchmen, Nick Englesis, actually traveled with Bradley to all of its road games, and Fordy Anderson, the team's coach, reported witnessing payments being made in the locker room. The rot in the Bradley program was not simply the result of players in the Catskills being duped into a gambling scheme. It was systemic. And it was concocted far from Madison Square Garden at a small private college in the supposedly impenetrable Midwest.

Throughout the growing ordeal, Adolph Rupp, one of Phog Allen's original players at the University of Kansas and by now a legendary coach at the University of Kentucky, looked on with disdain at the state of the college game. "The gamblers couldn't get to our boys with a ten-foot pole," Rupp told reporters. The Wildcats were under "constant and absolutely complete supervision while on the road," and "nowhere was that supervision more complete than in New York." *Sport* magazine's Woodward backed Rupp's assertions. Though the population was willing and eager to gamble on horse racing, the state's other obsession, Lexington, Kentucky, was "a small-town community, crazy about its basketball team, where there is little betting. The citizens of Lexington are probably as basketball-conscious as any men and women in the country. But they don't bet much, and there is absolutely no organized bookmaking such as you find in the larger metropolitan areas."

The Wildcat program was the most prominent in the country and the one with the most recent success. Kentucky won its first NCAA Championship in 1948, then repeated the following season. After CCNY's year of dominance, Kentucky would win its third national title in four years in March 1951, as players from City College were awaiting trial for their role in the scandal. The 1948 team, nicknamed "The Fabulous Five" by Rupp, was led by Ralph Beard and Alex Groza, dominant players revered by fans in a state obsessed with college basketball.

By 1951, both Beard and Groza were professionals, players and part-owners of the Indianapolis Olympians, and on October 20 they were arrested in Chicago by New York detectives. Another Kentucky player,

Dale Barnstable, was arrested in Louisville. All three admitted to sharing $2,000 to shave points in a 1949 NIT game against Loyola Chicago in Madison Square Garden, a game in which the Wildcats, who would go on to win the NCAA Championships, were upset as heavy favorites. Soon, other players like Jim Line, 1951 captain Walt Hirsch, and reigning National Player of the Year Bill Spivey were implicated. Everyone but Spivey, who was indicted for perjury, admitted involvement. Three gamblers were also indicted, including Nick Englesis, who had spearheaded much of the activity at Bradley. Englesis was a former Kentucky football player and used his connections with the school's athletic department to recruit players for the scheme.

Though the judge in the New York case, Saul Streit, was lenient on the players, he sentenced Englesis and the gamblers to prison. He also had harsh words for Kentucky's "evil system of commercialization and overemphasis." He argued that "intercollegiate basketball and football at the University of Kentucky have become highly systematized, professionalized and commercialized." The program was rife with "covert subsidization of players, ruthless exploitation of athletes, cribbing at examinations, 'illegal' recruiting, a reckless disregard for their physical welfare, matriculation of unqualified athletes by the coach, alumni and townspeople, and the most flagrant abuse of the 'athletic scholarship.'" Rupp in particular "failed in his duty to observe the amateur rules, to build character and to protect the morals and health of his charges." His coaching made the players "ripe for plucking by the Fixers."

As historian Charles Rosen explained, "Rupp's boys regularly received cash from either Rupp himself, or from the 'Boosters.' The sums ranged from $10 to $50, depending on how well the players performed. On the rare occasion of a UK loss, the ballplayers were lucky to get anything to eat." Rupp claimed "that any winning coach 'has to blur the line' in getting athletes, motivating them, and keeping them in school." Ralph Beard even admitted that payments from alumni for good games gave the players no reason to interpret fixing payments any differently. Dale Barnstable explained that the gamblers roped in the players by first having them win by more than the point spread, making the payments seem consistent with winning basketball. By the time that point shaving meant intentionally playing poorly, the players were in too deep to protest.

It was, in other words, a culture of graft at the University of Kentucky that created the conditions for abuse, and that culture began with its leader. Rupp was close friends with Lexington's most powerful bookmaker, Ed Curd, whose bar was only five blocks from the Wildcats' gymnasium. In direct contrast to the claims of Rupp and Woodward, former Kentucky sports information director Russell Rice argued that "Lexington was probably the biggest high school and college gambling center in the country," a place where "bookies from racetracks after World War II were moving into the intercollegiate field and the situation was bound to get worse." The players under indictment argued that Rupp coached to the point spread, using substitutions based on the perceived size of victory. While Rupp denied that charge, he did admit to calling Curd to ask about point spreads. He admitted that Curd had traveled with the team and dined with them on more than one occasion while Kentucky was in New York to play games at Madison Square Garden.

The power structure of the university and the state quickly rallied to support Rupp and to deny that any of his admissions or accusations against him were true. University president Herman Donovan went even farther. In 1952, he wrote a letter to Kentucky senator Thomas Underwood, audaciously asking if it would "be possible for you to obtain information from the FBI and from the Dye's [sic] Committee on the standing and status of Judge Saul S. Streit. If this information is available, the Board of Trustees, the Athletics Board, and many of us here at the University would like to have these data." The goal was clear: defame the messenger rather than fix the problems delineated in the message. It was an uglier, more official version of Clair Bee's talk with journalists in years past. Donovan also contacted the president of the University of Maryland. "Our mutual friend, President Humphry of the University of Wyoming, telephoned me a few days ago saying that he believed you had a file of information regarding Judge Saul S. Streit of New York City," he wrote. "I can use it to good advantage if you have such a file." He promised to "certainly protect you should you send me any data on this Judge who is so interested in reforming athletics in Kentucky and elsewhere, and so determined to protect gamblers and racketeers in his own bailiwick." The requests demonstrated the corruption at the highest levels of the University of Kentucky, but they also demonstrated that other universities, like the University of Wyoming, had similar systemic problems. College basketball was not simply being corrupted by the Gomorrah of New York City. Scandal wasn't reserved for smaller private institutions like Bradley. Kentucky and Wyoming were large state universities in states deemed affectionately as the country's heartland. And the corruption at Kentucky went from students, to the coach, to the university president.

The Southeastern Conference banned the Wildcats from conference play and postseason tournaments for one season. The NCAA placed the university on a one-year probation. The Kentucky players, all beyond their college eligibility by the time of the 1952 rulings, lost their careers. The punishments demonstrated the inequities of the collegiate system. While the players avoided jail time, unlike the gamblers who paid them, they suffered lifetime consequences while the other group who made money from their play, namely the coach and administration, completed their punishments in the course of one brief season.

Saul Streit, meanwhile, was also presiding over the trials of other indicted co-conspirators from the variety of universities caught in Larry Hogan's wide net. Streit's broad rulings cited payment to players, corruption in recruiting, the manipulation of high school transcripts, grade fixing, forgery, and other forms of fraud as being endemic in collegiate basketball throughout the country. "The naivete, the equivocation and the denials of the coaches and their assistants concerning their knowledge of gambling, recruiting and subsidizing would be comical were they not so despicable," he argued. "The acts of these defendants are merely the symptoms of the disease."

That disease was obviously much larger than the players entrapped by the effort at a cure, and it was larger than just college basketball. College administrators, those not actively part of the cover-up, understood that the NCAA Sanity Code was an obvious failure, but there was disagreement about what kind of powerful executive there should be. The NCAA was seen by many as part of the problem, not part of the solution. At the 1950 NCAA convention, for example, a motion to suspend seven colleges cited for noncompliance with the Sanity Code could not get the two-thirds majority it needed to pass. In what seemed to be a real leadership vacuum, college presidents even began discussing using the American Council on Education as a new regulatory body for college athletics.

In 1952, however, at the height of the point-shaving scandal, the NCAA recovered. The organization eliminated the Sanity Code and decided to permit "full scholarships based only on athletic ability," relaxing the standard and ensuring that athletes didn't have to be in financial need to qualify for an athletic scholarship. The colleges also extended the NCAA's power to impose sanctions upon colleges that violated the association's regulations. They named a full-time executive director, Walter Byers, who would serve until 1988, and established a national headquarters. The group also used the meetings to impose its sanctions on Kentucky and Bradley. When the colleges left the 1952 convention, the NCAA was a major athletic regulatory body.

But it still remained unable or unwilling to stop the gambling problem. All told, thirty-five active and ex-players stood accused of accepting bribes and fixing at least eighty-six games from 1947 to 1951. Twenty players and fourteen gamblers were indicted and convicted. Ten years later, however, another scandal surfaced, demonstrating that despite the NCAA's new regulatory system, the practice of point-shaving and game-fixing had continued relatively unabated. After two years of arrests following a similar controversy in 1961, more than fifty players at twenty-seven universities were shown to have fixed games for gamblers.

The scandals ensured that college basketball would carry with it a scarlet letter into the second half of the twentieth century. Streit's emphasis on the "evil system of commercialization" in collegiate basketball programs like Kentucky and City College, and even in smaller programs like Bradley, ensured that the collegiate game itself, rather than just a handful of top teams, would be associated with graft and corruption. Its image was similar to that of boxing and horse racing in the public mind, as one of the corrupted sports whose outcomes were just as likely to be predetermined than not. It was a problem that could only be solved by a dynastic program with unqualified success and a clean reputation. As it turned out, in the first full season after Streit's rulings, John Wooden's UCLA Bruins engaged in its first undefeated Pacific Coast Conference season, finally losing in the NCAA tournament to the University of San Francisco, led by center Bill Russell. A new day was dawning, and for collegiate players willing to buck the trend of corruption, there were also new professional opportunities waiting for them after graduation.

7

The Birth of the National Basketball Association

MAX KASE WAS BORN in Yonkers, New York, in 1898, when basketball was still in its infancy. He grew up loving the game, along with every other sport, and became a sportswriter and, ultimately, a sports editor at the *New York Journal American*. He had watched in awe at the original collegiate triple-header at Madison Square Garden in 1931 and then Ned Irish's lucrative doubleheaders that successfully followed throughout the heart of the Great Depression. Kase had also seen the drawing power of teams like the Original Celtics and the Renaissance Five, along with the various stops and starts of early professional leagues. He had witnessed professional teams based in New York begin with promise before finally disbanding. But the success of college basketball at Madison Square Garden, combined with the success of other professional team sports leagues, convinced Kase that professional basketball could be a stable and profitable reality. During World War II, he promoted a charity game for war relief at Manhattan Center that drew an overflow crowd. He was convinced after that 1944 contest that the country was ready for stable, organized professional basketball.

His first approach was to Walter Brown, president of the Boston Garden and an influential part of the Arena Managers Association of America, which controlled thirteen of the most important arenas in the country. All but one made the bulk of their money from professional hockey, with teams either competing in the American Hockey League (AHL) or the National Hockey League (NHL), supplemented with other traveling events that arrived in cities like Boston, Providence, Philadelphia, Pittsburgh, Indianapolis, St. Louis, New York, and others. Brown, whose principal interest was in the Boston Bruins, was intrigued by Kase's idea, which would fill more dates at member arenas, but told the eager promoter that any action would need to wait until after the war, when a peacetime economy and a returning soldiery would create a more fruitful basketball market.

Meanwhile, Kase approached Ned Irish, principal promoter for Madison Square Garden and the New York Rangers NHL team. He asked the sports mogul about renting the Garden to create a professional basketball team in his new league once a new one actually formed. Irish was less receptive, explaining that his regular collegiate doubleheaders already saturated the New York market. In addition, a binding agreement between members of the Arena Managers Association ensured that if the group got involved in a basketball league, the Garden, not Kase, would own the New York team. It was a reality that pushed Kase out of any potential leadership role, but his idea and influence still lingered. Walter Brown pitched Kase's plan to other association members, leading Al Sutphin, owner of the Cleveland Arena and the AHL's Cleveland Barons, to take the organizational lead. At the end of the war, the city's professional football team, the Cleveland Rams, had left for Los Angeles, and Sutphin saw a possibility in the move for a new audience for basketball.

It was part of a larger shift in the trajectory of professional sports. The Rams' move from Cleveland would be the opening salvo of what would become a decade-long migration west of professional teams to the burgeoning postwar Sun Belt. In 1953, Major League Baseball's Boston Braves moved to Milwaukee; in 1954 the St. Louis Browns moved to Baltimore. In 1955, the Philadelphia Athletics moved to Kansas City. Finally, in 1958, the Brooklyn Dodgers and the New York Giants moved to Los Angeles and San Francisco, respectively. "When the Dodgers left Brooklyn," recalled a fan twenty-five years later, "we lost our innocence forever. Love and loyalty, we were shattered to hear, were only so much mush to the people in power." Dodgers owner Walter O'Malley was reviled in Brooklyn, but he did have relatively legitimate reasons for moving the team, all centering around the changing American urban dynamic. Teams wanted nicer facilities, more prosperous neighborhoods, and better parking.

Such would become the professional norm, as metropolitan areas began vying for established and expansion franchises. But for those cities without a Chavez Ravine, room to put new stadiums was scarce. Instead, many cities built outside of downtown areas in suburban satellite communities. The argument was that suburban sites offered easier access to cars and wealthier fans. They also provided an escape from the congestion, dirt, and perils of the inner city. Critics worried that moves into the suburbs encouraged the decay of downtown areas. Such stadiums, they argued, inherently favored the privileged few over the rest of the city.

In making such moves, professional sports were following larger national economic and social trends. Though suburban communities had been around since the nineteenth century, it was in the wake of World War II when they began to dominate. The suburbs pulled both jobs and more prosperous families out of the city. Freeways, automobile sales, and federal subsidies for homeowners all encouraged the building of these cities outside the confines of urban spaces. And when baseball and football franchises moved, businesses moved along with them to take advantage of the cleaner air, larger space, and suburban money. Those moves ensured that sports like baseball and football would be associated with the wealth and whiteness of the suburbs. Though professional hockey stayed in urban arenas, its early city tenure before the war and the whiteness of its players maintained its associations with suburban ideals. Professional basketball, meanwhile, was organizing to fill those urban arenas at the same time that White flight to the suburbs was changing the landscape of other, more established professional sports. It was an intersection of time and place that would cast a long shadow over professional basketball among many White sports fans.

Back in 1946, however, league organization was still theoretical. Al Sutphin contacted Arthur Wirtz, the most powerful member of the Arena Managers Association, about the possibility of a new league. Wirtz owned the Chicago Blackhawks and Detroit Red Wings of the NHL, and the Detroit Olympics and St. Louis Flyers of the AHL, along with the arenas that housed them. As went Wirtz, so would go the possibility of the new potential league, and Wirtz proved interested. By late spring, all the arena owners were in agreement. A new professional basketball league was in the works.

The leader they chose to head their new organization was Maurice Podoloff, a Ukrainian immigrant and graduate of Yale Law whose principal sports background was in hockey. Podoloff had a relationship with several of the group's founders in his capacity as president of the American Hockey League (AHL) but was worried when approached about the new opportunity that he had no knowledge of basketball. The organizers, however, were unconcerned. He was a good manager, and he was someone they could trust. Still, in his seventeen years as the leader of professional basketball, Podoloff never learned much about the game itself and never found it as compelling as hockey.

In the organizational meetings for the new group, Podoloff proposed using the AHL's constitution as a base. The group established franchise fees, a playoff system, and gate receipt distributions. They also debated a name for the new organization, ultimately deciding on the Basketball Association of America (BAA). The most influential voices at the meeting were Irish, Sutphin, and Eddie Gottlieb, who had made his name with the Philadelphia SPHAs. They worked out player eligibility standards and decided that exhibition games could not be played with teams from the rival National Basketball League (NBL) and American Basketball League (ABL), as any losses to those teams might serve to devalue the viability of the new organization. Similar worries were reflected in the group's prohibition of franchises fifty miles from one another, as well as in its concern about radio and television. Everyone agreed that radio broadcasts could only be beneficial, drawing potential fans to the arena after hearing descriptions of the games. Each team would be free to negotiate local radio contracts as they saw fit, but television was seen as more problematic. "We ought to agree here that no club will do anything with television," Sutphin argued. "Televising games only keeps fans away from the games. We can only get involved in a television deal if we do it on a leaguewide basis."

Pushback came from Ned Irish, whose team would be in the country's largest market. "There are currently only six thousand television sets on the entire Eastern Seaboard, and probably by the end of the season, that number might be doubled under the most optimistic forecasts," he argued. "The extra revenue, if available, would be most helpful, and I don't see any difference between radio and television broadcasting."

The extra revenue would definitely be helpful, but there was a decided difference between radio and television. "And so the monumental change began in our lives and those of millions of other Americans," said one man about his family's purchase of their first television in 1950.

"More than a year passed before we again visited a movie theater. Money that previously would have been spent for books was saved for TV payments. Social evenings with friends became fewer and fewer still." There were only six thousand sets on the Eastern Seaboard in 1946, but by 1956, three-fourths of all families in the United States owned televisions. Those families watched an average of thirty-five hours of television a week.

Nothing was more central to the history of organized sports during the second half of the twentieth century than television. The meaning of sports is generated by those who watch, who invest themselves in the games. With television, the fans at home rather than those in the stadium became the ultimate arbiters of organized sports. There were a variety of pragmatic draws to television broadcasts, like graphics, music, and announcers. Eventually, rule changes would allow television timeouts, and leagues would develop lengthy playoff systems for national championships, all made for television audiences. But the advent of television did more. It fundamentally changed what sports were. Sports had always been local, building team loyalties centered around a regional base. But televised sports provided a new form of immediacy. Attendance at sporting events dropped in the 1950s, and the continuous success of games like basketball was going to increasingly depend upon a national rather than local constituency. A final consequence of the move to television, one that the organizers of the BAA could never have imagined, would be the growth of athletic salaries. As television and commercial sponsorship began bringing millions and millions of dollars into games, athletes, who were increasingly known because of television, began demanding a larger cut of the revenue.

The first televised sports broadcast was in 1938, but television's initial impact came in the 1950s when networks began taking advantage of better technologies. Irish might not have been able to predict the growth to come, but he knew there was money in television. Ultimately, teams in the New York and Chicago markets were allowed two television broadcasts per season, setting a precedent for what would become the core of professional basketball's revenue stream in decades to come.

The final debate at those original meetings ended in a unanimous agreement that teams in the association would include no Black players. Team segregation had been the trend in the professional game from its early days, though segregated teams had often played games against one another. That was the plan for the BAA. The association hoped to play preliminary exhibition games against Abe Saperstein's Harlem Globetrotters, and worried that hiring Black players for their own teams would draw talent away from Saperstein and leave him refusing to play games against the BAA. The Globetrotters were far more popular than any of the would-be teams being proposed, and the revenue from such exhibitions was seen as vital to the league's viability. Thus it was that a good faith effort to encourage games with the nation's premier Black team led to the banning of Black players on league teams. Jackie Robinson was already playing under a Brooklyn Dodgers contract in Triple-A affiliate Montreal. The world was changing. But professional basketball, largely because of its deference to the Globetrotters, would require several years to catch up.

Along with broader issues, the league organizers established eleven teams for that first season, banned zone defenses, and lengthened the game to forty-eight minutes, eight longer than games played by collegians. Since doubleheaders like those promoted by Irish were unworkable for the professionals, a longer game would give more show for paying customers. The teams spread as far west as Chicago and St. Louis and as far north as Detroit and Toronto, though most of the franchises spread up and down the Eastern Seaboard, from the Boston Celtics, which Walter Brown named after buying rights to the appellation from the former manager of the Original Celtics, down to the Washington Capitols.

The franchises of the Celtics and Capitols began their tenures in different ways. The Celtics, coached by Honey Russell, struggled that first season, losing their first five games and remaining at the bottom of the standings for the bulk of the season. The Capitols, on the other hand, hired a young high school coach and former naval officer who convinced the organization that he was up to the task of leading a professional team. His name was Arnold "Red" Auerbach, and he led the Capitols to the best record in the association during its first season.

That first effort featured a sixty-game schedule, the first of the contests taking place in Ontario between the Toronto Huskies and New York Knicks, a game recognized by the modern NBA as its inaugural event. At the Maple Leaf Gardens, 7,090 fans watched, where a makeshift court had been laid over the hockey ice, condensation creating a slippery surface for the players. "It was interesting playing before Canadians," explained one New York Knick. "The fans really didn't understand what was going on at first. To them, a jump ball was like a face-off in hockey. But they started to catch on and seemed to like the action." Toronto sportswriters described fouls as "roughing" or "cross checking" to maintain the hockey comparison. And while basketball wasn't hockey, the newspaper coverage and more than seven thousand fans made that first game an undeniable success.

Most of the contests that first season were unable to top seven thousand paying customers, but the teams muddled through on at least relatively stable ground. A bizarre playoff setup that had the top teams in each of two divisions play each other in the first round, then receive a bye to play the winner of a four-team playoff between the two second- and third-place teams, eliminated the league-leading Capitols in the first round. Ultimately, the Philadelphia Warriors faced the Chicago Stags for the championship, with the Warriors winning in five games to become the first BAA champion.

While the Celtics watched that first playoff from the outside, the franchise remained on stable footing thanks to Walter Brown and Boston Garden. Other teams, however, found their financial situation more precarious. The Detroit Falcons, Pittsburgh Ironmen, Cleveland Rebels, and even the Toronto Huskies found themselves unable to field a team for the BAA's second season. The American Basketball League (ABL), centered on the East Coast in the same territory that had proved powerful for most of the teams in the new organization, had foundered in the face of competition, and in response, the league's best team, the Baltimore Bullets, left to join the BAA. The ABL would continue operating until 1955, but it was, after the Bullets' secession, a decidedly minor league for its last years of life.

Meanwhile, with only eight teams for its second campaign, the BAA reduced its schedule to forty-eight games. The players, however, refused to accept a corresponding reduction in pay, and with other leagues still active, owners had little choice but to agree. It made the season a difficult one financially, but there were other difficulties for the association. The Bullets, for example, amassed the second-best record in the league and went on to win the playoff championship, manifesting the fear that organizers had been fretting over since banning exhibition games with teams from rival leagues. A team associated in most minds with the ABL had won the championship of the BAA, making it difficult, particularly with the shortened season and the financial problems that accompanied it, for association officials to claim superiority over its rivals. Only adding to concerns over league inferiority, the NBL had George Mikan, the game's unquestioned star, who had won the championship that season with his Minneapolis Lakers.

Podoloff was no basketball expert, but he was an expert in league rivalries, operating a hockey organization in direct competition with the NHL. He understood the fragility of the BAA exposed by the success of the Bullets and Lakers, but he also understood that the association's superior arenas and superior markets gave it an advantage over its competitors. With the ABL all but defunct, operating as a nonthreatening minor circuit, Podoloff turned his attention to the NBL. He knew that the Lakers would have no immediate need to join the BAA, as it was already clearly dominating its current league, so he started instead by approaching Indiana teams in Fort Wayne and Indianapolis. The Zollner Pistons in particular had been professional basketball's dominant team from 1944 to 1946, but they had found less success in the following seasons, making their owner Fred Zollner willing to consider a jump. The other Indiana franchise, the Indianapolis Kautskys, were owned by grocery store magnate Frank Kautsky. The team had never experienced success like that of the Zollner Pistons, but it appealed to Podoloff because of its location in the state's largest city. Both of the Indiana teams, one with a big name, the other with a big market, agreed after Podoloff's urging to join the BAA.

It was a theft that fundamentally weakened the NBL, and after creating the weakness, Podoloff used it as leverage to go after the biggest prize, George Mikan and the Lakers. The franchise was operated by Max Winter, who was susceptible to Podoloff's message. Being the best team in a minor league would always be less profitable than participating at any level in a major league, so the Lakers, too, absconded. The team just behind the Lakers in the NBL standings was the Rochester Royals, who had earlier unsuccessfully tried to join the BAA, organizers assuming that Rochester was an inferior market and worried that the team owners did not simultaneously own their arena. But the Royals were good, and in Podoloff's move to weaken his rival, they now met a lesser standard for admission. With the Indiana teams, the league's two best teams, and

Mikan all abandoning the NBL for the BAA, the project of diminishing the association's competition was complete.

"We weren't much better off than the NBL until he came along," one association official said of Mikan. "It's no exaggeration to say he saved the league." With both the NBL and ABL operating as minor leagues during the 1948–1949 season, the BAA had no need to apologize for the success of its new entries. The Indiana teams changed their mascots to the Pistons and Jets, removing their owners' surnames, but they remained at the bottom of the BAA standings. Rochester and Minneapolis, however, would dominate the association, amassing the two best records in what returned to a sixty-game schedule. Mikan's Lakers, though the Royals outpaced them during the regular season by one game, easily dominated the playoffs and won the championship.

A decidedly diminished NBL, meanwhile, played its own season by adding several smaller entries to fill out an eight-team league season, one ultimately won by the Anderson Duffey Packers. The Duffey Packers, from comparatively tiny Anderson, Indiana, played home games in the local high school gymnasium. Several teams proved financially unable to complete the season. The NBL, critically wounded by Podoloff's raiding, finally succumbed, and its remaining teams merged with the BAA.

The BAA was eager for the growth. Its Indianapolis Jets had failed, as had the Providence Steamrollers, but the association was able to add NBL champion Anderson, along with teams from Sheboygan, Wisconsin; Waterloo, Iowa; and Denver, Colorado. The association absorbed the remaining and willing NBL teams, even those from small markets, because leaders wanted assurances that they wouldn't be vulnerable to antitrust lawsuits by franchises left out of the merger. They also added the more desirable Syracuse Nationals and Tri-Cities Blackhawks, both of whom would remain in the NBA until the twenty-first century. In addition, the association created a new expansion team in Indianapolis to replace the Jets, giving them a seventeen-team league. To acknowledge the merger and create a sense of recognition among the fans of the western teams, the BAA also merged the names of the two organizations, rechristening the group the NBA.

That first season under the association's new name, Mikan's Lakers again dominated, the game's most powerful player winning yet another championship in yet another professional organization. Still, the new teams performed well. Minneapolis's opponent in the championship series was the Syracuse Nationals. Indianapolis, Tri-Cities, Anderson, Fort Wayne, and Sheboygan all made the playoffs. The additions demonstrated that the NBL teams were decidedly worthy of inclusion, but the seventeen-team format was unmanageable, and all teams were not created equally. Anderson, Waterloo, Sheboygan, and Denver were unable to survive after that first season, and original BAA teams Chicago and St. Louis also dropped out. It dropped the second season's roster to ten teams, which was substantially more manageable.

It was also during the 1950–1951 season that the association began staging a midseason all-star game, following the lead of its fellow professional sports leagues. Just as attaining a professional sports franchise was an emblem of respectability for growing Sun Belt cities in the wake of World War II, all-star contests were similar representations for professional leagues themselves. The NBA was far from the most popular American sports organization, but Podoloff and others understood that the one benefit the league had in relation to sports like football, whose players wore helmets, and baseball, whose players wore caps, was easily visible players in close proximity to the fans who came to watch them. What the association lacked in established history, it believed it could compensate for by elevating visible stars as attractions for would-be spectators. During a Lakers contest in New York's Madison Square Garden, for example, the marquee announced: "Tonight! George Mikan vs. Knicks." Even in its earliest days, leaders of the NBA realized that it would be stars who drove the game.

And the league had stars. Mikan and Jim Pollard of the Lakers, Dolph Schayes of the Syracuse Nationals, Ed Macauley of the Celtics, and Dick McGuire of the Knicks all became draws in their individual markets. So, too, were Alex Groza and Ralph Beard of the upstart Indianapolis Olympians, but their tenure would be cut short by the collegiate point-shaving scandal that engulfed the country in 1951.

The scandal would also touch the professional ranks. Jack Molinas, a rookie player for the Fort Wayne Pistons, was discovered to have gambled on games. One of the league's referees, Sol Levy, admitted taking bribes to fix contests. Both he and Molinas were banned from the association. The NBA realized that the fiasco taking place in the collegiate ranks could actually serve as a boon to the pros if Podoloff and the association's board of governors took swift, decisive action that gave the professional game the moral high ground. Not only did the association ban Levy and Molinas, but it banned Groza, Beard, and Bill Spivey, all of whom had been caught in the sting operation at the University of Kentucky. The league already had a powerful executive while the NCAA was still searching to find its footing and saw the college calamity as a zero-sum gain.

No less influential was the effect the scandal had on Madison Square Garden. The loss of college basketball's popularity, particularly in New York, the heart of the scandal, was a boon to the NBA. The Knicks originally played some of their games in the Garden, but many contests were played in a local armory because dates for the larger venue were taken by Irish's doubleheaders. When the profitability of those college games dipped after the gambling controversies, the Knicks were able to move into Madison Square Garden full-time, only bolstering the team's appeal and legitimacy.

There were, then, real successes for the fledgling organization, but the 1950–1951 season wasn't without calamity. Red Auerbach had been the glue holding the Washington Capitols together, but prior to the start of the 1950–1951 campaign he moved to Boston to begin coaching the Celtics. Without its leader, Washington struggled and would not survive the season. Boston, meanwhile, would achieve the league's fourth best record, beginning its nascent ascent to league dominance. It was a rise that would be aided by another collapse that season. In the association's 1950 collegiate draft, Auerbach controversially used Boston's first pick, and the first overall pick in the draft, on Charles "Chuck" Share, a center from Bowling Green. In so doing, he overlooked the local hero from Holy Cross, Bob Cousy. Cousy instead landed in Chicago, but the Stags never made it to the season, leaving its players to be picked over by other teams. Even then, Auerbach wanted Chicago's established star, Max Zaslofsky, but in a lottery, he was left with Cousy. Boston was on its way.

Meanwhile, the league still belonged to George Mikan, who annually led the association in points. During the 1950–1951 season, though, despite his Lakers' regular season dominance, the team fell in the championship series to the Rochester Royals after Mikan fractured his leg. It would be Mikan's last season without a championship. His Lakers would dominate the next three seasons, leaving Minneapolis with five championships in six years before Mikan retired in 1954.

In a league of stars, Mikan towered over them all. His dominance of the association led Minneapolis to become its first real dynasty, which brought with it both positive and negative effects. On one hand, the dominance of stars like Mikan ensured that the league would be noticed by the readers of American sports pages. It would benefit attendance at venues like Madison Square Garden that advertised his presence over and against that of his team. At the same time, however, the consistent annual dominance of one player and one team disincentivized fans of rival organizations from attending games that didn't include the association's biggest stars. One of the core determinants of paid attendance in local markets was the belief by fans that their team had a chance to win. With the 1951 Finals upset by Rochester as the one exception, the Minneapolis Lakers dominated every season of the early NBA.

In an effort to fix what could be legitimately seen as a potential problem for the association, Podoloff and the governors widened the foul lane from six feet to twelve feet while maintaining the three-second rule about continuous time in the area. The new regulation, known as the "Mikan Rule," didn't stop the Lakers center from maintaining his league lead in points and rebounds, but it did, as many had hoped, reduce the distance between Mikan and everyone else, adding a measure of equity to the association's schedule. Still, he and his team would dominate the standings and the playoffs for the next three seasons. In 1954, however, Mikan retired. "I had a family growing, and I decided to be with them," he later explained. "I felt it was time to get started with the professional world outside of basketball." He was only twenty-nine years old.

The country he entered was in the process of an unprecedented economic boom built from the success of World War II and the passage of the GI Bill, which provided unemployment insurance for returning veterans unable to find work, money for veterans' postsecondary education, and low-interest loans with no down payment requirement for real estate purchases. Millions of veterans took advantage of the GI Bill, sparking education and housing booms that changed both the economic welfare of the American people and the country's physical landscape. An explosion in the construction industry was fed by standardization in housing and home appliances that created prefabricated neighborhoods symbolized most famously by Long Island's Levittown development. High tax rates kept government services available to those who needed them. The economy also created free time and disposable income for families, allowing them to participate in extracurricular activities like attendance at professional basketball games. Public transportation could take residents from neighborhoods like Levittown to arenas like Madison Square Garden, creating a new generation of professional fans.

Much of that boom was facilitated by the Republican administration of Dwight Eisenhower, and Mikan attempted to ride that Republican wave into his own political career. He lost a Minnesota congressional race in 1956 before one ill-fated season as the Lakers' coach. He then turned to a career in real estate law in Minnesota, taking advantage of the postwar construction boom in and around Minneapolis. Basketball, however, would always call him back.

Back in 1954, one of the other principal reasons for Mikan's retirement was a history of injury. He regularly played through pain, fracturing at least ten bones in his playing career and sustaining a variety of other maladies. The early NBA was a violent game, with frequent fights and hard fouls the norm. For some fans, that physical play was a draw, a recapitulation of hockey on hardwood, its own version of "roughing" and "cross checking," just as the fans from the association's original game in Toronto had interpreted. For others, however, the violence took something away from basketball's beauty, and the fouls that resulted from such violence took away from its pace. Many games turned into frustrating free throw contests, particularly at the end of games.

The pace was also slowed intentionally by the players themselves, as they often strategically held the ball to keep it out of the hands of superior players like Mikan. In one notorious contest between Fort Wayne and Minneapolis, the Pistons passed the ball back and forth on the Lakers' home court for long stretches, driving both their opponents and the Laker fans crazy. Spectators threw debris at the players; many demanded a refund. With four minutes left in the game, Fort Wayne was losing by one point, so they held the ball for the remainder before setting up a final shot to win the contest. It was the lowest scoring game in NBA history, the Pistons winning 19–18, and while it worried the board of governors, nothing Fort Wayne did was against the rules.

The combination of frequent fouling and intentional slow pacing hurt the game's ability to take full advantage of the postwar economic boom. Still, there were opportunities. The NBA had long given up the BAA's original fear of television and sought opportunities to grow the game through the medium. In 1953, the ABC network developed Major League Baseball's Game of the Week, the first network series devoted to sports. CBS would take over the series two years later, growing a desire, if not an expectation, among sports fans for weekend athletic programming on the major American networks. Still, the channels didn't really consider sports programming critical to their overall success in the 1950s; comedies and dramas were far more valuable. And the popularity of baseball and football left little room for professional basketball broadcasts.

Adding insult to injury, when the NBA did manage to include some of their games on national television, they did not highlight the best aspects of the game. In one contest during the 1953–1954 season, a national telecast ran out of time and cut the contest before its conclusion. The constant fouling and slow play led the game to last more than three hours. With so few opportunities to take advantage of national television, Podoloff and the board of governors realized that something had to be done. It was Danny Biasone, owner of the Syracuse Nationals, who came up with a solution to the problem. "I looked at the box scores from the games I enjoyed, games where they didn't screw around and stall," Biasone explained. "I noticed each team took about 60 shots. That meant 120 shots per game. So I took 2,880 seconds (48 minutes) and divided that by 120 shots. The result was 24 seconds per shot."

The new shot clock would speed up games and create more scoring for an association seeking momentum after the retirement of its most popular attraction. Scores would rise and new teams would have an opportunity for success. In the four seasons following Mikan's retirement, four different NBA teams won championships. The Syracuse Nationals won in 1955, followed by the Warriors and the Celtics. Boston's 1957 championship, its first, would begin an unprecedented run of dominance, but before the team's multiple years of consecutive titles, it would fall to defeat in 1958 to St. Louis.

Ben Kerner and Leo Ferris founded the team that would become the St. Louis Hawks as the Buffalo Bisons in 1946, the same year the Celtics and Knicks joined the BAA. From Buffalo, Kerner moved the team to the Mississippi River, locating in the area of Rock Island and Moline in Illinois and Davenport in Iowa, renaming the team the Tri-Cities Black-hawks after the area's infamous Black Hawk War.

From the Tri-Cities it was on to Milwaukee, a larger market that Kerner hoped could provide more profit; there the newly named Hawks suffered through a span of losing seasons. Those losses ensured that profit would not come, and in 1955 the team moved again, this time to St. Louis. Under the leadership of general manager Marty Blake and the play of star Bob Pettit, the team began to have real success, making the NBA Finals in 1957, its second St. Louis season, before losing in seven games to the Celtics. The following year, the Hawks improved again, winning the franchise's only championship after a six-game series with the Celtics.

It was the last time in the next eight seasons that the Celtics would lose an NBA Finals series. But the Hawks' championship in 1958 would be substantial for another reason, as well. The club from St. Louis would be the last all-White championship team in the NBA.

8

Integration

DESPITE THE BASKETBALL Association of America's (BAA) agreement that Black players would not participate on association teams, the Buffalo Bisons, which would become the St. Louis Hawks, included on their 1946 roster William "Pop" Gates, former star of the Renaissance Big Five. Gates, who played his college basketball at Atlanta University, integrated the team and the league the year prior to Jackie Robinson's 1947 Dodgers debut, and thus the team that became the Hawks, the team that would later become the last all-White NBA champion, began, if briefly, the original blackening of the National Basketball Association (NBA).

When Ben Kerner moved his Buffalo team to the Tri-Cities border of Iowa and Illinois, however, he found an area with a small-town mentality, with no hotel in Moline willing to house Gates. Kerner would not invite him back for the 1947–1948 season. The play of Pop Gates with the 1946 Bisons was significant, but his time with the team was short and not mimicked by Buffalo's competitors, the result of the BAA gentlemen's agreement between team owners. Such segregationist restrictions, however, would not last long.

Nor was Gates's play with the Bisons the genesis point of professional or collegiate basketball's desegregation. Unlike baseball, which had distinct leagues for White and Black players prior to a clear segregationist Rubicon crossed by Robinson in 1947, basketball's integration was more complex, more fraught with a history of urban play and racial interconnectedness building from the early work of YMCAs. Without specific Black professional leagues, early pro teams like the Rens and Globetrotters played a large number of their games against White teams. It created an early situation that preferenced team segregation over game segregation.

Early university basketball inverted that paradigm. While professional baseball and basketball, as well as institutional YMCAs, maintained a stark color line in the early twentieth centuries, several White colleges accepted talented Black athletes. Fenwick Watkins, for example, joined the University of Vermont basketball team as early as 1905, playing both forward and guard for three seasons. He would later join other athletic teams at the university. Wilbur Wood joined the basketball team at the University of Nebraska two years later, the consensus best player for the Cornhuskers from 1907 to 1910. In 1909, Cumberland Posey, who would become influential in both Black professional basketball as a player and in professional baseball as a team owner, played for Penn State's basketball team for two seasons, then later played for Duquesne, in violation of eligibility requirements, from 1916 to 1918. Perhaps most famously, Paul Robeson, who would go on to a career in theater, film, music, and civil rights activism, played football and basketball at Rutgers from 1915 to 1919, despite being one of only three Black students enrolled at the school.

The inclusion of Black players at predominantly White universities was important, but it was by no means integration. Watkins, Wood, Posey, and Robeson were exceptions to a broadly accepted though usually unstated rule against including Black players on White college teams. And even when team segregation was breached, game segregation was not. Historically Black colleges and universities developed substantial basketball programs in the early twentieth century, but the network of schools served as a series of league formations, creating an organized structure of opponents that ensured that White college teams—or, on occasion, predominantly White college teams—would play other White teams, and Black college teams would be restricted to opponents from other African American universities.

The impetus for segregation in professional and collegiate basketball fed from the impetus for segregation in national life. As part of its project of post-Reconstruction retrenchment, the states of the former Confederacy began in the late nineteenth century to minimize or eliminate the Black right to vote. Violence was always part of that effort, but state legislators moved to institutionalize the process with literacy tests, property qualifications, and poll taxes. Grandfather clauses in some states ensured that poor, illiterate White voters would be able to bypass the restrictions. And the efforts at disenfranchisement would have a crippling effect, codified by the Supreme Court's *Williams v. Mississippi* ruling in 1898. In Louisiana's 1896 election, for example, 130,000 Black men voted. By 1904, that number had been reduced to 1,300.

Another part of that retrenchment required regaining control of Black lives and bodies, so southern states began passing "Jim Crow" laws, mandating segregation in almost all public facilities. The imperative for segregation would take over every facet of southern life, but the domino effect of state action began on railroads. In 1889, for example, Black Baptists from Savannah bought first-class tickets to travel to a convention in Indianapolis. News was telegraphed ahead, and the riders were confronted by a White mob at a railroad stop in Georgia, where they were threatened and beaten. In the circular logic of southern conservatism, such violence was cited as reason to make segregation into law. Tennessee mandated segregation on railroad cars in 1881, Florida in 1887. Other states followed suit.

Louisiana took its turn in 1890 with the Separate Car Act, a law that mandated separate train cars for White and Black passengers. The following year, a group of concerned Black business leaders in New Orleans formed a citizens committee and planned a test case to challenge the law's constitutionality, a case that after years of litigation finally ended in the Supreme Court's *Plessy v. Ferguson* decision in 1896. The court's decision validated segregation, arguing that "legislation is powerless to eradicate racial instincts or to abolish distinctions based on physical differences. . . . If one race be inferior to the other socially, the Constitution of the United States cannot put them on the same plane."

After *Plessy*, southern states were emboldened to segregate every aspect of White and Black social life. But along with disenfranchisement and segregation, southern states also instituted the convict lease system, renting convicts to private contractors like coal-mining firms, railroads, and planters. The state got paid, and the companies got cheap labor they could treat like slaves. The convicts were ill-fed, ill-clothed, and worked almost to death. The mortality rates of prisoners in some states were more than 25 percent, and more than 90 percent of prisoners leased were Black.

Added to such formalized indignities were episodes of horrific violence. In 1886, in Washington County, Texas, for example, masked Democrats tried to steal ballot boxes in a Republican precinct. Armed

Black men resisted and shot one of the White men, leading to eight Black arrests, and three retributive lynchings. In Phoenix, South Carolina, in 1898, a White Republican candidate for Congress tried to convince Black voters to fill out affidavits claiming they were denied the right to vote. White Democrats responded violently, shooting the candidate, then going on a rampage killing an uncertain number of Black men. Meanwhile, in Wilmington, North Carolina, race relations were tense. Alfred Moore Wadell, a former Confederate and US congressman, vowed in a speech to "choke the Cape Fear [river] with carcasses." When Alex Manly, the editor of the local Black newspaper, the *Daily Record*, pushed back against such rhetoric, a White mob destroyed the newspaper office. At least a dozen Black men were murdered; more than a thousand Wilmington residents fled.

Riots in these and other cities were horrific open wounds, but more routinized lynchings created death by a thousand cuts. Between 1889 and 1932, 3,745 people were lynched, an average of between two and three every week. And in the 1890s alone there was an average of more than 180 lynchings per year.

Many in the South responded to the violence, both vigilante and institutional, by leaving. The Great Migration out of the South started slowly. In the 1910s, for example, 90 percent of Black Americans still lived in the South. But the migration would develop momentum, sparked in particular by events like World War I. Between 1910 and 1940, 1.75 million Black people left the South, doubling the Black population outside the region. Most went to urban hubs in the North like Washington, Philadelphia, New York, Pittsburgh, Cleveland, and Detroit. Upon arrival, however, they found that while Jim Crow laws didn't exist in the cities, a version of Jim Crow did. It kept Black workers from better paying factory jobs and shunted them into segregated enclaves.

That residential segregation, however, led to the creation of strong, all-Black neighborhoods. As urban racism limited options for Black skilled workers, entrepreneurs turned to the segregated sections of cities as a potential escape from that bigotry. As White collusion kept African Americans from residency in certain neighborhoods, Black neighborhoods would need a thriving business community to keep them afloat. Real estate agencies, funeral homes, doctors' offices, newspapers, groceries, and restaurants soon opened for business, making their money selling solely to a Black customer base.

Segregation, then, was associated most violently with the American South, but it was practiced in various ways throughout a country that based much of its thought and action on White supremacy, keeping the majority of college basketball teams segregated in the interwar period following World War I. There were, however, exceptions to that rule. Ralph Bunche, for example, who would go on to become a diplomat and Nobel laureate, played for UCLA in the early 1920s. George Gregory captained the Columbia University basketball team in the late 1920s and became the first Black All-American in 1931. David DeJernett starred at Indiana Central before signing with the Rens in 1936. And then there was Jackie Robinson himself, who played for UCLA beginning in 1939. Though he is best known for collegiate football and track, Robinson also played basketball for coach Wilbur Johns.

In 1944, there was even progress, no matter how secretive, in the South. On Sunday, March 12, while most of Durham, North Carolina, was in church, the medical school team of Duke University slipped off campus to the gymnasium at North Carolina College for Negroes, led by legendary coach John McLendon. There were no fans and no fanfare. Duke's administration didn't know about the game. But in the segregated South, Black and White college teams played one another, and North Carolina College for Negroes routed the Blue Devils by 44 points. It wasn't a racial reckoning, however; it was a mutual love of basketball. After a period of rest, the two teams decided to play again, this time creating new teams from each school, two integrated groups playing college basketball on a sunny Sunday in North Carolina. Both teams kept the game secret and Durham police never discovered the violation.

While Duke wouldn't desegregate its basketball team until 1966, there were a variety of factors that led various universities outside the region to desegregate their basketball teams much earlier. There was, for example, broad national criticism of the southern Closed Society and the racial violence that permeated the region. The actions of the Nazi Party in Germany in the years leading to World War II made many wary that there was a similar segregationist oligarchy in the United States. In sports, Jesse Owens had given lie to White supremacist doctrine by dominating the 1936 Berlin Olympics while throngs of Nazi spectators looked on.

It made Owens, a Black man, a national hero after successfully competing against White athletes. Then there was Joe Louis. In 1936, as Owens was dominating in Berlin, Louis fought German champion boxer Max Schmelling and lost. But two years later, and two months after Hitler annexed Austria, Louis fought Schmelling again. This time he won, knocking out Schmelling in the first round and figuratively defending America in the process. Two-thirds of the American population heard the fight on the radio.

Finally, Robinson himself would take hold of the national consciousness when he took the field for the Dodgers in 1947. Of course, baseball's integration was not the only outgrowth of the intersection of sports and race. In the fall of 1946, as Pop Gates began his brief tenure with the BAA's Bisons, the National Football League's (NFL) Los Angeles Rams hired Black players and integrated the NFL. The Cleveland Browns did the same for the All-America Football Conference. In 1949, the American Bowling Congress allowed Black competitors. Such moves, of course, were not an immediate driver of universal integration or acceptance of Black players. It was in 1959, for example, twelve years after Robinson integrated the Dodgers, that the Boston Red Sox hired a Black player, finally desegregating every Major League Baseball team.

Back in 1947, college basketball was left with the immediate impact of Robinson's arrival in Brooklyn. At the end of the 1946–1947 season, as Robinson was in Dodgers' spring training, another UCLA player, Don Barksdale, became the first Black consensus All-American. As the 1947–1948 season approached, the Missouri Valley Athletic Conference agreed to desegregate its teams. It was a significant move, but Missouri Valley was not one of the major conferences; it didn't have the national profile of organizations like the Big Ten, but there would also be progress in that conference.

The Big Ten, founded as the Western Conference, long maintained an agreement between member universities to only include White players on their teams prior to World War II. Indiana high school basketball was less restrictive and included desegregated teams well before its universities. Bill Garrett, for example, was a Black star who led Shelbyville High School to the 1947 state championship but originally had to enroll at Tennessee A&I, a historically Black college, because Indiana's major universities did not recruit him. Garrett and his Black Shelbyville teammates

suffered a variety of racial attacks. Indiana had been a hub of Ku Klux
Klan activity in the 1920s, amassing more than half a million members in
the terrorist organization in its second wave of popularity following the
group's reformulation in the 1910s. But it was also a state obsessed with
basketball, one with a large YMCA presence that encouraged the game's
integration. And it had Indiana University, source of the state's national
basketball pride, the president of which was amenable to desegregating
the Hoosier team. Garrett would ultimately join the state's flagship after
negotiations between leaders of the YMCA, Indiana's administration,
and Branch McCracken, the Hoosiers' head basketball coach, desegregated Indiana and with it the Big Ten.

Meanwhile, sixty miles east of Bloomington at the Indiana State
Teachers College in Terre Haute, the basketball team had already
desegregated, led by a young coach named John Wooden. Wooden's
team played in the National Association of Intercollegiate Basketball
(NAIB), a division dedicated to small college teams. After qualifying
for the NAIB's tournament in 1947, Wooden, in his first season with the
team, refused the invitation because the association did not accept Black
players. When Wooden's team earned an invitation the next season, led
by Black star Clarence Walker, the NAIB abandoned its Whites-only
policy, making Walker the first Black player to compete in a postseason
tournament. Indiana State made it to the 1948 championship game, ultimately losing to the University of Louisville. In the summer after Indiana State's run, UCLA's Barksdale played on the US Olympic basketball
team, becoming the first Black player to win a gold medal in the sport.
And he did so after practices scheduled in the segregated South under
the leadership of Kentucky's Adolph Rupp, coach of the Olympic team, a
racist who had never coached a Black player and wouldn't again until the
last seasons of his career.

The accumulated momentum would ultimately lead both the NCAA
and the National Invitation Tournament (NIT) competitions to desegregate two seasons later, first allowing Black players to participate in
1950. Prior to the move, John McLendon said, "The NCAA may mean
National Collegiate Athletic Association to some people, but to us it
means No Colored Athletes Allowed." The colleges were sensitive
to such criticism and thus made the tournament change, and it was a
change with immediate consequences. The City College team that won

both the NCAA and NIT tournaments that season, and which would later become mired in scandal, started three Jewish players and two African American players. The group's unprecedented dominance of the 1950 postseason could not have happened without the desegregationist rule changes. Black players first had a chance to play, and they promptly won every available championship.

The changes in the collegiate game would be hard for the professionals to ignore. Though the gentlemen's agreement had kept Black players out of the game after the brief stint of Pop Gates, it did not extend to all non-White athletes. In the 1947–1948 season, a Japanese American point guard from the University of Utah, Wataru Misaka, played for the New York Knicks, breaking a different color barrier in the professional game. Misaka's collegiate play, first at Weber State, then at Utah, took place against the backdrop of severe anti-Japanese sentiment during World War II and internment camps that imprisoned more than 130,000 Americans of Japanese descent. Becoming a professional just two years after the closing of those camps was both an act of courage and a necessary advancement for the association.

Black players, however, were still barred. That would change after the 1950 NCAA and NIT tournaments. In the 1950 NBA Draft, Red Auerbach's Boston Celtics drafted Chuck Cooper from Duquesne University, the first African American selected in the NBA. The draft took place on April 25. The following day, the Washington Capitols signed Harold Hunter, a guard from North Carolina College who had helped his team win the 1950 Colored Intercollegiate Athletic Association Tournament. Though Hunter was cut in training camp, his signing itself was an important milestone. One month later, the New York Knicks signed Nathaniel "Sweetwater" Clifton. Sweetwater had played collegiately at Xavier University of Louisiana, a historically Black college in New Orleans, but he came to professional prominence with the Renaissance Big Five, then the Harlem Globetrotters, which led to his signing by the Knicks. West Virginia State's Earl Lloyd, who had been drafted in the ninth round of the 1950 draft by the Capitols, became the first Black player to participate in a game, playing on Halloween night. The following day, Chuck Cooper played. Three days after that, Clifton played.

Attempting to take advantage of the new acceptance of Black players, Kerner's Tri-Cities Blackhawks decided to try again with his desegregationist sentiment, signing Hank DeZonie from Atlanta University. DeZonie had played with the Dayton Rens, an NBL team that had collapsed before the merger, and in December he signed with the Blackhawks. The provincial Tri-Cities, however, had not abandoned the racism that eliminated Gates from professional play. "The coach didn't know basketball, and I couldn't bother with segregation," DeZonie remembered. "They put me up with an old woman who chewed tobacco and the snow was up to the ceiling. I was past that." He played five games with the Blackhawks before leaving the team.

DeZonie's experience was a reminder that desegregation was no cure-all for White supremacy. Despite the prevalence of racism, however, most of the early Black players stayed in the association. And many of them thrived, despite the bigotry they faced. In 1953, for example, Don Barksdale broke yet another barrier by becoming the first Black NBA All-Star.

That same year, the man who would not simply be an All-Star, but the first legitimate Black professional superstar, was beginning his first collegiate season at the University of San Francisco (USF). Bill Russell had not been a great high school player, but he had size, potential, and a feel for the game. Under the leadership of USF coach Phil Woolpert, Russell became legitimately great. Or, perhaps, despite Woolpert. The Dons' coach emphasized fundamental, organized play that often worked against the instincts of Russell and Black teammates like KC Jones and Hal Perry. But as Russell grew, both in stature and on the court, the team continued to improve. Russell made everyone around him better.

There were, however, obvious and inevitable problems, particularly when the Dons played road games. Racist jeering from fans was a consistent concern. When an Oklahoma City hotel refused to allow the team to stay during a 1954 tournament, White and Black players moved to a local collegiate dormitory. It was one in many defining racial indignities for Russell that would drive him to succeed. The following two seasons, Russell, Jones, and the Dons captured back-to-back national championships, winning fifty-five consecutive games in the process. USF was not a traditional basketball power. It was a small school with a modest program, but Russell made it a powerhouse. Or the powerhouse of Russell carried the Dons to the program's most successful seasons. John Wooden, who had moved from Indiana State to Westwood, California, and the

Bruins of UCLA, called Russell "the greatest defensive man I've ever seen."

When he entered the 1956 NBA Draft, the paradigm shifted. Now a Black player was the most coveted asset for professional teams. Red Auerbach wanted Russell for the Celtics but had a low draft choice because of his team's recent success. He convinced the Rochester Royals, who had the first pick, not to draft Russell by reminding them of the signing bonus he would command and by offering to bring the Ice Capades, owned by Walter Brown, to Rochester. Kerner's St. Louis Hawks drafted Russell with the second pick, and Auerbach agreed to trade All-Star center and St. Louis native Ed Macauley, along with Cliff Hagan, for the San Francisco star. Auerbach had already used the team's territorial compensatory pick on Tommy Heinsohn and later drafted Russell's teammate KC Jones. In one night, the Celtics acquired two Black stars and three players who would eventually join the Hall of Fame.

In less than a decade, the association had moved from reluctant desegregation to team-building with Black stars. In the first Celtics season of Russell and Jones, Boston would win its first NBA championship. The following season, the Celtics would lose in the Finals to St. Louis after a foot injury kept Russell from two games. The Hawks were the last all-White team to win the title, and their path was cleared by an injury to the game's dominant Black star. Times had decidedly changed. The Celtics, led by Russell, would win the next eight NBA championships, from 1959 to 1966, one of the most successful dynasties in the history of professional sports.

The way for that progression had been paved by civil rights activists who had worked to publicize the negative consequences of segregation. In 1954, as Russell and his teammates were being turned away from an Oklahoma City hotel, the Supreme Court's *Brown v. Board of Education* decision overturned the *Plessy* ruling from 1896. "We come then to the question presented: Does segregation of children in public schools solely on the basis of race, even though the physical facilities and other 'tangible' factors may be equal, deprive the children of the minority group of equal educational opportunities? We believe that it does." But if "separate educational facilities are inherently unequal," as the ruling stated, then segregated facilities more broadly were also inherently unequal. *Brown*, then, wasn't just a blow to White southern conceptions of public education, but to White southern conceptions of public life.

In 1955, as Russell led the Dons to their first NCAA Championship, the court issued its *Brown II* ruling, demanding that state and local governments move "with all deliberate speed" to integrate the schools. White southerners reacted violently, a retrenchment represented most publicly by the August murder of Emmett Till in Money, Mississippi. The Black South, however, pushed back. In December, after Russell had begun his second collegiate championship season, Rosa Parks refused to give up her seat on a Montgomery bus, sparking a boycott that would last 381 days and introduce a powerful new voice to the nation. Martin Luther King Jr. built on his success in Montgomery by creating the Southern Christian Leadership Conference (SCLC) in early 1957. Months later, the Celtics would win their first championship, and the semester following the win would see the civil rights movement spread to Little Rock, Arkansas, when nine students attempted to desegregate the city's Central High School.

In early 1960, as the Celtics dynasty progressed, four Black students at North Carolina A&T College in Greensboro sat down at a local drugstore lunch counter and asked for service, the opening salvo in what would become known as the sit-in movement, where young activists challenged local segregation laws by demanding equal access to public facilities. That movement would lead to the creation of the Student Nonviolent Coordinating Committee (SNCC). Together with the Congress of Racial Equality, SNCC then launched its next attack on segregation by conducting "freedom rides" across the South, taking integrated busses across southern state lines in 1961 to force the federal government to take action.

By 1963, the civil rights movement had moved to Birmingham to take advantage of the racist violence of the city's police commissioner, Eugene "Bull" Connor. In April, King and his SCLC began "Project C" to take advantage of an official who they knew would respond harshly to their tactics, thus ensuring the media attention they needed to facilitate government action on desegregation. It was an incredibly violent summer. White police officers unleashed dogs and water hoses on Black marchers. Four young girls were killed when Birmingham's Sixteenth Street Baptist Church was bombed. When thousands of Birmingham residents protested the city's lack of action after the bombing, the Birmingham police killed two more protesters in the resulting melee. Perhaps most importantly, the violence was televised, making the nightly news all over the country and all over the world. President John Kennedy went on national television to address the situation, arguing that racial violence was "retarding our nation's economic and social progress and weakening the respect with which the rest of the world regards us."

Still, he wanted calm more than anything else. The Kennedy administration was reluctant about the possibility of a late summer "March on Washington for Jobs and Freedom," but when it realized there was no way to stop the gathering, Kennedy endorsed the event. Thus it was that on August 28, 1963, an integrated group of more than two hundred thousand people marched through Washington to the Lincoln Memorial, where King gave his famous "I Have a Dream" speech.

Kennedy, for his part, had already begun working on legislation that would address many of the concerns of movement organizers, and after his death Lyndon Johnson shepherded the Civil Rights Act of 1964 to passage in the legislature. The law strengthened federal remedies against job discrimination, prohibited racial discrimination in public accommodations, and even barred discrimination based on sex. While legislators debated the bill, however, civil rights workers in Mississippi began a voter registration drive they called "Freedom Summer." It was an action that provoked even more retributive racial violence, segregationists murdering six civil rights workers over those hot summer months. Johnson would make use of the national sympathy resonating from the Mississippi violence to get the other important piece of civil rights legislation passed, the Voting Rights Act of 1965, which mandated federal oversight of local elections in the South.

The push against segregation conditioned team owners, college administrators, and basketball fans for the racial changes afoot in the game, but so, too, did the play of the new Black stars, whose talent generated their opportunities. In 1958–1959, for example, as the Celtics were beginning their dynasty, another talented Black center, Wilt Chamberlain, left the University of Kansas after his junior year and joined the Harlem Globetrotters for a season while waiting for eligibility for the NBA Draft. Chamberlain was a statistical marvel, named the Most Outstanding Player of the 1957 NCAA Final Four even though his team lost to North Carolina in the championship game. After his year with the Globetrotters, he was drafted by the Philadelphia Warriors and stayed with the team after its move to San Francisco before finally being traded to Philadelphia's new team, the former Syracuse Nationals, now known as the 76ers. Chamberlain and Russell dominated the NBA throughout the 1960s, the former winning individual statistical awards and the latter winning championships. Together they filled the role that Mikan once served, the most visible and overwhelming stars of the period who captured the imagination of basketball fans across the country. In the process, and unlike Mikan, they normalized Black dominance and celebrity in the game during the age of civil rights.

Meanwhile, the number of Black players in high-level college basketball continued to increase. As the Freedom Rides commenced in 1961, the University of Cincinnati won the NCAA Championship with three Black starters. The following season, they repeated the feat with four Black starters. The 1962–1963 season was dominated by Loyola Chicago, another team that started four Black players. Like San Francisco before them, the Ramblers' program was modest compared to the titans of college basketball, but the team, led by players like Jerry Harkness, Vic Rouse, and Les Hunter and coached by George Ireland, found magic in 1963, Rouse making a game-winning shot in overtime of the championship game as the clock expired.

The game most remembered during the tournament that season, however, was a second-round contest, when Loyola Chicago faced Mississippi State University from the segregated Southeastern Conference. When Mississippi State was offered an invitation to the tournament, there was debate about whether the school would accept. After a student petition demanding the team play, and hundreds of letters from fans across the state, university president Dean Colvard agreed to allow the team to participate "unless hindered by competent authority." The competent authorities in Mississippi, however, were avid White supremacists, and they were concerned. The year prior, James Meredith had desegregated the state's other major university, Ole Miss, sparking the ire of Governor Ross Barnett, who promised Mississippi's White citizens, "We will not surrender to the evil and illegal forces of tyranny." After John Kennedy intervened, however, Meredith entered campus, sparking riots from students and others, forcing Kennedy to send in the National Guard, which led to a spate of violence known as the Ole Miss War. Forty-eight National Guardsmen were injured, and twenty-eight federal marshals were wounded by gunfire. Two people were killed, one of whom was a French journalist covering the story for the international news.

Such was the context in which university leaders were making decisions about the Mississippi State basketball team. In a controversial meeting of the state college board, with protesters on both sides waiting outside, officials voted to let the team play. But Barnett and other Mississippi politicians were vehemently opposed, and two state senators obtained an injunction against the team's travel to East Lansing, Michigan, where the game against Loyola would take place. The Aggies' coach, Babe McCarthy, worried that authorities would enforce the injunction and so spirited his team away, traveled to Michigan, and played the game against Loyola, the first time a team from the Deep South played an integrated contest. Harkness remembered later the significance of the game. "The flashbulbs just went off unbelievably," he said, "and at that time, boy, I knew that this was more than just a game. This was history being made."

Months later, the March on Washington would bring King's "I Have a Dream" speech to the nation. One season later, in 1964, Elvin Hayes and Don Chaney, two Black high school prodigies from Louisiana, would desegregate the University of Houston's basketball team. One season after that, Don Haskins's Texas Western team started five Black players in the NCAA championship game against Adolph Rupp's segregated University of Kentucky team. In one of the most celebrated games in collegiate history, Texas Western, led by Bobby Joe Hill and Dave Lattin, defeated a Wildcat team led by Louie Dampier and Pat Riley at the University of Maryland's Cole Fieldhouse. It was a symbolic victory, one that encapsulated for many the racial progression developing in basketball and in the nation as a whole over the previous decade. Less celebrated but just as symbolic, while Texas Western and Kentucky played in Maryland, Brigham Young University and NYU played on the same night, March 19, for the NIT championship in Madison Square Garden. Brigham Young won the game, the last time an all-White college team achieved a national championship.

The racial politics of March 19, 1966, mattered. The games in Maryland and New York seemed to many fans to signal an irrevocable shift in college basketball, but in reality, the games were symptoms of a shift that was already taking place. Later that year, for example, Charlie Scott would join the University of North Carolina, another dominant school in

the former Confederacy, to desegregate its basketball team. The following season, Perry Wallace would join the basketball team at Vanderbilt,
finally desegregating the Southeastern Conference (SEC). The rest of the
conference would slowly, reluctantly follow suit, with the final team to
desegregate ironically being Mississippi State in 1972. But for all the scrutiny given to the championships of 1966 and the slow southern change
they helped produce, the year was a brief respite from the dominance of a
team that had long been integrated.

John Wooden's UCLA Bruins had won the NCAA Championship in
1962, 1964, and 1965. The season after Texas Western won the title, the
Bruins added sophomore sensation Lew Alcindor, who led the team to
an undefeated season and another championship, the first of what would
become ten consecutive NCAA titles. In 1968, Alcindor's UCLA Bruins
traveled to Houston's Astrodome to play Hayes, Chaney, and the University of Houston in what became known as the Game of the Century.
The first nationally televised regular season college basketball game had
more than fifty-two thousand fans in attendance to witness Houston end
UCLA's forty-seven-game winning streak.

UCLA would have its revenge against Houston in the NCAA tournament, winning another in its long line of championships, and Alcindor
would lead the team and the nation in all three of his collegiate seasons.
He was one of the most dominant players the college game had ever
known, averaging more than 26 points and more than 15 rebounds per
contest. His three NCAA Championships set a standard that would help
the Bruins win seven more consecutively after his graduation.

There was concern by many pundits that the collegiate dominance of
UCLA and the professional dominance of Boston was diminishing competition and driving fans of other teams from attendance at games. But
there was no longer concern about the viability of basketball's integration. Alcindor's race was not the problem it would have been decades
prior. Prominent collegiate teams had successfully normalized blackness
as a part of organized basketball, further darkening the feeder system for
the professional ranks in the second half of the twentieth century. The
full acceptance of Black players, however, was less universal, and many
White powerbrokers worried that the continued blackening of the game
would drive away White fans. And while Alcindor's blackness was no
longer a problem, those same powerbrokers, league and team officials in

both the NBA and NCAA, often derided his performance of blackness in public spaces and the unapologetic activism of athletes like Alcindor and Russell.

9

Race and Civil Rights

"BASKETBALL WAS ORIGINALLY invented as a white man's game," wrote philosopher and diplomat Michael Novak, but in the post–World War II culture, its "mythos became more than urban. It became in a symbolic and ritual way uniquely black." Such was the result of its sophistication, its flashy showmanship, and its association with urban cityscapes. "Basketball, although neither invented by blacks nor played only by blacks, came to allow the mythic world of the black experience to enter directly, with minimal change, into American life." Baseball was a game with Black athletes, as was football, where at least the quarterback was going to be White. Basketball, by contrast, was a Black game. Both baseball and football featured position differences and assumptions about intelligence that allowed fans to maintain their racial prejudices and still identify with teams featuring Black players. But no professional sport would come to be associated with blackness as was basketball.

Basketball was tethered to ethnicity almost from its inception, as in the 1890s "inner-city settlement houses became the breeding grounds for future interscholastic, collegiate, and professional stars," explains historian Steven Riess, "almost all drawn from inner-city ethnic groups." As teams began professionalizing in the 1920s, the game grew from those ethnic enclaves, where Jewish teams like the B'nai Brith All-Stars and the Philadelphia SPHAs, Irish teams like the Original Celtics, and African American teams like the New York Renaissance Big Five dominated.

It was that urbanity, Riess notes, that ultimately drew Black players at or below the poverty line to the game and consequently drove the perception of its blackness in the postwar period as it had its ethnicity prior to World War II. "Other young athletes may learn basketball," wrote historian Pete Axthelm in 1970, "but city kids live it." Basketball "is considered a city game in a society which romanticizes the pastoral," wrote Jeffrey Sammons a generation later. "It has no Ruth, Gehrig, Cobb, Dimaggio, or Matthewson, icons of a white athletic dominance of years gone by. Although basketball is probably far more American than baseball in its pace of play, constant action, and undeniably urban foundations, no enabling mythology has been created for or seen in it historically. Moreover, it is now a black game in numbers, superstars, culture, and symbols."

That being the case, professional basketball's relationship to protest was ingrained in the racial coding given to the game in the process of its evolution. Inevitably, however, when placed within that particular crucible, protest in professional basketball would encompass far more than simply participation in the games themselves. American professional players would fight within the structure of their leagues, and they would use the prominence provided by those leagues to fight for broader civil rights outside the boundary lines created by their wealth and prestige. It was for Black professional basketball players a two-front war, a Double V campaign against discrimination created by the game and discrimination just outside the doors of the arena. That fight would leave a legacy of protest in professional basketball that redounded to those in subsequent generations who leveraged the gains from within created by those players who came before them to continue the clarion call for racial equality outside of it.

It could be a fraught endeavor for players, owners, and fans in the civil rights decades following World War II. When Black professional basketball teams, the Harlem Magicians and the New York Olympians, hanging on to the segregated celebrity of teams like the Rens and the Globetrotters, scheduled a game in Birmingham in January 1957, for example, the requirement that White and Black audiences had to attend separately drew protests from the Birmingham Baptist Ministers Conference and rights organizations like the Alabama Christian Movement for Human Rights and the Emancipation Association of Birmingham, all of whom petitioned promoters to cancel the game unless everyone could attend the same contest. The petitions went unheeded, the separate games played, much to the dismay of many Black residents of the region. One letter-writer from Tuscaloosa pointed out that four Black churches and two ministers' homes had recently been bombed "because of their fight against segregation. I am sure if these outstanding athletes knew that Negroes are now making great sacrifices for first-class citizenship," the letter explained, "they would not come South to stamp their approval on segregation by playing to segregated groups."

Also in 1957, the Georgia state legislature narrowly failed to pass a new sports segregation law that prohibited any integrated competition in the state and began making another effort to revive the attempt in 1958. A frustrated Marion Jackson, sports editor of the *Atlanta Daily World*, argued that "the white folks of Georgia are willing to surrender their civil liberties in obedience to the idol god of jimcrow [*sic*] rather than to take a stand for decency and tolerance." He pointed out that southern legislatures passed no legislation beneficial to Black residents following the *Brown* decision, and that new segregation laws like Georgia's sports effort still proliferated, even though they were cutting off the state's nose to spite its face, prohibiting both good competition and legitimate revenue. In 1961, seven Black men were arrested in Savannah after playing basketball on a municipal court designated as Whites only. The Georgia NAACP, which was monitoring the case, claimed that it was impossible to tell whether or not the action was intended as a protest because the city did not have any municipal courts that were not designated for Whites.

Such racial inconsistencies also existed at the national level. As Damion L. Thomas noted in the decade following World War II, the State Department "attempted to develop a relationship" with the Harlem Globetrotters, hoping to encourage Black Americans to see the American Dream as "available to individual African Americans despite segregation." The State Department did so, Thomas argued, because it saw "the Globetrotters' cooning as well as their degrading caricatures of African Americans" as reflecting "the behavior, attitudes, and mind-set of most black Americans. Hence, State Department arguments simultaneously stressed racial progress, but also the notion that African Americans' 'unsophisticated behavior' made them unfit or at least ill-prepared for full equality." It was a situation that led even Black basketball success to work against integration, against the full participation of Black players with White, a situation even sponsored by the federal government.

That being the case, the desegregation of the NBA in the 1950s was significant, but it also signified the looming issue that race would remain in the new organization. The *Pittsburgh Courier*'s Jack Saunders, for example, took the Philadelphia Warriors to task in 1953 for being one of the last professional basketball holdouts in hiring Black players. "Apparently the Philadelphia Warriors have too many good white players to give Negro players a break," wrote Saunders facetiously, despite the fact that "the Warriors had lost 27 of 33 games played." There were many who accused the team of prejudice. "If that be true the owners of the Warriors think more of prejudice than they think of money." The paper cast most of the blame on Eddie Gottlieb, the former SPHA and the Warriors' owner and coach, who was rumored to consider quitting because of the team's lack of success, a situation, Saunders argued, that could have been avoided by incorporating talented Black players.

"Has the National Basketball Association the strength to protect its players from segregation practices in biased cities?" asked *World* sports editor Marion Jackson. The answer, as of February 1959, seemed to be yes. In response to segregation in West Virginia, Minneapolis Lakers' star forward Elgin Baylor refused to play in an exhibition game in the state's capital. "A pro basketball player dunked a free throw through the hoop of segregation," proclaimed the *Los Angeles Sentinel* in a confused metaphor. When Baylor's Lakers were scheduled to play Cincinnati in Charleston, West Virginia, the city assured Minneapolis president Bob Short that there would be no segregation in the city, but the local hotel refused to accommodate Baylor and his Black teammates. The team moved in its entirety to a Black hotel, and Baylor refused to participate in the game. "Such is the stuff men are made of," gushed the *Sentinel*. A local promoter for the American Business Club, which sponsored the Charleston game, demanded that the NBA punish its young star for not playing, but the association defended Baylor and responded to the incident with a staunch anti-segregation policy, President Podoloff announcing that before any NBA team played in a nonleague city, "we will insist on a clause to protect players and clubs from embarrassment." The Lakers agreed, Short announcing that the team would play no further neutral-site games "unless we are guaranteed common facilities for rooming and feeding all our players." The *Sentinel* praised Short, as well, but Baylor was the story. His "refusal to compromise with all the evil that segregation stands for is a tribute to his character and should give the faint-hearted something to think about. He has shown the way."

Baylor's actions "will do much to topple ole Jim Crow from the sports picture," guessed Black press columnist Brock Brockenbury. "This was an act that even Jackie Robinson might have hesitated to pull." Such was a common theme. Columnist Dan Burley claimed that Baylor "overnight has become the 'Jackie Robinson' of pro basketball in his strictly one-man crusade against southern Jim Crow." Brockenbury encouraged his readers to send letters of thanks to both Baylor and the Lakers to assure officials that "what they did is appreciated by us."

Baylor was grateful for the support. "I've appreciated the many replies I've received from various parts of the country," he announced. "I want it understood, however, that I didn't take this stand to become a hero. I just felt it wasn't right for me to play in a town where I couldn't be treated on an equal basis with the rest of the team."

While Baylor's refusal to play was new, the segregated treatment of NBA teams was not. Just weeks prior to the West Virginia fiasco, in December 1958, a similar incident occurred when the Lakers played the Boston Celtics in Charlotte, North Carolina. Black players for both teams, including Baylor and Bill Russell, were forced to eat at different restaurants and stay in different lodgings than their White teammates. Both played in the Charlotte game, but neither was happy. "I don't care if we ever go back," said an angry Walter Brown, owner of the Celtics. "I know one thing—I'll never do anything to embarrass my players." Richard Short was similarly upset, just as he would be again in February. It was after the Charlotte incident that Baylor told the team owner that he would not play if a similar incident occurred.

Though Russell had not been in Charleston for Baylor's refusal to play, he supported him unequivocally. "Elgin didn't do what he did for himself alone," he told the *New York Post*. "He did it for me and every other Negro player in the league." Russell described his own similar experiences in junior college and on the Olympic team. "This is a white man's world," he explained. "They take us and they educate us. They say: 'You're going to help. Be on your best behavior.' They give us their religion, their code of ethics, their way to dress and to live and then they don't live up to it." It was high-order betrayal. "They draw a line and we're not supposed to go over it. What do you think it does to a person inside? Do you think you ever get over it?" The justifiable anger of the mistreated players was a cut that would leave a scar for all Black players in the league.

Even on professional teams with liberal management and general rapport between Black and White players, explained columnist Brock Brockenbury, "subtle prejudice pops up in little ways, in the conversation of the players, in their habits, in the little involuntary groupings and the like." Those continued problems led Russell in 1962, just three years after the West Virginia incident, to announce that after his playing career he planned to move to Africa. It was that season that Russell experienced yet another indignity, this time at a segregated restaurant in Lexington, Kentucky. After being refused service at a restaurant in Lexington, five Celtics players and two from the St. Louis Hawks booked tickets on the next flight out of town and did not play. "The people of Lexington, who had a double standard at that time, were not offended at the game that evening," wrote Russell. "They got just what they apparently wanted— a lily-white basketball game." While the manager of the hotel where the incident occurred claimed that the fiasco was a misunderstanding, Celtics coach Red Auerbach took the players to the airport himself. "I couldn't possibly order them to play," he said. Around that same time, Oakland was scheduled to play an exhibition in Houston, and, as Russell explained, "the NAACP asked the Negro players to refuse to play under the segregated seating laws that were in force." There was no such request from the NAACP in Lexington, but there was a frustrated Russell, which served much the same function.

The same was true when college players came through the region. Chet Walker, a Bradley University standout in 1960, described horrendous treatment when his team made a swing through the South. His coach told the Black players "to expect racism and offensive treatment, that it was just the way things were and there was nothing he or we could do about it. Implicit was the idea that we better not cause any incident that would reflect badly on the team or on Bradley. The message was that the South was going to be different because we were different: this is your lot, accept it, don't make waves if you want to play."

With such racial incidents mounting—prominent and melodramatic in the South but present in myriad ways throughout the country—a new upstart promotion, the American Basketball League (ABL), began play in 1961. The new league, created by Abe Saperstein, owner of the Harlem Globetrotters, put teams in non-NBA cities in the northeast and far west, including one in Hawaii, as well as directly challenged the association in Chicago and Los Angeles. The ABL was a product of the Globetrotters' owner and emphasized its commitment to Black basketball. Saperstein's organization would even be, among other things, the first professional league to feature Black head coaches. Its Pittsburgh franchise even called itself the Rens. The ABL did not last long, collapsing in 1963 with roughly $2 million in losses, unable to compete with the NBA in the west and northeast and struggling with an unwieldy travel schedule that included Hawaii. It was a venture that seemed a signpost for future attempts, failing in business but succeeding in the promotion of a more robust Black basketball presence.

The *Pittsburgh Courier* announced in August 1963, just after the ABL's collapse, that professional basketball had "grown by leaps and bounds down through the years and Negro stars have grown with it." It described Elgin Baylor, Bill Russell, Wilt Chamberlain, and Oscar Robertson as the unquestioned leaders in the game. What the *Courier* did not include in its celebration, however, was that a roster of Black stars was, in the perception of NBA leadership, a drain on the league's popularity.

That month, August 1963, the NBA board of governors held a series of meetings designed to dramatically improve the long-term health of the league. The association had played during the previous season without a television deal and had suffered financially as a consequence. At those meetings, the board replaced the association's original president, Maurice Podoloff, with former Harlem Globetrotters publicity director and mayor of Stamford, Connecticut, J. Walter Kennedy, who initiated a platform of strict discipline to sanitize the NBA's reputation. "Few professional athletes ever bother to read their contracts," Kennedy explained, because there was "one specific line in their contract which gives me unusual power—the power to ban them from the NBA for life for conduct I feel detrimental to basketball." Podoloff had used the line during the collegiate betting scandal, and Kennedy threatened to do the same. The players were told not to socialize with gamblers. "They have been told to check carefully before allowing their picture to be taken with people they don't know. And if any NBA players do get into trouble, they can expect no mercy from me." Kennedy even fined Red Auerbach for not leaving the floor after receiving two technical fouls during a game.

The board also expanded the maximum active roster from eleven to twelve, placing an extra uniformed player at the end of professional benches. With those changes, the association managed a new television contract for a Game of the Week beginning in January 1964. Podoloff, retiring but seeing much progress in the moves, also formed a committee to examine the possibility of expansion to ten teams the following season. Of all such corporate maneuvering, the most curious of the moves was the roster expansion, as all the others were designed to increase revenues while the roster expansion would only limit them. The assumption of many, including some of the association's Black players, was that as the association's talent became blacker, it became less marketable, and thus the roster expansion was a maneuver to create another active roster spot for a White player to make the teams more marketable. "The NBA has apparently purged itself of the quota system," Bill Russell wrote in 1970, indicating his belief that, though it went without official documentation, one clearly existed. "The day in 1965 that Red [Auerbach] started five blacks—and we went on to win the title—that was the end of the quota system."

August 1963 was seminal for the NBA because of the association's board of governors' meeting, but the month was better known for a different meeting, the March on Washington, attended by, among more than two hundred thousand others, Baylor, Russell, and additional Black players. That month, it was also announced that Baylor would play a Nigerian delegate to the United Nations in Bob Hope's new movie, *A Global Affair*, demonstrating that Black stars were a lucrative commodity and thus the NBA's racial concerns were ultimately unnecessary.

That season was dominated by Baltimore Bullets rookie Gus Johnson, a Black power forward from the University of Idaho who would eventually make the NBA's All-Rookie First Team. Johnson was routinely cited by Black players as an exemplar of the extra work it took for African Americans to succeed in basketball. Johnson was an Akron high-school standout but was always overshadowed by Jerry Lucas from Middletown in the southern part of Ohio. The White Lucas got a scholarship to Ohio State while Johnson settled for Idaho. When the two got to the NBA, Johnson always made playing against Lucas a priority. "Gus eats him alive, and Jerry doesn't do much against Gus," said one player. "You can see Gus out there and I know he's thinking: 'I had nothing in my life, never had, and this big white kid had everything. I'll show him, I'll show him.'"

It was Du Bois's double-consciousness writ onto basketball gymnasiums around the country, and it could be motivating or utterly disheartening, depending on the player. "I consider my life up to the present time a waste," Russell explained in April 1963. "I don't consider anything I've done as contributing to society." Playing basketball was "marking time, the most shallow thing in the world." He demonstrated a frustration with race relations that was uncompromising. "I accepted things I shouldn't have," he said. "Little things. Like the fact that a police car stopped every time it went by and a few of us were talking on the corner. I thought it stopped for everybody. Now I know it only stopped for US."

The racial reality for Black players and the racial hand-wringing by White owners would become more prominent in February 1966, when *Sport* magazine published one of its most controversial articles, an investigation into NBA executives' fears about race. Journalist John Devaney delved into what he called "pro basketball's hidden fear." The exposé began with a provocative question by Howard Cosell to Wilt Chamberlain. "Are we reaching the point," Cosell asked in a WABC radio interview, "where perhaps there are too many Negro players in the National Basketball Association for box office appeal?" It was an intentionally provocative question from an intentionally provocative self-promoter, but Chamberlain's answer was even more surprising: "I definitely think that probably we have."

Seven of the ten starters in the association's 1965 All-Star Game, for example, were Black. "Nobody wants to say anything, but of course the owners are worried," admitted one NBA coach. "How are you going to draw with eleven colored players on your team?" It was a worrisome question to many in the association, while others found it ridiculous. All, however, agreed that the league was blackening. In the 1955–1956 season, six of the NBA's eighty players were Black, and one, Maurice Stokes, made the All-Star Game. Ten years later, the association had ninety-nine players, and forty-seven were Black. Of that number, thirty-one were starters and fourteen made the All-Star Game. Almost half the players, two-thirds of the starters, and three-quarters of the All-Stars were African American, in a league where fans were close to the players, and where those players wore no hats or helmets, far more visible than in any other professional league. Devaney also noted that the best collegiate players in every class were Black, meaning that the trend would only continue.

The problem, argued Devaney, was "race prejudice," and it was everywhere. "The fear of NBA owners, the question that worries them is: in a society that is 90 percent white, is this prejudice—this inability of some white spectators to identify with Negro athletes—deep enough and widespread enough to hold back NBA growth?" The answer of both NBA publicity director Haskell Cohen and commissioner Walter Kennedy was an unqualified no. Both pointed to rising attendance over the same decade that included the rise of the Black superstar. "When a team wins, it draws," Cohen explained. "When it loses, attendance falls off. It's as simple as that." The counter to such claims came in examples such as Boston. The Celtics had been champions for seven straight seasons. The team's average attendance in the 1960–1961 season was 7,448 per game. Four years later, the team averaged 8,779 fans per game. It was, to be sure, an improvement, but the team's arena held 13,909. Chamberlain, in his interview with Cosell, chalked up such relative stagnation amid overwhelming success to the continued blackening of the team, as White stars like Bob Cousy and Bill Sharman were replaced with Black stars like Sam Jones and KC Jones. "Why should a team with a record compiled such as it has not draw to capacity crowds," asked Chamberlain, "whereas the hockey team fills the house almost every night?"

Another consideration was television, the viewers beyond the arena. ABC television paid the American Football League $2 million for sixteen football games and paid the NBA $750,000 for seventeen basketball games. "In broadcasting circles," Devaney claimed, "it was said that the reason for the disparity in prices was the lack of a White NBA star." Kennedy, of course, denied such claims but was not in the broadcasting business. ABC's ratings for professional basketball were not bad, but Devaney seemed to be on to something. "I'm only being realistic," a television executive told the reporter, "when I say that if a white center were to come along to challenge Chamberlain or Russell, the ratings for those games would jump fifty percent."

One of the certain victims of the racial worry in the NBA was the Black fringe player. One NBA official explained that "up to 1960 or so, you kept a colored player as your ninth or tenth man. You had to pay him only $6500 or so, a lot less than you had to pay a white boy. But not anymore. Now the tenth and 11th players are white boys, to balance out the squad." Teams replaced White players with White players, Black players with Black players, keeping a racial consistency that would maintain fan expectations. Stories were myriad of team executives being told by management to draft White players to mollify a fan base, ultimately missing out on Black players who would become stars. So, too, were the stories of marginal Black players losing jobs at the end of an NBA team bench.

Such was, so the rumors went, the reason rosters had expanded to twelve players in 1963. "Times have changed—for the better—but prejudice did not die with the Civil Rights Act of 1964," wrote Devaney. "The NBA knows it is facing a problem." Again, a solution seemed to be expansion, but this time with more teams, rather than more players on the end of the bench. "The thinking is that at least 50 percent of these new jobs would be filled by Negroes, but others would be taken by whites who otherwise would be shut out of the NBA." In addition, expansion would allow the association to divide into four divisions, "giving better balance and more winners. And winners usually do well at the box office."

The suggestion of expansion, of course, portended a possible move to the supposedly recovering Jim Crow South. Both New Orleans and Atlanta had applied for new NBA franchises, for example, and the prospect of such a move seemed at least potentially successful by the mid-1960s. The St. Louis Hawks, a team "with seven Negroes on the squad," scheduled eight of its games in the 1965–1966 season in Memphis, and those games averaged a respectable 7,501 fans. "An NBA club would go over in the South with 50 percent Negro players," a White southern player explained, "but the team would have to be a winner." It was a curious assessment, both ominous and optimistic at the same time.

The exposé turned out to be "one of the most controversial stories we have ever run." *Sport* was inundated with mail parsing every conceivable issue related to race and professional basketball, but the magazine vigorously stood by its story. "We heard that there was a fear, an anxiety, among the powerbrokers of the NBA," *Sport* responded several months later, "that pro basketball wasn't growing the way it should because there were too many Negroes in the league." The Devaney investigation had proven such rumors true. "He found out that some people in the NBA felt that the preponderance of Negro players was hurting the game. He found out that some people feared an almost-total takeover of the NBA by Negroes."

The fear of the NBA was real, but so were the changing times that surrounded it. New voices in the civil rights movement began to emerge. The early radicalism of groups like the Nation of Islam gave leaders like Malcolm X a prominent platform in the first half of the 1960s. The year after his 1965 assassination, Huey Newton and Bobby Seale founded the Black Panther Party in Oakland and Stokely Carmichael of the Student Nonviolent Coordinating Committee began the call for what he termed "Black Power." The new militancy of this Black Power movement held dramatic sway in sports. In 1960, for example, Cassius Clay won the light heavyweight gold medal at the Rome Olympics. He capitalized on his success by going pro and beginning a rapid climb to the heavyweight championship. He was handsome, enthusiastic, and charismatic, and thus he garnered attention. Before his fight for the title versus Sonny Liston in 1964, he famously proclaimed, "I am the greatest!" After he defeated Liston and became the champ, he shocked his fans by renouncing his "slave name," Clay, in favor of Ali and announced his conversion to the Nation of Islam.

In 1966, during the Vietnam War, Ali refused his draft notice into the army on religious grounds. He faced a possible prison term, was suspended from boxing and stripped of his title, and engendered the contempt of many White fans. But he inspired the Black population as well as civil libertarians and opponents of the war. Despite his troubles, Ali was unquestionably the most famous athlete in America, whether people loved him or hated him, and his actions helped trigger a larger Black revolt, principally among those in amateur sports.

In 1967, for example, Harry Edwards, a Black sociology professor at San Jose State, organized a movement to boycott the 1968 Olympic Games in Mexico City, demanding that Ali's crown be reinstated, notorious racist and anti-Semite Avery Brundage be ousted as president of the International Olympic Committee, apartheid states South Africa and Rhodesia be barred from the Games, and Black coaches be added to the American team. Edwards gained the support of prominent civil rights leaders but wasn't successful in convincing the majority of Black athletes to participate in the actual boycott. The most prominent exception was UCLA's Lew Alcindor, who boycotted the Games, used his prominence to support civil rights causes, and would later follow Ali in joining the Nation of Islam, renouncing his own slave name, changing it to Kareem Abdul-Jabbar.

Meanwhile, in the pros, Russell still led the way in both celebrity and activism. The Celtics center was one of those principally responsible for both stabilizing the NBA and beginning the process of its blackening. When Russell debuted, there were only fifteen Black NBA players, and he would be the first iconic national Black figure in the league. He became a representation of the race in his chosen sport, and his rivalry with Chamberlain drove the success of the NBA through the 1960s. "Never before have so many people taken an active interest in professional basketball," wrote *Sport* magazine's Barry Gottehrer. "Suddenly, housewives and college coeds who generally avoid athletic events with a passion are taking sides in this battle between the giants."

It was then Russell's rise to professional prominence, along with that of Chamberlain, Oscar Robertson, Elgin Baylor, and Connie Hawkins—a group historian Nelson George has called "standard-bearers for the Black athletic aesthetic"—that normalized the Black presence in professional basketball in the late 1950s, "years marked by acceptance and infamy for Blacks." The Chamberlain-Russell rivalry dominated coverage of professional basketball and thus contributed to the assumption by Whites that the NBA was a Black league, turning many White fans who felt alienated by the successes of the civil rights movement away from the sport. Meanwhile, Russell unapologetically used his success to participate in the movement, leading marches in Boston and joining others around the country. He participated in Mississippi's Freedom Summer in 1964. "I don't like most white people because they are white," Russell famously announced in the early 1960s. "Conversely, I like most Negroes because they are black. Show me the lowest, most downtrodden Negro and I will say to you that man is my brother." By 1965, almost half of the NBA's players were Black. Television ratings were up, as was the NBA's overall popularity, but the blackness of the league, combined with statements like those of Russell, only stoked the racial skepticism of White sports fans about the viability of the NBA.

Russell's least favorite place to play was St. Louis, considered by many in the 1950s and early 1960s to be the most racist NBA city. Before the Celtics and Lakers became championship rivals, the Hawks dominated the Western division and provided an annual challenge for the Boston juggernaut. The two played for the NBA championship in 1957, 1958, 1960, and 1961. In December 1956, the Celtics played a game in St.

Louis's Kiel Auditorium. "The ball went up and Bob Pettit of the Hawks and I jumped for it," recalled Russell.

"Coon."

"Go back to Africa, you baboon."

"Watch out, Pettit, you'll get covered with chocolate."

"Black nigger."

"There was no doubt who the fans were yelling at," Russell said. "I was the only Negro athlete on either team."

It wasn't the kind of reaction that encouraged management to invest in Black players, but ultimately the Hawks would have no choice. St. Louis was still an ostensibly southern town with segregationist policies in much of the city. The fan base was White and had racialized expectations of its team. Lenny Wilkens was the second Black player in St. Louis history, arriving in 1960 to join Sihugo Green, who signed the year prior. The Black players, despite their talent, were expected to rebound the ball and pass to the White stars. Most of the Hawks' White players, like LSU's Bob Pettit, Kentucky's Cliff Hagan, and Kansas's Clyde Lovellette, had never played with Black teammates.

When Green, for example, turned over the ball, as David Halberstam noted, "the whites would not say anything, they would simply raise their eyebrows as if to say, *what can you expect, that's the way they are.*" Away from the court, things weren't much better. Wilkens once received $25 for a promotional event in St. Louis, while his White teammates Bob Pettit and Cliff Hagan received $75. "That was St. Louis," wrote Halberstam.

St. Louis was also particularly difficult for visiting Black players. It could be "the loneliest town in the world." Bill Russell had experienced brief racial attacks in college, "but in St. Louis it was 'baboon . . . nigger . . . black bastard.' Not from the players. Never have I heard a professional ballplayer say anything about race in a game. But the fans were using it as a weapon." It was, for Russell, "the St. Louis of my bitter memories," and the city was notorious throughout the league, some seeing it as an exception, others as an outsized example of slightly milder bigotries in every NBA market.

Because of such incidents, there was, in the late 1960s and early 1970s, a broader critique of the traditionally understood notion that sports was a character-building endeavor. Russell's autobiography in 1966, Harry Edwards's *The Revolt of the Black Athlete* in 1969, Jim Bouton's *Ball Four* in 1970, Dave Meggyesy's *Out of Their League* in 1971, and Jack Scott's *The Athletic Revolution* in 1971 each in their own way gave lie to the myth that sports was a cure to the ills of society. At the same time, however, sports were also marshaled as a check against such countercultural messages by the likes of Richard Nixon, Spiro Agnew, and Ronald Reagan. That check coincided with a rise of sports in the Sun Belt, as new cities in the expanding South and West sought to burnish their reputations with professional teams. In turn, those teams would, at least in the popular mind, take on the conservative values of those cities.

The St. Louis of Russell's bitter memories would watch as their NBA team moved to Atlanta in 1968, which initially problematized that transition by placing a Black team from a Black league into the heart of the Deep South at a time of significant racial unrest. Still, following a business model that played not to its employees, but rather to the racial assumptions of its clientele, Hawks management steadily eroded the talent of the team in order to make its appearance more palatable to those conservative Sun Belt values. Or, as David Halberstam surmised, Atlanta's management, "anxious not to offend its white fans (or, more accurately, hoping to locate them), had broken up a very successful, virtually all-black team, and drafted [white LSU guard Pete] Maravich out of college." That being the case, "primarily for racial reasons, [Atlanta] remained a troubled franchise for a decade to come."

The NBA's most immediate reckoning with race and solvency, however, came not from its lone outpost in the Deep South, but instead from a new rival that embodied the efforts of Saperstein's ABL, celebrating Black players and flashier style in an effort to compete for fans with the established professional circuit.

IO

The American Basketball Association and the Merger

LEADERS OF THE NBA may have spent much of their time wringing their hands over the growing presence of Black players in the association, but that worry, made public by the *Sport* exposé, provided an opening for a new organization with a more progressive view of race and a more creative view of what the game itself could be.

Professional sports in the 1960s had grown substantially by taking advantage of the postwar economic boom, expansion to the burgeoning Sun Belt, and the metastasizing television market. And it was a growth that allowed new competitors to take advantage of the same phenomena. While Major League Baseball's federal antitrust exemption kept competitors from really challenging its regimented market control, Podoloff's American Hockey League had served as an early competitor to the National Hockey League and demonstrated that organizational rivalries could be stable enterprises.

And then there was football. By the mid-1950s, televised professional football was attracting millions of new viewers, filling relatively vacant Sunday afternoon programming. One of the principal reasons for its popularity was television's ability to simplify the game. Football's complicated rules and subtle decisions were difficult to understand without prior knowledge, but with television announcers explaining the rules and intricacies of the game, more people could enjoy it. In 1963, CBS debuted a new technology, instant replay, that would also become a boon to televised basketball coverage. When combined with the ability to show the action in slow-motion, another technology introduced soon afterward, cameras could pinpoint specific events on which to focus and evaluate their nuances. Then came color television. Teams moved to brightly colored uniforms with the names of players on the back of their jerseys. Football organizations, both college and pro, put emblematic logos on their helmets to take advantage of the new technology. Football truly became a television sport. As critic Richard Kostelanetz noted, compared with telecast games, "live games now seem peculiarly inept, lethargic, and pedestrian."

League organizers, then, were essentially creating new television shows, and the newest of those shows came in 1960 with the creation of the American Football League (AFL), rival to the National Football League (NFL). When the older league ruled against Dallas's Lamar Hunt and Houston's K. S. "Bud" Adams obtaining expansion franchises in the NFL, they announced in 1959 the formation of their own group, the AFL. The new league began play with eight teams, four of them in NFL cities. Though it struggled financially in its early days, Harry Wismer, owner of the New York Jets, persuaded AFL owners to sell league television rights to ABC, with all the teams dividing the receipts equally, which kept the fledgling organization afloat. By 1964, the NFL's CBS deal was worth $14 million. NBC responded by awarding the AFL a five-year, $42 million deal, giving the upstart a new store of cash, which it promptly used to begin buying college players away from the NFL. The resulting bidding war led salaries to rise, and owners in both leagues wanted it to stop. In 1966, they met and decided to merge, establishing a common player draft and agreeing to play a championship game. Hunt and Adams had found a backdoor into the NFL.

The year of the professional football merger was the same year as the controversy surrounding the *Sport* exposé, leading several would-be basketball franchise owners to see an opportunity to take advantage of both a lucrative television market and the NBA's weakness on race to create their own rival organization, with the ultimate goal of using a Hunt-Adams strategy to force a merger that would allow their teams to finally join the established association. The NBA, they reasoned, was the youngest representative of the four major professional American sports, without its own federal antitrust exemption, and thus particularly susceptible to new competition. The relatively small number of players included on each team assured them that there would be plenty of available, talented players. Abe Saperstein's ABL had already attempted the feat earlier in the decade, failing largely because of logistical problems that new leaders believed they could solve.

Dennis Murphy, Southern California promoter and the mayor of Buena Park, California, had already attempted to organize a rival professional football league but was forced from the idea by the success of the AFL. After failing to secure a football team in that league, he had to move on. "There was only one hockey and one basketball league. So why not have another?" he asked. "Since I knew nothing about hockey, but basketball was my favorite sport, I figured I'd pursue the idea of a basketball league. I saw that the NBA had 12 [teams]. It seemed like there should be more teams. Why? I don't know. What the hell, it was worth a shot."

"What the hell, it was worth a shot" was the clarion call of the American Basketball Association (ABA). "They were so disorganized it was almost beyond belief," remembered Gary Davidson, legal counsel for the ABA and its first president. "They knew nothing whatsoever about starting a league or running one." Murphy worried about the swift failure of Saperstein's attempt, contacting Bill Sharman, a former star player and later coach in the ABL. Sharman explained that the real problem with the league was that Saperstein had largely bankrolled the operation himself, owning most of the teams outright, and wasn't prepared to take the heavy losses inevitable in the creation of a new organization. Murphy's effort, he argued, would need individual owners for each team who could absorb early financial losses for the promise of future profit. But it was a task easier said than done. "All anyone had to do to get a franchise was to say he had money, to appear to have money, and to say he wanted a franchise and was prepared to support one until it succeeded," said Davidson.

The collection of those who fit the bill was diverse. Davidson and Murphy were joined by people like singer Pat Boone, who was part of the Oakland Oaks ownership group, and Morton Downey Jr., who would go on to pioneer vulgar right-wing television talk shows after helping found the New Orleans Buccaneers. When the cast of characters was finally assembled, the group gathered in January 1967, meeting for two days at New York's St. Regis Hotel. They decided, among other things, to solicit George Mikan to become the new association's commissioner. Mikan was interested, and after he finally agreed, the introductory press conference in February was able to announce not only the league, but the leadership of one of the game's greatest legends. The owners also sought to separate the new organization from its would-be rival. The group announced that there would be a 3-point shot in the ABA game. The ball would be red, white, and blue. "We had no plan," explained Indiana's Dick Tinkham of the ABA's formation. "Sure, we wanted to merge with the NBA. That was a goal. But a plan? We had none. We went by the seat of our pants and made it up as we went along."

The red, white, and blue ball was Mikan's idea, a way to make the league stand out from the NBA. Many opposed it as a gimmick that would keep many fans from taking the ABA seriously, but it was a decidedly genius stroke. Not only did the ABA ball become the clear symbol of the group, but it added additional revenue from sales of replicas across the country. Then Art Kim, owner of the Anaheim Amigos, proposed a longer, thirty-second shot clock and a 3-point shot, a "homerun" basket that would add a new element to offensive strategy and allow losing teams to equalize a score more quickly. It was another gimmick, but when combined with six additional seconds of offensive time, one that opened the floor, pulled defenders away from the lane, and encouraged not only longer shots, but flashy plays at the basket with fewer bodies in the way. It, too, would become a defining feature of the ABA.

Armed with a colorful ball and rules that encouraged open play, the league set off on its maiden season. Organizers wanted to rival the NBA and encourage a merger, so they wanted cities that did not already have NBA franchises. They put teams that first year in Anaheim, Oakland, Denver, and Pittsburgh. The South also fit that particular bill, and so despite the league's reluctance to go to the Deep South, still in the throes of racist retrenchment following the Civil Rights Act of 1964 and the Voting Rights Act of 1965, it did place teams in Dallas, Houston, Louisville, and New Orleans. Even with that strategy, however, the league unapologetically identified itself racially. While the NBA had Black stars like Chamberlain and Russell, it had struggled with race and its relationship to fans, as the *Sport* article made clear. The ABA, however, actively pursued Black players. As historian James Whiteside has noted, the league was founded "in the immediate wake of the most active and successful period of America's civil rights struggle." The league also wanted a more flamboyant, less fundamental style that officials believed Black athletes could bring. Just as the ABA would play in different cities than the NBA, it would attempt to play to a different audience, as well. "The ABA," explained historian Tom Dyja, "helped to shift the balance of power in professional basketball to African-Americans by basing its existence on them and not pretending otherwise."

The star of that first season was Connie Hawkins, a New York high school legend from the Bedford-Stuyvesant section of Brooklyn. Hawkins accepted a scholarship offer from the University of Iowa in 1960, but in his freshman year was implicated in the second major collegiate point-shaving scandal. He had borrowed $200 from a New York attorney at the center of the scandal, a sum for school expenses that Hawkins's brother paid back—but the sweep of the 1961 moral panic matched that of the one ten years prior and arrested even more conspirators. Even though Hawkins didn't even participate in varsity basketball, prevented from doing so by an NCAA rule that kept freshmen from the team, Iowa hoped to avoid controversy by expelling the young player. Other colleges refused to sign him for fear of being tainted by scandal, and Kennedy's NBA banned him from play there, as well. Left with few options, Hawkins joined Saperstein's ABL, playing for the Pittsburgh Rens and winning the league's Most Valuable Player award. From there, he joined the Globetrotters, also a Saperstein organization, playing with the barnstorming group for four seasons before returning to Pittsburgh to play for the city's entry in the new ABA. It was a strategic move for Hawkins, who during his time with the Globetrotters filed a lawsuit against the NBA. The association had unfairly banned him from participation, he alleged, because he had never been demonstrated to have been associated with gambling. Joining the ABA, his lawyers suggested, would prove his level of play was worthy of NBA competition.

That it was. He won the new group's regular season and playoff MVP awards and led the Pipers to the inaugural ABA championship. After an injury-truncated second season and a series of media accounts highlighting Hawkins's lack of complicity in the betting scandal, the NBA decided to settle the lawsuit and remove the ban against him. It paid Hawkins more than $1 million in damages and assigned his rights in 1969 to a new expansion team, the Phoenix Suns.

Meanwhile, the ABA continued without its consensus best player. The other premier player in the league that season didn't actually play.

Rick Barry had been a star at the University of Miami before joining the NBA's San Francisco Warriors in 1965. There he immediately improved a struggling team and won the association's Rookie of the Year award. In his second season, he carried the Warriors to the NBA championship series, where he averaged more than 40 points per game. He also led the league in scoring. After only two seasons, Barry was one of the NBA's best players, but there were troubles behind the scenes. Warriors owner Franklin Mieuli, known as a relative skinflint, refused to pay Barry incentive money the player felt was due him. Meanwhile, when the ABA put a franchise across the bay in Oakland, the team hired Bruce Hale, former University of Miami coach and Barry's father-in-law, as its coach, a gambit to convince the Warriors star to jump to the new association. Those factors, combined with a massive financial offer that made Barry one of the highest paid basketball players in the game, including an ownership stake in the team and a percentage of home game ticket sales, convinced him to become the first NBA star to leave the league for the ABA.

The NBA, like its counterparts in other professional leagues, included a reserve clause in its player contracts. It was a rule that had been around since the founding of baseball's National League in 1876, the creation of William A. Hulbert, a baseball owner who had made his money owning and regulating coal mines. Under the reserve clause, teams had the right to renew a player's contract every season, thereby keeping them in perpetuity. The clause was upheld by the Supreme Court in 1922 in *Federal Baseball Club of Baltimore, Inc. v. National League of Professional Baseball Clubs*. Oliver Wendell Holmes spoke for a unanimous court, arguing that baseball was not interstate commerce. Other leagues followed suit, and when Barry's jump challenged the rule's validity, the NBA sued, forcing Barry to sit out the 1967–1968 season. Instead, he served as a radio broadcaster for the Oakland Oaks as Connie Hawkins dominated the association.

Two years later, the St. Louis Cardinals' Curt Flood would make a similar attempt in Major League Baseball, becoming reviled in the process. Flood's trailblazing effort was met with a revulsion colored by racism against a Black player in a historically White league. While Barry, a White player, received none of the racial animus, the move did earn him an undeserved reputation as a money-obsessed dilettante, even after other NBA players followed his lead. Though his first season on the court for the ABA was cut short by injury, Barry still led the league in scoring average and helped the Oaks win the second association championship in 1969.

After the season, the ABA made one of its most auspicious decisions. Spencer Haywood, a college player from the University of Detroit, left school after his sophomore season in 1969. He was barred from the NBA by a rule that required players to have completed four years of college or to be four years beyond high school. The ABA saw in the restriction a new possibility and instituted a "hardship" rule, arguing that players should be able to enter professional play early if guided by financial or family exigency. Haywood signed with the Denver Rockets and immediately led the association in both points and rebounds in its third season of play and was named its Most Valuable Player.

Both the NBA and the NCAA were unhappy, as the move threatened the viability of both competitors. So, too, was Haywood, who filed an antitrust suit against the NBA, arguing that the association was colluding in a "group boycott" to keep qualified players from work in violation of the Sherman Antitrust Act. Meanwhile, Haywood jumped after his MVP season to the NBA's Seattle Supersonics, who hired him against the wishes of the league, which threatened to void the player's contract and impose a variety of sanctions on the team. But the United States District Court for the Central District of California ruled in Haywood's favor. "If Haywood is unable to continue to play professional basketball for Seattle," the court argued, "he will suffer irreparable injury in that a substantial part of his playing career will have been dissipated, his physical condition, skills, and coordination will deteriorate from lack of high-level competition, his public acceptance as a super star will diminish to the detriment of his career, his self-esteem, and his pride will have been injured and a great injustice will be perpetrated on him." Though the NBA was able to have the injunction reversed at the Ninth Circuit Court of Appeals, Haywood and the Supersonics appealed to the Supreme Court, which ruled in their favor in January 1971.

As Haywood was entering his first and only season in the ABA, Julius Erving was entering his sophomore year and his first varsity season with the University of Massachusetts. Erving was a prodigy. In two collegiate seasons, he averaged 26 points and 20 rebounds per game before leaving after his junior season to become a professional. Using the Haywood hardship exemption, Erving signed a four-year contract with the Virginia Squires. He played well in his first season, finishing second in the ABA's Rookie of the Year voting to Artis Gilmore, but like Barry and Haywood before him, Erving's early career would be shaped by contract disputes as much as play on the court.

After Erving discovered that his agent was employed by the Squires, he demanded to renegotiate his contract for fair market value, arguing that his agent's conflict of interest gave him a lower salary than his production commanded. When the Squires balked, and because he was now four years removed from high school, Erving signed a lucrative $1 million contract with the Atlanta Hawks, hoping to jump to the NBA. In the NBA's draft, however, Erving was selected by the Milwaukee Bucks, creating a dispute between three teams in two leagues over his services. Though the Bucks already had both Kareem Abdul-Jabbar and Oscar Robertson, and the addition of Erving would have created an unbeatable leviathan, the Squires star joined the Hawks training camp to fulfill the lucrative contract he signed with Atlanta. He even played exhibition games with the team, combining with former Louisiana State University star Pete Maravich in preparation for what he thought would be his first NBA season. But commissioner Kennedy ruled that the Bucks held Erving's NBA rights; as such, the Hawks would be fined $25,000 for every game Erving played with them. The player appealed the commissioner's ruling, but the owners sided with Kennedy.

Meanwhile, the Squires sought an injunction against Erving playing with any NBA team, arguing that their rights superseded both Atlanta's contract and Milwaukee's draft choice. In October 1972, a judge agreed, issuing the injunction and sending Erving back to Virginia. Though he may have been displeased with the ruling, the player known as Dr. J thrived back in the ABA, averaging 32 points in his return season. But his success could not pull the Squires out of their financial doldrums. Cash-strapped and desperate, the team sold its best player to league rival the New York Nets in a complicated deal that also included financial compensation for the NBA's Atlanta Hawks. In his three seasons with the Nets, the last three in the life of the ABA, Dr. J dominated the association, leading his team to two championships while statistically overwhelming his opponents. In the 1975–1976 campaign, Erving finished the season in the top ten in points, rebounds, assists, steals, and blocks per game; he was in the top ten in free throw percentage and free throws made, in 3-point field goal percentage and 3-point field goals made.

While Erving's Nets ended their ABA tenure on top, the association's most successful team was the Indianapolis Pacers, which won three championships and appeared in the playoff finals five times under the leadership of coach Bob Leonard and the play of forward George McGinnis and center Mel Daniels. The Kentucky Colonels made it to three Finals, winning one, led by University of Kentucky standout Dan Issel and Jacksonville University center Artis Gilmore. It was clear that the ABA, for all of its organizational confusion, financial trouble, and player contract disputes, was able to create star players and talented teams. It began the move away from the professional college graduation requirement and created the 3-point shot. It created a bidding war for players that ultimately drove salary expansion and ensured that core elements of the professional game would play out in court rather than on the court. Finally, in the association's final All-Star Game in 1976, it introduced one more of its lasting legacies, a slam dunk contest to showcase the athleticism and artistry of its players. To encourage participation, the league offered a $1,000 prize and a stereo system to the winner. The contest might have been nothing more than a footnote in the ABA's brief history, but that night Erving won the event by jumping from the free throw line, flying to the rim and dunking. The slam dunk contest would become another legacy of the ABA.

By the time of the first slam dunk contest, the association was already negotiating a merger with the NBA. Merger, of course, had been the ABA's goal from the outset, but the effort had been delayed. As early as 1970, just three years into the ABA experiment, the NBA's board of governors had voted in favor of accepting some teams from the rival league into its own, an effort led by Supersonics owner Sam Schulman, at that time fighting the association over the Spencer Haywood contract. Schulman's bitterness over the deal was such that he even threatened to take his team to the ABA unless a merger was approved. After the vote, it seemed as though a merger was inevitable. "The war is over," wrote *Basketball Weekly*. "The Armistice will be signed soon."

The one group who hadn't had a say, however, were the players. Fourteen years prior in 1954, as George Mikan retired and leadership in the NBA shifted to a new generation of players, Bob Cousy and his agent,

Joe Sherry, organized the players to petition the association for a variety
of rules changes. They wanted independent arbitration, a limit on exhibition games, and pay for promotional appearances. Despite the early
intransigence of the league, the effort ultimately served as the genesis
for the National Basketball Players Association (NBPA). In 1957, Cousy
approached the AFL-CIO for guidance and the players threatened a
strike. It finally earned the Players Association recognition by the board
of governors but didn't earn them the concessions they were hoping for,
and Cousy's frustration led him to cede control of the group to his Celtics
teammate Tommy Heinsohn, who had little more success in the following years.

Things came to a head in 1964, when Heinsohn organized a wildcat
strike of that season's All-Star Game, the first to be nationally televised
live. The players wanted a pension plan; they wanted athletic trainers
for every team; they wanted the elimination of Sunday afternoon games
immediately following Saturday night games. The players understood
that live television provided them a rare, immediate leverage, and despite
threats and protests from owners, commissioner Walter Kennedy bowed
to the pressure and met the players' demands. They had been waiting in
the locker room for twenty minutes, but finally took the court after Kennedy's concession.

Six years later, the Players Association was faced with a potential
merger that it saw as a violation of antitrust laws. The players filed a
class action lawsuit to block the merger and end basketball's version
of the reserve clause. Oscar Robertson, as head of the NBPA, was the
lead plaintiff of 479 total petitioners, winning an injunction against the
merger as the case winded its way through the justice system. With that
avenue temporarily halted, the two associations turned to Congress for
an antitrust exemption in 1972. The effort failed, as did a similar bill in
1973.

In response to the legislative failures, the ABA hired a new commissioner, Mike Storen, tasked by the league with aggressively pursuing
the merger. It was an aggression that *Sports Illustrated* saw as problematic. "The tactics Storen says the ABA will employ sound a good deal
more like those used by AFL commissioner Al Davis in the last days
of the football war than a plan for peaceful coexistence," the magazine
announced. "The ABA has reinstituted its $300 million antitrust suit

against the NBA. It also may move some franchises into better TV markets, an ill-advised maneuver that will mean going against established NBA teams on their home turf. And for the first time since 1970 the ABA will go after established NBA players." It was aggression as risk, a risk that also appeared in exhibition games between the two leagues. Beginning in 1971 after merger efforts had been stalled by the courts, the interleague exhibitions would either demonstrate a functional equivalency between the associations or expose the ABA as an inferior outfit. Again, however, the risk paid dividends; the ABA won just as often as it lost in such contests, only fueling momentum for a merger.

While ABA competition had proven equal to the challenge of measuring up to the NBA, many of the teams' finances did not. Prior to the 1975–1976 season, the Denver Nuggets and New York Nets attempted to join the NBA without their fellow ABA teams, a move ultimately stopped by court order. During that final season, several ABA teams folded, as monetary concerns kept them from completing their schedules. The association ended that year with only six teams. When the Players Association class action was settled in 1976 and the possibility of a merger became a reality, the NBA announced that it would only absorb four of them.

The Kentucky Colonels, despite being one of the most successful teams in ABA history in both victories and fan attendance, were not included among the four. Owner John Y. Brown Jr. began selling several of his players as the season came to a close, which made the team less attractive, but the real cause of its exclusion was ownership of the NBA's Chicago Bulls, which held the rights to the Colonels' Artis Gilmore and stood to benefit if the team didn't survive the move. Brown, seeing the writing on the wall, allowed the ABA to buy him out for $3 million and sold Gilmore's rights to Chicago for another $1 million. The Spirits of St. Louis, despite having less success in both victories and attendance, managed an even better deal. Owners Daniel and Ozzie Silna accepted more than $2 million in cash and a one-seventh share of television revenue for the four surviving teams in perpetuity. The Spirits folded, but the Silna family still receives and will continue to receive millions of dollars annually from the association.

The NBA absorbed the four remaining teams—the Denver Nuggets, San Antonio Spurs, Indiana Pacers, and New York Nets—but classified them as expansion teams, requiring them to pay millions of dollars in expansion fees for the privilege of membership. They were barred from receiving television revenue for three seasons and from choosing players in the 1976 NBA Draft. The Nets' liability was even greater, as they had to pay more than $4 million to the Knicks to compensate for moving into the team's territory. To raise the cash, Nets ownership sold the rights to its best player, Julius Erving, to the Philadelphia 76ers, mortgaging years of future success to join the NBA.

The deal was punitive, to be sure, but when it was done, the NBA had moved to more markets and its competitor was gone. The first season after the merger was dominated by the Portland Trailblazers, led by a former part of John Wooden's UCLA collegiate dynasty, Bill Walton. The center had been the first overall draft pick in 1974 and was one of the most talented players in the association, but his first two seasons had been marred by foot injuries. Joined by Lionel Hollins and coached by Jack Ramsay, the Trailblazers were already poised for a good season if Walton's feet cooperated. Then the team acquired Maurice Lucas in the ABA dispersal draft from the Spirits of St. Louis, adding to an already strong roster.

Walton led the league that season in rebounds and blocks, but foot injuries limited his play in the regular season. Still, the Blazers managed to earn the third seed in the NBA's Western Conference and Walton's return aided a playoff run to the Finals, where the Trailblazers defeated Dr. J's Philadelphia 76ers. The team was one of eight different champions in the decade of the 1970s, the only period in the association's history without an established dynasty. No decade had more champions, more hope among the various fan bases of the league that their team could win a title. Conventional thinking dictated that such parity would drive increased interest in the league, but the NBA's ratings and attendance subsided in the 1970s.

Parity, however, wasn't the NBA's only problem. The season following Portland's championship run, in December 1977, an on-court incident encapsulated the association's troubled relationship with violence and race. Kermit Washington was a role-player for the Los Angeles Lakers, known primarily in a professional game recognized since its earliest days for rough play and fights as an enforcer, similar to the traditional hockey goon. *Sports Illustrated*'s NBA preview for the season highlighted the role of enforcers in the association, depicting Washington, among other players, under the heading, "Nobody, but Nobody, Is Gonna Hurt My Teammates." He and other teammates, including Lakers star Kareem Abdul-Jabbar, had been in several fights already in the early season, but on the night of December 9, things changed.

The Lakers played the Houston Rockets. After an early second-half missed shot, Abdul-Jabbar, Washington, and Houston's Kevin Kunnert battled for the rebound, which ultimately led to violence. Kareem pulled Kunnert off Washington as Washington landed a punch to Kunnert's head. Watching the melee and hoping to stop it, Houston forward Rudy Tomjanovich ran to help his teammate. Tomjanovich was a star in his own right, a standout at the University of Michigan before joining the Rockets franchise in 1970. He had been an All-Star selection four consecutive years. Perhaps more importantly, he was White, as was Kunnert.

Washington saw Tomjanovich coming, assuming in the moment that he was coming to participate rather than stop the fight. He swung at Tomjanovich, fracturing the bones in his face, breaking his jaw and nose, and leaving him lying in a pool of his own blood. Tomjanovich was able to walk off the court under his own power, but blood and spinal fluid were leaking into his skull. It was a stroke of fortune that he did not die.

Television cameras recorded Washington's punch, but they missed the fight that preceded it, which meant that the extensive coverage of the shocking event only depicted Tomjanovich's calamity, a large, angry Black man almost killing a relatively defenseless White one. For a league that often struggled with race, that lagged decidedly behind the other major professional leagues in attendance and television time, the incident came to symbolize the problems of the NBA in the minds of many. The association realized, argued chief counsel David Stern, that "you couldn't allow men that big and that strong to go around throwing punches at each other." To save face, the association suspended Washington for sixty days and fined him $10,000. He played several more seasons but carried the incident with him as a metaphorical scarlet letter for the rest of his career. "Kermit was fighting a battle he couldn't win," said Red Auerbach, whose Celtics hired Washington for a portion of the following season. "Nothing he could say or do was going to change the way people perceived him because of that moment."

The response to the punch also returned race to the public spotlight in interpretations of the association, popular sympathy for Tomjanovich taking a decidedly racial tone. An All-American White player had been viciously attacked by a degenerate Black player. The narrative was wrong, of course. Washington was no degenerate and everyone in the league, White and Black, brawled with one another during games. But it helped destroy Washington's career; it also hurt an NBA coded as the blackest of professional leagues.

It was a reputation exacerbated in 1981 when David Halberstam published *The Breaks of the Game*, an account of the 1979–1980 Portland Trailblazers' season. Readers were able to read about the injury troubles of Bill Walton and the struggles of a team seeking to reclaim the glory of years past, but race also played a central role in Halberstam's account. He described the travails of Washington in the seasons following the Tomjanovich punch and the racism in team leadership of various organizations such as the St. Louis and Atlanta Hawks. "Race was always there," wrote Halberstam, "blacks tending by and large to go off with one another and whites with each other." He argued that there was a perception among some coaches that Black players who had grown up in the South and gone to southern schools played (and interacted with teammates) with less assertiveness than Black players from elsewhere, attributing the difference to the stifling racial climate of the region where they had been raised. Such racial assumptions were then exacerbated by television. In 1964, professional basketball left NBC for ABC, becoming a sport with a national draw under the leadership of Roone Arledge. That second contract, a four-year deal beginning in 1969, was only worth $6 million in its final year. It was paltry by the standards of other professional leagues, but ratings continued to increase. It was that growth that led to massive expansion, from nine teams at the beginning of the ABC years to seventeen in the early 1970s. Television also, however, emphasized racial disparities. "Just as the camera had caught and transmitted the true intensity of old-fashioned rivalries in the earlier days of the league," Halberstam explained, "so it now caught with equal fidelity the increasing lethargy and indifference of many players in regular season games, a lethargy and indifference now seen by a largely white audience as at least partially racial in origin."

And so the NBA ended the decade with the legacy of both the ABA and its earlier racial reckoning. The season that was the subject of Halberstam's account witnessed the NBA add the 3-point shot to its rules. Four years later, in 1984, it added a slam dunk contest to its All-Star festivities, a contest that almost exclusively showcased the association's Black talent. It was a confused relationship with race, one that would only continue in the next decade as two new stars emerged to capture the imagination of fans. One was White, one Black. Their popularity would forever change the trajectory of the league.

II

Magic and Larry

IN THE FIRST MONTHS of the 1979–1980 season chronicled by David Halberstam, professional basketball was at a crossroads. The parity of the 1970s had given way to a variety of new champions, but it had also witnessed the nadir of the pro game's popularity. Basketball's television ratings were at their lowest point, and while the teams of the NBA were financially stable in a way that those of the previous American Basketball Association (ABA) never were, the economic doldrums that resulted from low attendance and sparse viewership portended a potential slide into relative oblivion for an association that had overcome a variety of struggles since its nascent successes in the immediate wake of World War II.

The slide was even more pronounced in that final year of the decade. *Sports Illustrated*'s John Papanek published a report on the association's problems in February 1979, interviewing Larry O'Brien, who put on a brave face. "I wouldn't say we have no problems in the NBA," he said, "but you can see from my empty desk here that there certainly is no crisis. In fact, for the first time in my four seasons as commissioner I can say that the NBA is stable. Stable is the best word that can be used to describe the NBA." O'Brien had replaced Walter Kennedy in 1975 after serving as postmaster general under Lyndon Johnson and head of the Democratic National Committee. He helped shepherd the merger through its legal thickets but found it difficult in the following years to raise the game's national profile. As explained in *Sports Illustrated*, "Twelve of the 22 teams are drawing fewer fans than they did a year ago for the same number of playing dates. League-wide, attendance is down 3%," and that number would have been markedly worse had Buffalo not relocated to San Diego and Detroit not moved operations to the Pontiac Silverdome.

"The most alarming news is that attendance in the big four markets of New York, Los Angeles, Chicago and Philadelphia is down drastically" and "national television ratings are down a whopping 26%."

And while the broadcast choices of CBS, which acquired the NBA after ABC's contract expired, certainly played a role, and while a long playoff made the regular season less interesting to many, it was undeniable that at least part of fan disinterest was conditioned by racial concerns. "It is a fact that white people in general look disfavorably upon blacks who are making astronomical amounts of money if it appears they are not working hard for that money," said Seattle's Paul Silas, the Black president of the Players Association. "Our players have become so good that it appears they're doing things too easily, that they don't have the intensity they once had." Al Attles, coach of the Warriors and one of the first African American coaches in the NBA, was similarly skeptical. "A lot of people use the word 'undisciplined' to describe the NBA. I think that word is pointed at a group more than at a sport. What do they mean by it? On the court? Off the court? What kind of clothes a guy wears? How he talks? How he plays? I think that's a cop-out." One anonymous executive told Papanek that "the teams are too black. The question is are they [the black players] promotable? People see them dissipating their money, playing without discipline. How can you sell a black sport to a white public?" The Phoenix Suns, Papanek reported, were the league's only team with a majority of White players. "This is something we must no longer whisper about," said Nuggets general manager Carl Scheer. "It's definitely a problem and we, the owners, created it. People see our players as being overpaid and underworked, and the majority of them are black. What can we do about it? Just try to get people who will work hard, and I don't think we'll have a problem."

The *Sports Illustrated* exposé was a recapitulation of the racial hand-wringing of the *Sport* report a decade and a half prior, and to fix the "problem," O'Brien and the board of governors paid $500,000 to a public relations firm, exploding the league's public relations budget in an attempt to reverse what they interpreted as a negative and at least partially racially-motivated downturn. Public relations, however, only worked if there were players to publicly relate, and at the start of the 1979 season, the NBA had two new players who would carry the association into the next decade and, with the right marketing, stop the ratings and attendance slide.

The potential for that slide didn't disappear on December 28, 1979, but the potential to stop it finally seemed to exist. The game at the Los Angeles Forum that night was not nationally televised, but the hype surrounding it was real, bringing the arena's first sellout since March 1978. Fans flocked to see two rookies revive a collegiate rivalry.

Earvin Johnson was born in Lansing, Michigan, the child of hardworking parents who had been part of the Great Migration, coming from the South to find work in the country's industrial heartland. As a child, he idolized Bill Russell and became a star junior high player. For high school, however, he was bused to a White institution, one of the common mechanisms in the 1970s to comply with court orders for northern school districts to desegregate. Residential segregation in the North kept school districts zoned by geography racially separated despite no formal ordinances mandating the practice. One of the ways that many districts complied with court orders was to bus students of one race to a school of another. The quintessential showdown over busing came in Boston, when a federal lawsuit filed by Black parents led to a district judge's ruling in 1974. The schools in Boston were vastly unequal, with far less funding for Black schools. Responding to the court ruling, Boston chose to begin busing thousands of White students to Black schools in Boston's Roxbury district. White parents revolted with boycotts and protests intended to prevent their children from being sent to Black schools. Clashes with police led to dozens of arrests and violence continuing for years.

Johnson's high school career coincided with Lansing's own effort at busing, enacted at the same time as the violence in Boston commenced, and it sent Johnson into a decidedly racist situation accompanied by a variety of arguments and fights. "The first few months, I was miserable at Everett [his predominantly White high school]. But being bused to Everett turned out to be one of the best things that ever happened to me," Johnson later remembered. "It got me out of my own little world and taught me how to understand white people, how to communicate and deal with them." It was there that, as a sophomore, he earned the nickname "Magic" after amassing a triple-double in a local victory. By his senior season, he led his team to a state championship.

His talent earned him scholarship offers from universities across the country. Collegiate basketball in the first half of the 1970s was dominated by UCLA, and John Wooden offered Magic a chance to play for the Bruins, but the second half of the decade provided a similar parity to that of the professional ranks, with Bob Knight's Indiana Hoosiers, Al McGuire's Marquette Warriors, and Joe Hall's Kentucky Wildcats all winning NCAA Championships. Dean Smith's North Carolina Tarheels, Bill Foster's Duke Blue Devils, and Norm Sloan's North Carolina State Wolfpack moved the axis upon which college basketball turned from Southern California to the coastal South. Johnson, however, chose to stay home to play for Jud Heathcoate's Michigan State Spartans.

In his freshman season, Magic led his team to a Big Ten Championship and the NCAA tournament quarterfinals, known colloquially as the Elite Eight. In his sophomore campaign during the 1978–1979 season, he led the Spartans to the NCAA championship game, where they would take on the comparatively small Indiana State University Sycamores, led by their own collegiate sensation.

Larry Bird was also born to hardworking parents who struggled to make ends meet, but tiny French Lick, Indiana, was far from the urban climbs of Lansing. Bird's parents divorced while he was in high school, and his father committed suicide a year later. Basketball became both an outlet and an escape from problems at home. At Springs Valley High School, Bird became a phenomenon in a state obsessed with basketball since the years preceding the Franklin Wonder Five in the early 1920s. As a senior, Bird averaged 31 points and 21 rebounds per game. The small-town star didn't have the national profile of Johnson, but he also didn't have to suffer racial inequities and busing.

Bird received a scholarship from Bob Knight to play with his home state's beloved Hoosiers, but he dropped out after a month on campus. The student body population was larger than his hometown and adjusting to what Bird saw as the big city of Bloomington was difficult, if not overwhelming. He went back home and worked several different municipal jobs during the 1974–1975 season before enrolling at Indiana State, a smaller school in the smaller town of Terre Haute. The university had been the early coaching home of John Wooden, and in 1975, the school found itself almost accidentally accepting one of the game's greatest players. Bird averaged more than 31 points and more than 13 rebounds in his three seasons at Indiana State, and in his senior season, he took his small school, one that hadn't even been ranked in preseason polls, all the way to the finals of the NCAA championship tournament, where it would meet Magic Johnson's Michigan State.

The championship was played in Salt Lake City's Special Events Center, and along with the fifteen thousand fans in attendance, roughly forty million fans watched from home. Two of every five households in the country tuned in to the game, the largest American audience by percentage to ever witness a game of basketball. The game itself may not have lived up to the hype it received in the run-up to the contest—Bird did not shoot well, and Michigan State won by 11 points—but the interest it drove helped create the modern tournament, leading to two different field expansions and larger venues in the coming seasons.

Part of the game's draw was the racialized symbolism it presented, with a flashy Black star contending against a rural White phenom who served as "The Great White Hope." The racial element of the rivalry would continue after the season. Bird was a senior and Johnson a sophomore, but both became professionals after the championship game. Bird had already been drafted the previous year; his rights held by Boston. Johnson was drafted first overall by Los Angeles. It was Bird, however, the loser of the NCAA contest, who signed a $3.25 million five-year contract, the most lucrative rookie deal in all of American organized sports. It was a contract that laid bare the racial worries of *Sports Illustrated*'s exposé. If NBA administrators were worried about the lack of a dominant White presence, they now hoped they had one in Bird.

The racial politics of basketball, the ratings success of the NCAA championship game, and the storied history of both the Celtics and the Lakers made the night of December 28, 1979, so auspicious for those at the Los Angeles Forum. It was the first contest between Bird and Magic since the NCAA championship game in March. Already in the season's first two months, the two rookies had seemingly restored success to their legendary franchises. Bird's Celtics had the best record in the NBA and Magic's Lakers led the Western Conference. Asked before the game about the role of the new players in what was hoped to be a renaissance for professional basketball, Bird was circumspect. "I'm sure [fans] are tired of hearing about me and Magic, but I think we're the two guys that can help it," he said. "Since our teams are doing so well right now, you gotta do as much as possible to help the NBA out."

Like the NCAA championship game before it, the first professional meeting of Magic and Bird was anticlimactic, Magic outscoring Bird 23 to 16 and the Lakers winning the game with relative ease. But also like the NCAA Championship, the contest portended the success of the organization that the rivalry touched. Not only were the Lakers and Celtics leading their respective conferences, but attendance at venues visited by the teams markedly increased, fans across the country hoping to see the two new stars who would elevate the association in the 1980s. As that first season ended, Magic averaged 18 points, 7 rebounds, and 7 assists; Bird averaged 21, 10, and 4. The Celtics reached the conference finals before losing to Julius Erving's 76ers. The Lakers would meet Philadelphia in the NBA Finals, defeating them in six games and winning the franchise's first championship since 1972. In the deciding game, Johnson replaced an injured Kareem Abdul-Jabbar at center, playing all five positions during the game and scoring 42 points en route to earning the Finals' Most Valuable Player award.

The following season, Johnson missed forty-five games with torn cartilage in his knee and the Lakers were victims of a first-round playoff upset. Meanwhile the Celtics advanced to the Finals, where they defeated an upstart Houston Rockets team for the franchise's first championship since 1976. The rivalry was decidedly renewed.

Still, there were obstacles to building the kind of interest in the NBA that accrued to the NCAA tournament. CBS broadcast four of the six finals games between the Celtics and the Rockets on tape delay after the late local news of affiliate stations. Only games 3 and 4, played on a Saturday and Sunday, were broadcast live, and the Sunday contest was scheduled for one o'clock in the afternoon eastern time, ten o'clock in the morning in Los Angeles, so that the network would have time to broadcast a golf tournament following the game. It was the lowest-rated finals series of the twentieth century, despite the star power of Bird and the Cinderella story of Houston. It would be the last finals series to be broadcast on tape delay.

There was clearly more work to be done. In past decades, league popularity was driven by dynasties, and the Magic/Bird rivalry was able to drive new viewership after the dismal 1981 Finals by sustaining two simultaneously. Every NBA Finals series in the decade included either the Lakers, the Celtics, or both. Led by Magic and Abdul-Jabbar, along with North Carolina's James Worthy, Los Angeles won the Western Conference eight times in the 1980s and won five NBA Championships. The Celtics won the Eastern Conference five times and won three titles. Bird was joined by Kevin McHale, drafted by the team from the University of Minnesota, and Robert Parish, whom the Celtics acquired in a trade with the Golden State Warriors. Both the teams would dominate the decade, and their rivalry, combined with the rivalry between Magic and Bird in particular, would drive a new popularity for the game that only grew from the doldrums of 1981.

It also drove the professional development of the stars themselves. "When the new schedule would come out each year, I'd grab it and circle the Boston games," Magic remembered. "To me it was The Two and the other 80. During the season I'd check out Larry's line first thing. If he had a triple double, I knew what I'd want that night. But what would get me would be his big ones—say, when he had 20 rebounds. I'd say, 'I'd better get me 20 assists tonight.'" Bird was no different. "The first thing I would do every morning during the season was look at the box scores to see what Magic did. I didn't care about anything else." Both players understood that despite the opponent that each played on a given night, they were always playing against each other.

The public interpreted the meaning of the rivalry, as well. Attendance at NBA games rose 42 percent in the 1980s, more than any other professional league. Between 1979 and 1984, the association's television ratings rose, while those of the other professional leagues stayed static or dropped. CBS, which had played Finals games on tape delay and originally treated the NBA as a second- or third-tier product, responded to the rise by signing the association to a new four-year contract worth $173 million in 1985. Advertising revenue correspondingly increased, and the new visibility of players like Magic and Bird meant that the athletes themselves would feature prominently in those campaigns. In 1985, as the NBA signed its new CBS deal, Converse created a television commercial starring the two rivals. Bird is shown shooting baskets on a dusty outdoor court in French Lick, when a stylish limousine speeds through the rural area and pulls up in front of him. Magic steps out and challenges his rival about the Converse shoe created in his name, announcing his own Converse shoe as a competitor. The advertisement encapsulated the public perceptions of the two: Bird, the rural, diligent worker; Magic, the flashy, braggadocious star. It played on the racially coded assumptions of fans described by Papanek before their first meeting in the 1979 NCAA tournament.

Despite the rivalry, the two really didn't know each other. But the Converse commercial provided a new opportunity. Magic said, "Larry and I sat down for lunch, and I tell you, we figured out we're so much alike. We're both from the Midwest, we grew up poor, our families [are] everything to us, basketball is everything to us. So that changed my whole outlook on Larry Bird." Still, the respect they had for one another did not grow into a real friendship until later. "I always thought you had to keep the edge," said Bird. "You don't want to get too close to a person because you will get a little soft. Once me and Magic left that commercial shoot in Indiana, it was back to business, believe me. We both had a burning desire to win championships. And once we got with our teams, all of that was forgotten until we retired."

That desire to win championships combined with the talent of both to drive their success and, ultimately, their celebrity, with help from the association's public relations and corporate sponsors like Converse. The NBA's new emphasis on the star power of its players was driven by its new commissioner. David Stern began his career in basketball as lead attorney for the firm that represented the association in its fight against the class action lawsuit brought by Oscar Robertson and the Players Association. He also helped negotiate the terms of the ABA merger before joining the NBA officially as legal counsel in 1978. In that position, he helped create a salary cap and revenue-sharing program for the league and also instituted the NBA's first drug-testing program, a response to the reported use of cocaine by many of the players. Much of that concern was racially coded, as well, but cocaine was also a legitimate problem in professional sports and drug testing served both to limit its use and bolster the reputation of the league by assuring fans that it was trying to stop it.

Buoyed by those successes, Stern took over as NBA commissioner in 1984 following the retirement of Larry O'Brien. He proceeded to put the association's marketing emphasis on its star players, who would be the driving force of the game's growth in the decades to come. He also began a broad attempt to expand basketball's reach, offering inexpensive high-light packages to other countries to grow the game in foreign markets.

It was a successful strategy, but not without its pitfalls. The NBA Draft, like that of the NFL, had traditionally ordered its selections according to team records, with those maintaining lower winning percentages choosing before those with higher winning percentages. It was a practice that rewarded failure and encouraged those with little hope of reaching the playoffs to lose intentionally to secure a higher draft choice the following year. In an effort to prevent the phenomenon, known as "tanking," Stern created a new system for the 1985 draft. Teams that did not qualify for the playoffs were placed in a lottery, the seven franchises with the lowest winning percentages given an equal chance to win the top pick. Though the New York Knicks had barely missed the playoffs and did not have the lowest winning percentage, they were awarded the first draft choice, taking the consensus best player, Georgetown University's Patrick Ewing.

The televised event led to immediate speculation that the lottery was rigged to create a new contender in the NBA's largest and most historically viable market. Stern's emphasis on star players seemed to many to augur a desire for a new New York star. Stern had grown up rooting for the Knicks. The accounting firm that oversaw the lottery, Ernst and Whinney, was also the accountant for Gulf and Western, the company that owned the Knicks. Though there is no conclusive proof that the draft lottery was rigged, conspiracy theories began immediately, speculating on various scenarios that alerted Stern as to which envelope to choose. The controversy would ultimately move the lottery selections off television and led to the creation of a weighted system, whereby teams with the lowest winning percentages would have a statistically larger chance to win the first draft choice.

In 1985, however, the draft lottery seemed to highlight the principal problem with elevating star athletes as the core of the association's public relations. It could lead to potential corruption and an unfair advantage for teams with the most marketable players. But there were other problems to deal with, as well. Regulating drug policy by instituting a testing regime helped bolster the NBA's reputation, but it could not eliminate the actual problem of cocaine use among professional athletes. At the following year's draft, the Celtics had the second overall choice, using its pick on University of Maryland star Len Bias, who had averaged more than 36 points and 10 rebounds in his senior season with the Terrapins. Slated to be Boston's next great acquisition, a talent who would carry the Celtics dynasty into the 1990s, Bias was poised to be pushed by the league's promotional efforts to market its young stars to a new generation of fans. Bias had even begun negotiations with Reebok for a lucrative promotional contract. Two days after the draft, however, Bias died of cardiac arrhythmia exacerbated by a cocaine overdose.

The death of Len Bias shocked both the NBA and the entire American sports world. It demonstrated that drug abuse was not just a problem in professional sports, but in collegiate athletics, as well, and it was a blow to an association that had actively sought to build its reputation on drug testing and star players. But the death also had reach beyond the bounds of sports. Seven days after Bias's overdose, Don Rogers, a safety for the NFL's Cleveland Browns, died of a cocaine overdose. At the same time, crack cocaine was spreading across socioeconomically devastated neighborhoods throughout the country, creating a moral panic that a cheaper, more dangerous form of the drug would bring about the ruin of society. In response, federal legislators began crafting the Anti-Drug Abuse Act of 1986, colloquially known as "the Len Bias law." It created mandatory minimum prison sentences for crack and powder cocaine use as part of a larger War on Drugs promoted by the presidential administration of Ronald Reagan.

And just like almost everything else associated with the NBA since its integration, the law was coded in a decidedly racist way. Holding five grams of crack cocaine induced a mandatory five-year prison term, while holding five hundred grams of powder cocaine brought the same sentence. Len Bias and Don Rogers were both Black, but they were also wealthy, privileged athletes. The vast majority of powder cocaine was used by more affluent Whites, while Black users at or below the poverty line tended to opt for the cheaper alternative. The sentencing disparity created by the law exacerbated the blackening of the prison population at the same time as fostering its general explosion.

The War on Drugs was part of a broader reactionary conservatism that dominated politics in the 1980s. On one hand, the unequal, top-heavy economic prosperity brought by deregulatory Republican policies helped spur basketball's growth and the decade's emphasis on athletic celebrity, just as it had when similar deregulatory Republicanism had dominated in the 1920s. On the other hand, the economic success of the later decade helped wealthier Whites and largely left the working class out of its vision of financial prosperity. Efforts like the War on Drugs proved overly punitive toward Black defendants, and the Reagan administration and its congressional adherents were often accused of creating a new economic segregationism that mimicked the one that dominated during the height of the Great Migration. The administration also pushed back against affirmative action programs that sought to level a racially unequal playing field.

And then there was the administration's response to a new kind of health crisis that the United States and the world had never seen. AIDS first appeared in the United States in 1981. On June 5 of that year, the Centers for Disease Control and Prevention (CDC), reported on a rare kind of lung infection in five gay men in Los Angeles, who also had other rare or unusual infections. Coverage of the report appeared in several California newspapers, and soon the CDC was flooded with additional cases. At the same time, there were also reports of a cluster of cases of a rare cancer called Kaposi sarcoma among a group of gay men in California and New York. On July 3, the *New York Times* reported on the phenomenon, affecting forty-one gay men. By the end of the year, there was a total of 270 cases of "severe immune deficiency" in gay men, with 121 of them dying.

In January 1982, San Francisco established the first clinics and foundations to provide some kind of treatment to these men; a similar organization was soon formed in New York. In April, Congress held its first hearings on the disease, with the CDC estimating that it was affecting tens of thousands of people. In September, based on the hearings, Congress appropriated millions of dollars for surveillance and research, and on September 24, the CDC first used the term *AIDS*, Acquired Immune Deficiency Syndrome, to describe the malady. On December 10, the CDC reported the first case of AIDS in an infant who received a blood transfusion. By the end of the month, at least twenty-two more cases of similar infections in infants were reported, as well as the first cases of heterosexual hemophiliacs dying of AIDS.

Of course, even after the name AIDS was established, people still referred to it as the "gay plague" or "gay cancer." Because it affected homosexuals and intravenous drug users most often, there was a stigma attached to the syndrome that made many people initially reluctant to care about it. Dr. Joel Weisman recalled talking to one of his colleagues about the epidemic, the doctor replying, "I don't know what you're making such a big deal of it for. If it kills a few of them off, it will make society a better place." That was also the response of the Reagan administration, which completely ignored the problem in its first years. But by the end of 1983, there were more than 3,000 cases and more than 1,200 deaths. AIDS was becoming harder to ignore.

Still, the administration would try. Reagan wouldn't mention AIDS until September 17, 1985. "I have been supporting it for more than four years now. It's been one of the top priorities with us, and over the last four years, and including what we have in the budget for '86, it will amount to over a half a billion dollars that we have provided for research on AIDS in addition to what I'm sure other medical groups are doing." That was a lie, but it was, at least, an acknowledgment of the problem. He never advocated safe sex and condoms. Instead, Reagan pushed for a law to ban HIV-positive immigrants and for domestic abstinence programs. He was unable to stop his surgeon general, however, from issuing a frank 1986 report on the disease, encouraging parents and schools to talk about AIDS with their children.

Many groups believed that not enough was being done. They argued that if the epidemic were predominantly affecting straight people, it surely would have been handled differently. By 1988, there were more than eighty-three thousand cases and more than forty-five thousand deaths. It was only then when the government sent brochures to every household in the country to explain AIDS. Still, money, treatment, and help were scarce. There was still a stigma. In October 1985, popular actor Rock Hudson succumbed to AIDS, the first major figure to die of the disease. Hudson played a heterosexual leading man in movies, but his off-screen homosexuality kept American stereotypes in place. The slow turn away from the stigma began in 1990 when a clean-cut, heterosexual teenager, Ryan White, died of AIDS after a blood transfusion. White had become a spokesperson for awareness of the dangers of the disease throughout the 1980s, and his death reminded everyone that anyone could be susceptible to the syndrome. Nothing, however, compared to the coverage the year following White's death, when in 1991 Magic

Johnson announced that he had HIV, human immunodeficiency virus, the virus that caused AIDS.

Johnson discovered during a physical examination prior to the start of the 1991–1992 season that he had contracted the virus. Months prior, he had led his team to another appearance in the NBA Finals. His success had guided the association to new popularity in the 1980s. In his twelve NBA seasons, he averaged 20 points, 11 rebounds, and 8 assists per season. His personality and his talent made him the face of a growing league and a multifaceted marketing program that featured his personality and play, along with that of other star players. And then there was his storied rivalry with Larry Bird. Despite the hype surrounding the rivalry, the two only met in head-to-head competition thirty-seven times in those twelve seasons. Nineteen of those games, however, were in the NBA Finals, where Magic bested Bird in two of three series.

But now he had a new rival, a new opponent that was far more unforgiving. His announcement on November 7, 1991, landed like a bomb on the sport and the nation. In his press conference explaining the diagnosis, commissioner Stern was by his side as Magic announced his retirement from basketball. Many expressed their support, but backlash was inevitable in a country where response to the disease had been colored by bigotry for more than a decade. Rumors circulated that Johnson was gay, forcing him to admit that he had engaged in multiple extramarital affairs during his playing career. Eventually, he began to emphasize his infidelities in an effort to spread the word that heterosexuals could also contract HIV through sexual contact. He promised to devote himself to using his celebrity to battle the disease.

There was also pushback from some of the players. Despite his retirement, Magic was voted by the fans to play in the 1992 All-Star Game, prompting several, including, most infamously, Utah Jazz forward Karl Malone, to threaten a boycott for fear of possibly contracting HIV while playing. For the most part, however, the players rallied around Johnson. He did play in the All-Star Game, scoring 25 points and winning the game's Most Valuable Player award.

Most importantly, Magic's announcement and his work after it to raise awareness about the disease and money to fight it made HIV and AIDS matter to so many who had previously chosen to ignore it. And that new recognition was necessary. Ten years after AIDS was discovered, in 1991, the syndrome had become the second leading cause of death among American men aged twenty-five to forty-four, the same demographic that most regularly consumed professional and collegiate basketball. Money and treatment options continued to grow in the 1990s, much of it prompted by the work of Johnson.

Before he stepped in front of the cameras on November 7, Magic called his rival. "We'd been connected to each other since college," said Johnson. "We were always thinking about each other—what we were doing and how we were doing. I knew that he would want to know and also know from me. And I'm glad I was able to talk to Larry and let him know that I'm gonna be OK, and I knew he was going to be supporting me." He would be. "It was probably one of the worst feelings you could ever imagine," Bird remembered. "It was very difficult. We played against each other for a long time. At that time, HIV was known to be a death sentence. But for some reason, when he told me he was going to be fine, I believed him because everything he's ever said had really come to be true, as far as winning and winning championships. So I felt a little bit better. But still—I was a gamer, I loved game day; I couldn't wait to get down to the gym. But when I got that call that's the one time I can honestly say I didn't feel like playing."

The bomb that dropped on November 7 seemed to mark the end of an era. Larry Bird would play his final season in the months following Magic's announcement before retiring himself, a victim of chronic back problems. The two players who had sparked the revival of a game with diminishing attendance and television ratings left the stage they helped create, one loudly and one quietly, as befit their personalities. But even as they exited, there were new players who had proven that the professional game was in good hands. Magic's last full season, for example, the Lakers won the 1991 Western Conference but were bested in the NBA Finals by a new team starting a new dynasty with a new star. The Chicago Bulls would reign over the decade of the 1990s, and they would be led by the consensus best player the game had ever known.

12

The Jordan Rules

MICHAEL JEFFREY JORDAN was born in Brooklyn in 1963. When he was five years old his family moved to North Carolina, part of a broader phenomenon known as the Reverse Great Migration, wherein Black families in northern urban hubs pushed back into the burgeoning Sun Belt cities of the South, escaping the forced poverty of redlined, segregated enclaves for new opportunities in expanding markets, many with new professional sports franchises that bolstered their credentials and served as a draw for new arrivals looking for a fresh start. Jordan's parents became part of that new diasporic move in 1968, taking young Michael to Wilmington, where he attended Emsley A. Lamey High School. As a sophomore, he tried out for the varsity basketball team but was deemed to be too small. He was 5'11" in his second year of high school, and thus starred on Lamey's junior varsity team instead. After a substantial growth spurt over the summer, Jordan joined the varsity in his junior year, averaging 25 points per game and earning a place on the 1981 McDonald's All-American Team.

The McDonald's All-American basketball game began in 1977 as the premier contest for the best high school players in the nation, that first year headlined by Magic Johnson. Four years later, it was Lamey High School's Jordan who played in the game. He was universally acknowledged as one of the top high school players in the country and was offered scholarships by a variety of leading universities. Duke, Syracuse, and the University of Virginia were among the contenders, but Jordan ultimately chose to play for Dean Smith's North Carolina Tarheels. Smith had yet to win a national championship since arriving on campus in 1961, but he kept his team a perennial power and had made the NCAA championship game twice. In the late 1960s, his teams made the Final Four in three consecutive seasons. Playing for Smith's Tarheels gave Jordan an opportunity to play for a premier program only 150 miles from his home in coastal Wilmington.

It was a rapid ascent for the player, but despite his success in high school and his recruitment by some of the nation's best teams, missing varsity play in his sophomore season became part of the folklore surrounding Jordan's early years. Jordan's later celebrity was interpreted in popular circles as the result of overcoming an early inability or the crushing disappointment of high school failure. While Jordan was certainly disappointed over not making the varsity team as a sophomore, however, his talent never went unnoticed and his time on the varsity commenced when his size caught up to his ability. Still, the narrative of early failure, of greatness being overlooked by those in power, was a singular draw of the Jordan mythos.

Back in the 1920s, when Babe Ruth was the Michael Jordan of his day, much of the mythos surrounding his legend revolved around a similar ability to overcome difficulties in his youth. Ruth was an orphan who rose from an impoverished Baltimore background to become the best player in baseball. "In times past, we had been interested in and excited by prizefighters and baseball players, but we had never been so individually involved or joined in such a mass outpouring of affection as we did for Ruth," explained sportswriter Paul Gallico. He was "exploring the uncharted wilderness of sport. There was something almost of the supernatural and the miraculous connected with him too." Cleveland Indians catcher Chet Thomas was "not so certain now that Ruth is human. At least he does things you couldn't expect a mere batter with two arms and legs to do. I can't explain him. Nobody can explain him. He just exists." Still, his talent could not itself be transcendent. Historian Marshall Smelser has argued that Ruth "met an elemental need of the crowd. Every hero must have his human flaw which he shares with his followers. In Ruth it was hedonism, as exaggerated in folklore and fable." Jordan's folklore grew similarly, with much the same awe about superhuman play, though any hedonism—a penchant for gambling, in particular—would be decidedly downplayed by marketing agencies. Instead, much of that folklore surrounded Jordan being "cut" from his high school team, and though the narrative as presented publicly wasn't true, it was a transcendent athlete's orphan story, part of the narrative tale that made him the modern-day Babe Ruth.

At North Carolina, that narrative would only grow larger through Jordan's exploits, now played out on a much larger stage. In his freshman season with the Tarheels, Jordan combined with forward James Worthy and center Sam Perkins to take the team to the national championship game. There, North Carolina would meet a team with another freshman phenom, Patrick Ewing, and his Georgetown Hoyas. In a tightly contested game, Georgetown was ahead by one point when Jordan took what became the game-winning shot with fifteen seconds remaining, winning the national championship. It was Jordan's introduction to the nation.

But it was more than that; it was a turning point in the collegiate game. The 1982 NCAA tournament was the first since 1961 that did not include UCLA. The championship game, held in the New Orleans Superdome, was attended by 61,612 fans, almost doubling the previous record set a decade prior when the 1971 championship was played in Houston's Astrodome. The balance of power had shifted, and the popularity of college basketball was growing, aided by stars like Jordan. In his next two seasons, Jordan would be a first team All-American, and he concluded his junior year by being named the College Player of the Year. With nothing left to accomplish in his collegiate career, he forewent his senior season and entered the 1984 NBA Draft.

The first two draft choices that season belonged to the Houston Rockets and Portland Trailblazers, both of whom needed centers. Houston's Kevin Kunnert and Portland's Bill Walton had moved on, and both teams felt themselves in desperate need of large bodies to patrol the defensive lane, so they chose the University of Houston's Akeem Olajuwon and the University of Kentucky's Sam Bowie, respectively. Olajuwon had led Houston to two consecutive NCAA championship games in the years after Jordan's freshman championship season and played collegiately in the same city as the Rockets, promising not only team success but a hometown draw that would fill the arena. Bowie had been an Olympian in 1980, a star player who had led Kentucky to the Final Four in his senior season. Still, he had missed the previous two seasons with a tibia fracture that failed to heal properly, and many worried that his history of injuries would be an impediment to his playing career, despite his obvious talent and success when healthy. The Trailblazers already had Olajuwon's former collegiate teammate Clyde Drexler, and

Portland hoped that a healthy Bowie at center would complement its star guard.

With the centers off the draft board, that left Jordan for the team with the third choice, the Chicago Bulls. The Bulls didn't have the championship legacy of the Celtics, Knicks, or Lakers. They were the third association franchise to play in the city, following the original Chicago Stags, which folded in 1950, and the Chicago Packers, founded in 1961, which changed its name to the Chicago Zephyrs before moving to Baltimore to become the Bullets in 1963. The Bulls had been added to the NBA as an expansion franchise in 1966. Led by star Jerry Sloane in the early 1970s, Chicago had four fifty-win seasons and once made it to the conference finals but had since been unable to replicate that early success. Owner Jerry Reinsdorf had recently purchased the team, and he and general manager Jerry Krause decided to build their new franchise around the star guard from North Carolina.

And even in his early days, he was a star. Jordan averaged more than 28 points in his first season as a professional and played with a unique style that drove attendance at arenas around the association when the Bulls came to town. His immediate popularity led to a selection to the All-Star Game that year, though jealousy among the more established players led to an infamous "freeze out" during the game, wherein his fellow All-Stars refused to pass the ball to him. His revenge would be a Rookie of the Year award and the Bulls' first trip to the playoffs in several years. The following season would be anticlimactic, as Jordan broke his foot early in the campaign and missed sixty-four games. Still, after returning for the playoffs, Jordan scored a record 63 points against Larry Bird's Celtics, the eventual champion that season. In his third effort, the 1986–1987 season, a healthy Jordan averaged more than 37 points, scoring more than 3,000 for the season. Jordan's trajectory was one headed in a singular upward direction.

The 1987–1988 season would be his best to date. He averaged 35 points, winning the association's Most Valuable Player (MVP) award and its prize for Defensive Player of the Year. He also led his team, now including a rookie forward from the University of Central Arkansas, Scottie Pippen, out of the first round of the playoffs for the first time, winning an opening round matchup against the Cleveland Cavaliers before losing to the Detroit Pistons. The next season, the Bulls won two playoff rounds. They again faced the Cavaliers in the first round, and in a close fifth game with Cleveland up by one point, Jordan made what became known simply as "the shot," sliding to his left near the foul line to shoot at the buzzer over defender Craig Ehlo to win the game and the series, bringing the Bulls to the second round and heightening Jordan's profile all the more. After defeating the Knicks in the second round, however, the Bulls again lost to the Pistons. In the 1989–1990 season, the Bulls advanced to the Eastern Conference Finals, but for the third year in a row lost to Detroit.

The Pistons teams of the late 1980s were known as "the Bad Boys." Led by coach Chuck Daly, players Isiah Thomas, Joe Dumars, Bill Lambier, and Dennis Rodman engaged in a rough style of play with substantial hand-checking and defensive aggression that earned them a reputation as on-court bullies. It was a style, however, that earned them two championships in 1989 and 1990 after defeating the Bulls in earlier rounds of the playoffs. Their strategy against Chicago became known colloquially as the "Jordan Rules," employing double-teams and overwhelming defense against Jordan and forcing his teammates to outplay them. "If Michael was at the point, we forced him left and doubled him. If he was on the left wing, we went immediately to a double-team from the top. If he was on the right wing, we went to a slow double-team," Daly explained. "He could hurt you equally from either wing—hell, he could hurt you from the hot-dog stand—but we just wanted to vary the look. And if he was on the box, we doubled with a big guy. The other rule was, any time he went by you, you had to nail him. If he was coming off a screen, nail him. We didn't want to be dirty—I know some people thought we were—but we had to make contact and be very physical."

It worked and would be tried to lesser effect in future seasons by the New York Knicks. But the Bulls under second-year coach Phil Jackson, a former Knicks player, had a strategy to counter the Jordan Rules—the triangle offense. Developed by Jackson's assistant Tex Winter, the triangle was designed to better space the floor and allow players like Jordan to thrive in a more open system. In 1991, the Bulls again met the Pistons in the Eastern Conference Finals, but this time swept them in four games. The triangle had neutralized the Jordan Rules, and basketball's balance of power had shifted. In the NBA Finals that year, Jordan and the Bulls defeated Magic and the Lakers in Johnson's last full season before his HIV diagnosis. It was the one hundredth anniversary of Naismith's invention of the game, and a new star seemed to be inventing it all over again. Jordan averaged more than 31 points in the Finals and was named MVP of the series. The next season, the Bulls met the Trailblazers in the Finals. The team had long since moved on from Sam Bowie, who was now playing for the New York Nets, but star guard Clyde Drexler remained. He was not enough, however, and the Bulls won their second consecutive NBA championship. Jordan won another league MVP award and his second consecutive Finals MVP.

Before he and the Bulls could attempt another championship run, however, they had other business to conduct. Olympic basketball had long been a point of pride in the United States. It was invented in the United States, and Americans dominated it in international competition. Prior to the Barcelona Olympics in the summer of 1992, the United States had an almost unblemished record in Olympic play. But not entirely unblemished.

Entering the 1972 Summer Olympics in Munich, for example, no American team had ever lost in men's basketball, winning seven gold medals dating back to 1936. But in 1972, the United States met the Soviet Union in the gold medal game. The American team fielded a roster of college all-stars, while the Soviets had played more than four hundred games together. They were a team, a cohesive unit in a way that an all-star team could never be. The US players were led by Oklahoma State coach Hank Iba, who had coached the two previous Olympic teams to gold medals, and the 1972 iteration of the squad had little trouble reaching the finals of the tournament. Neither, however, did the Russians. A consistently close game in the gold medal contest led to an American lead, 50 to 49, with three seconds left to play. The Soviets inbounded the ball for a final chance, but the referees stopped the game with one second remaining after the USSR claimed to have called a timeout during two previous US free throws. Officials then ordered three seconds put back on the clock. The Soviets inbounded the ball again, and the horn sounded, apparently giving the Americans their gold medal. But the officials ordered the teams back on the floor because the timekeeper hadn't replaced the extra phantom two seconds on the clock. So the Soviets would now get a third chance to try to win the game. The Americans were dumbfounded. Mike Bantom, a forward on the US team, argued,

"It was like they were going to let them do it until they got it right." The Soviets threw a full-court pass, put in a layup, and won the game.

The United States filed a formal protest with the International Basketball Federation but were denied. *Sports Illustrated*'s Gary Smith noted that "everything progressed according to strictly Cold War politics. There were 3 Communist Bloc judges. It's a 3 to 2 vote. America loses. The Soviet Union wins the gold medal, and at that point the American players are facing a stark reality. Do they accept the silver medal?" They didn't. The United States did not participate in the medal ceremony, and the silver medals still reside in the Olympic vault in Lausanne, Switzerland.

The controversy was fed by the politics of the Cold War, a mistrust between the world's two superpowers beginning at the conclusion of World War II. Harry Truman's aggressive foreign policy and the arrival of the atomic bomb only exacerbated that mistrust, which fueled a global conflict that played out on the margins, in Greece and Korea and Vietnam, rather than in direct violent opposition between the two nations. One of the other margins upon which the rivalry took place was international athletic competition, making the Olympics all the more important. Medal counts became a measure of success. Jordan helped add to it in 1984 as part of the gold medal–winning amateur basketball team, but in 1988, during the final twilight of the USSR, the Americans again faltered, this time the basketball team losing to Russia in the tournament's semifinals. There was less controversy in the game, but that made the loss all the more demoralizing. The Americans left with the bronze medal, their worst result in Olympic history.

The problem the United States faced was that the International Basketball Federation (FIBA) barred NBA players from international competition, while groups like that of the Soviets could field international teams from domestic leagues. In 1989, however, FIBA changed its rules and allowed NBA players to compete. Though the decision proved a decided benefit to the United States, and though many US officials had pushed for the change, the Cold War was coming to an end, and the US contingent actually voted against the new allowance, influenced most immediately by leaders of collegiate and high school sports who saw the Olympics as a vehicle of their success. It was another battle in the long conflict between amateurism and professionalism in basketball, and as it had at so many other points in the game's history, amateurism lost.

USA Basketball, then, would include NBA players on its 1992 Olympic team. Jordan's play was a given, joined by Bulls teammate Scottie Pippen and other stars like John Stockton, Karl Malone, Charles Barkley, David Robinson, Patrick Ewing, and Chris Mullen. Magic Johnson and the recently retired Larry Bird were also on the team. The one major professional star not included was Detroit's Isiah Thomas, and rumors began almost immediately that his absence was prompted by Jordan's unwillingness to play with him. Thomas's Bad Boys Pistons teams had certainly played rough with the Bulls star, and they were by no means friends, but Thomas was unpopular with many of the players. Jordan's demand for his exclusion appears fictive. The other controversial exclusion was college center Shaquille O'Neal. USA Basketball wanted one collegian on the team and chose Duke's Christian Laettner over the Louisiana State University standout. Though O'Neal would be the NBA's first draft pick, Laettner had been named the College Player of the Year and had led the Blue Devils to consecutive NCAA National Championships.

Known popularly as the Dream Team, the Americans overwhelmed their Olympic competition, winning each game by an average of more than 43 points. It was, per *Sports Illustrated*, "arguably the most dominant squad ever assembled in any sport." The Dream Team grew the popularity of basketball overseas and drove a new popularity for the NBA at home.

With those new fans watching in the 1992–1993 season, Jordan's Bulls again dominated the association, meeting Barkley's Phoenix Suns in the Finals. Barkley won the season's MVP award over Jordan, and the Bulls star played as though he was trying to prove a point. He averaged 41 points during the series, winning both the championship and a third straight Finals MVP award.

Barkley was in many ways the antithesis of Michael Jordan, willing to speak his mind publicly on controversial issues. During that 1993 season, he riled many by arguing that athletes should not be role models. "A million guys can dunk a basketball in jail," he said. "Should they be role models?" He argued that artificially generated role models like athletes were creations of the media with a decided racial motivation. "It's as if they say, this is a young black kid playing a game for a living and making all this money, so we're going to make it tough on him. And what they're really doing is telling kids to look up to someone they can't become, because not many people can be like we are. Kids can't be like Michael Jordan." Nike turned the controversy into a commercial, Barkley announcing, "I am not a role model" in an iconic advertisement.

At the same time, however, Nike and other companies were also telling a generation of kids that they could indeed be like Michael Jordan. Nike created its first shoe for the Bulls rookie, the Air Jordan, in 1984, and advertised them with a series of commercials starring Spike Lee. As Jordan became more successful on the court, his endorsement deals continued to mount. He became a spokesman for McDonald's, Wheaties, Coca-Cola, Hanes, and Gatorade, among many others. Jordan, again like Babe Ruth before him, changed the relationship between athletes and the public, parlaying his basketball success into advertising revenue and earning far more money off the court than on it. In 1992, as the Bulls were beginning a campaign for their third consecutive championship, Gatorade created a series of commercials featuring a song and tagline that kids "want to be like Mike," a literal refutation of Barkley's comments. Jordan's advertising prowess is unmatched in the history of professional sports, but it created a model for other star basketball players in the decades to come.

At the same time, however, the reliance on public image required of an advertising icon kept Jordan from using his public platform to advocate for political and racial causes. As Jordan was winning his first title, the Clarence Thomas Supreme Court hearings demonstrated the double-bind of racism and sexism faced by women like Anita Hill. The following year, the Rodney King beating by the Los Angeles Police Department sparked an uprising in the city. Two years after that, the 1994 Violent Crime Control and Law Enforcement Act exacerbated mass incarceration and furthered the racial coding of judicial sentencing decisions. In 1996, a new welfare reform law limited public assistance for low-income families. There were, throughout the decade of Jordan's dominance, myriad social justice issues that would have benefited from his advocacy, but unlike Russell, Baylor, and Abdul-Jabbar before him, Jordan remained determinedly apolitical, despite calls for his voice. He hewed to his sole role as a player, despite criticism, because anything more would threaten his corporate relationships.

And so the only potential threat to his advertising prowess would be an extended absence from the game, which seemed after his third consecutive championship to be an impossibility. But it wasn't. On July 23, 1993, Jordan's father was murdered in a Lumberton, North Carolina, carjacking, his body dumped in a South Carolina lake and not discovered until early August. The trauma of the event didn't immediately prompt his next decision, but it exacerbated his conviction that it was his best choice. On October 6, 1993, Michael Jordan retired from basketball. His desire to play was gone, he explained, the pressure of overwhelming fame more than he could handle in his grieving state. The shock of the retirement reverberated around the world, as had Magic's retirement two years prior. The surprise was compounded four months later, when Jordan signed a Minor League Baseball contract with the Chicago White Sox, also owned by the Bulls' Reinsdorf. He joined the team's 1994 spring training camp and ultimately landed with its double-A affiliate, the Birmingham Barons. He had a .202 hitting average with the Barons, playing respectably but not at an elite or major league level. In August 1994, as his first season in the minors was coming to a close, Major League Baseball players went on strike, cancelling that year's World Series and continuing into March of the following year. Missing basketball, missing being dominant, and worried that he would be used as a replacement player if the major league strike continued into the 1995 baseball season, Jordan issued a brief press release on March 18: "I'm back."

The Bulls in his absence had substantially declined. In the 1993–1994 season, the team made it to the second round of the playoffs before falling to Ewing's Knicks. At the time of Jordan's return announcement, the 1994–1995 iteration of the Bulls was mired in a 31–31 record, struggling for playoff contention. He took the court against the Indiana Pacers the day following his announcement, a grateful fan base making the televised contest the most watched regular season basketball game since 1975. He led the Bulls to thirteen wins and four losses after his return, qualifying them for the playoffs, where they made it to the Eastern Conference Finals, finally losing to the Orlando Magic and Shaquille O'Neal.

The defeat only motivated Jordan. In his first full season back in the NBA, he led the Bulls to seventy-two wins, a record number of victories at the time. The team lost only four playoff games en route to its fourth championship. Jordan won the league MVP, the All-Star Game MVP, and the Finals MVP awards, a feat only New York's Willis Reed had previously accomplished. The following season Jordan lost the MVP voting in favor of Utah's Karl Malone, and as happened when Barkley won the award, he found himself in the playoff Finals against Utah. He outplayed Malone and the Jazz and the Bulls won another championship in six games. In the fifth game of the series, Jordan scored 38 points despite a debilitating stomach virus that left him feverish and dehydrated. Known colloquially as the "flu game," the Jordan mythos only grew as a result.

In the 1997–1998 season, Jordan again managed to win all three MVP awards, leading his team back to the Finals to again play the Utah Jazz. In the sixth game of the series, leading three games to two and down by one point, Jordan performed a crossover dribble against defender Byron Russell and made the game-winning, championship-winning shot with five seconds remaining, giving the Bulls their sixth championship in eight seasons. He retired for a second time in January 1999, defining a decade and bringing the NBA a new level of popularity. His last Finals series versus the Jazz had the highest television ratings of any Finals series, and the deciding game was the highest rated contest in the history of the association.

That popularity would play out in other ways, as well. Again, like Babe Ruth before him, Jordan would translate his athletic and advertising prowess into film. In 1992, during the Bulls' second championship season, a Nike commercial during the Super Bowl featured Jordan playing basketball with Warner Brothers' cartoon character Bugs Bunny. Four years later, the original advertising concept led to a feature film, *Space Jam*, that combined live action and animated sequences. The plot involves Jordan being recruited by Bugs and his cartoon friends to help them win a basketball game against a group of monsters trying to enslave them in a theme park. Charles Barkley, Larry Bird, Patrick Ewing, and other NBA stars also have roles in the story. *Space Jam*, like most of Jordan's efforts in the 1990s, was a phenomenon, the highest grossing basketball film of all time. Fifteen years prior, the NBA Finals were being shown on tape delay to miniscule audiences who proved largely unconcerned with the outcome. Now a basketball film was grossing more than $230 million worldwide.

Times had clearly changed, with the typical debits and credits that came with such seismic shifts. In 1995, for example, the association finally returned to Canada. The sport invented by a Canadian and the league that played its first game in Canada placed new expansion franchises in Toronto and Vancouver. It had been almost half a century since the Toronto Huskies played in that first contest against the New York Knicks, and now the city had a new team, the Raptors, to represent it in an NBA it helped create. The push north was part of a larger expansion project under the leadership of David Stern. In 1988, the association added teams in Miami and Charlotte; in 1989, it expanded to Orlando and Minneapolis, returning an NBA team to Minnesota for the first time since the Lakers absconded for Los Angeles in 1960.

If expansion was an undeniable signpost of success, however, labor relations issues were a reminder that the collective affluence it generated was distributed unequally. In the 1995 off-season, owners locked out the players in a labor dispute, the first work stoppage in association history. Lasting from July to September, the stoppage did not cancel any regular season games. Three years later, however, the NBA would not be so lucky. Negotiations between players and owners for a new collective bargaining agreement reached an impasse in June 1998. While a salary cap had long existed in the league, a carve-out existed known as the "Larry Bird exception," wherein teams were not capped when resigning their own players. Owners wanted an end to the exception and a change to rookie contract regulations that allowed players to become free agents after three seasons. Meanwhile, the Players Association opposed eliminating the exception and wanted a raise in the mandatory minimum salary for marginal players. The impasse culminated on July 1, when the owners again locked out the players, attempting to force them into accepting ownership's proposals.

August negotiations broke off when Stern and the owners balked at a Players Association request for more revenue sharing. During the first two months of what should have been the season, no games were played, but the owners were in no rush to compromise. A federal arbitrator ruled that they did not have to pay their players during the lockout, despite the fact that teams still received television revenue even when games were cancelled. Armed with that leverage, Stern refused to compromise with the players, telling them in late December that if a deal was not reached by early January, he would cancel the season. The heavy-handed tactics understandably splintered opinions among the rank and file. Most NBA players would never be affected by the Bird exception; they weren't superstars and needed their salaries. Tense meetings among the players divided along class lines, with lower-paid players wanting to accept Stern's offer and play. Led by Players Association president Billy Hunter, the group decided in a tense vote to accept the proposal. The new agreement capped player salaries for the first time in professional sports; it instituted a rookie wage scale that set deals for new additions based on draft position; the Bird exception remained and the minimum salaries were increased, but a new drug-testing policy ensured that players would be tested for both performance-enhancing drugs and marijuana.

The deal was a win for the owners and left a residue of tension between various groups of players and between players and owners. The wrath and acrimony engendered by the new collective bargaining agreement were perhaps the inevitable effluvium of the success that had redounded to the NBA and its players throughout the decade. The deal also signaled the end of an era. Jordan retired during the lockout before play resumed. The game's transcendent star left the stage in the middle of a fight scene. It seemed to portend a confluence of new problems as the professional game moved into the twenty-first century.

At the same time, however, there were signs that the game was in good hands. The San Antonio Spurs won the championship of that truncated season, but during the summer of 1999, Phil Jackson, coach of the Bulls dynasty, moved from Chicago to Los Angeles, where he took over a team that featured Shaquille O'Neal, one of the association's most dominant players, and Kobe Bryant, a rising star who had joined the NBA directly from high school in 1996. A new dynasty was in the making.

The success of the NBA in the 1990s, led by Michael Jordan, led to both new profits and new problems, and it also redounded to the men's collegiate game, which witnessed its own series of profits and problems as the century turned.

13

College Basketball at the Millennium

Jordan's game-winning shot in the 1982 NCAA Championship brought renewed interest in the association's tournament, but the collegiate game's popularity in the 1980s was also driven by the development of parity, with teams not considered traditional powers winning championships. It was a move facilitated by expansion of the tournament field to allow more teams to participate. The desire to include more schools was an inversion of the logic of the professional game, which saw its least popular decade in the time of most parity. Growing the field and providing more fan bases a chance to be included, however, proved for the NCAA to be a boon to both its tournament and the television product it generated.

And one of collegiate basketball's advantages over its football counterpart was its number of individual fan bases. Basketball required fewer scholarships and less equipment than football. It was a cost-effective way for many schools that either didn't play or didn't emphasize football to have high-level collegiate athletic success. Schools like Villanova, Seton Hall, St. John's, Providence, La Salle, and Holy Cross in the northeast; Drake, Bradley, Creighton, Butler, Wichita State, and St. Louis in the Midwest, all found a devoted following built almost solely on their basketball prowess. In the Midwest, many of those schools found a home in the Missouri Valley Conference, founded as the Missouri Valley Intercollegiate Athletic Association in 1907, while powerhouse basketball programs like Chicago's DePaul University and Milwaukee's Marquette University remained independent.

Teams in the Northeast had devoted followings and athletic success, but as of the late 1970s had little conference organization. Schools participated in an annual tournament hosted by the Eastern College Athletic

Conference (ECAC) to earn bids to the NCAA tournament. The ECAC was an organizing body for hundreds of schools across all NCAA divisions rather than a hub for a small number of equivalent universities. While the group's annual tournament provided exposure and NCAA bids to its best teams, it did not provide the organized scheduling and competition that more localized conferences provided. Thus it was that in 1979 a group of those schools created the Big East Conference to create a more formal organization for some of the leading basketball schools in the region. Connecticut, Georgetown, Providence, St. John's, and Seton Hall joined Boston College and Syracuse, schools that also had storied and successful football programs, to create a basketball-only conference. Villanova joined the following season, Pittsburgh two years after that.

The ability of smaller colleges to create successful basketball programs not only spread the game's popularity to all parts of the country, but it spread the possibility of success to those fan bases, making collegiate basketball a far more democratic game than collegiate football, a sport dominated by a handful of powerhouse programs. By concluding the college season with a championship tournament, basketball gave the fans of included teams a legitimate opportunity to hope for a national title.

The original NCAA tournament in 1939 featured eight teams. In 1951, the total doubled to sixteen, then moved to twenty-two teams two years later. In 1969, the slow expansion continued, raising the number to twenty-five. Starting in 1975, however, the NCAA embarked on a decade of exponential growth. That year, its men's basketball tournament field expanded to thirty-two, in 1979 to forty. In 1980, the tournament included forty-eight teams, and in 1983, the year after North Carolina's victory in the Superdome, it moved to include fifty-two. The following year the tournament added an additional team before evolving to sixty-four entries in 1985, where it would stay for the rest of the century.

"March Madness," as it came to be known, provided an easily consumable television product that drove revenue for both the NCAA and the universities and gave rise to terms like "Sweet Sixteen," "Elite Eight," and "Final Four" that transcended collegiate basketball and became part of the national lexicon. There were some doubters who worried that larger tournament fields would trivialize the regular season. Since March Madness games were played at neutral sites and regular season games took place on campus, any lessening of the regular season's meaning threatened to reduce attendance at the games that provided direct revenue to the schools. The draw of the tournament, however, only increased fan interest in the sport, which increased local interest in college teams that had a greater and greater possibility of inclusion in the field with each tournament expansion.

More teams meant more possible winners. The other benefit of the NCAA's parity principle was that it allowed for Cinderella stories, lesser or unknown teams able to win several games, capturing the interest of fans rooting for the underdog. And sometimes those Cinderella stories actually won the tournament. The year following Jordan's championship shot, the most successful team entering the tournament was the University of Houston, coached by Guy Lewis and starring a group known as Phi Slama Jama. Clyde Drexler, Akeem Olajuwon, and Michael Young played with a fast-paced, flashy style that emphasized creative and powerful dunks. The Cougars were the consensus top-ranked team entering the tournament, the odds-on favorite to win the championship. The North Carolina State Wolfpack, on the other hand, had finished in fourth place in the Atlantic Coast Conference before winning the postseason conference tournament. NC State was coached by the charismatic Jim Valvano, who had led the program since 1980. The team earned the sixth seed in one of four regional brackets of the tournament, meaning that prior to 1969, the Wolfpack would not have even been included in the field. They were a long shot, at best, but managed to arrive at the championship game through tense moments and close victories. Their reward for that success was a date with Phi Slama Jama, with whom the Wolfpack played another even contest. With five seconds left and the score tied, point guard Dereck Whittenburg heaved a long shot that fell short of the basket. Center Lorenzo Charles, however, was waiting for it, jumping, grabbing the ball, and dunking it with no time remaining for North Carolina State's first national championship since 1974. It was one of the most shocking upsets in collegiate basketball history, performed in the most exciting way possible. As millions watched on television, cameras followed Valvano as he ran around the court in search of someone to hug after the victory.

For the Wolfpack, the win meant a national championship; for the NCAA, the win was a validation of the expanded field and a precedent for hopeful fans in search of Cinderella stories in the years to follow. They would find another two seasons later, when the Villanova Wildcats posted a similar resumé to that of North Carolina State. The team had finished fourth in its conference, the Big East, and had finished its last ten games with only five wins. The Wildcats, led by coach Rollie Massamino and forward Ed Pinckney, ultimately earned an eighth seed in one of four regions. The winners of the Big East that season were the defending national champions, the Georgetown Hoyas, coached by John Thompson and led by center Patrick Ewing. The Hoyas began the season ranked number one and ended it the same way; they seemed destined to repeat as NCAA champions. The tournament progressed as it had two years prior, with the favorite winning its games with relative ease en route to the championship game, while the upstart Wildcats played several close contests before miraculously reaching the finals. But they weren't expected to actually win. Villanova had already lost to Georgetown twice during the regular season, but in the championship game the Wildcats were able to earn a close victory, winning by two points and taking the school's first national title.

Cinderella stories, however, could come in a variety of forms. The University of Nevada, Las Vegas, for example, only joined the top division of the NCAA in 1970, an obscure western university often pilloried as "Tumbleweed Tech." In 1977, however, the school earned a trip to the Final Four and repeated the feat ten years later. The Runnin' Rebels were led by coach Jerry Tarkanian, who joined the program in 1973 and built it from scratch. In the 1989–1990 season, UNLV featured star players Larry Johnson, Stacey Augmon, Greg Anthony, Anderson Hunt, and George Ackles. It entered the NCAA tournament with a 29 and 5 record and a number one regional seed, winning its games with relative ease and taking the national championship contest against Duke by 30 points. Johnson, Augmon, and Anthony would all be chosen in the first round of the NBA Draft. The Runnin' Rebels were a powerhouse, but they were also, in their way, a Cinderella story. Not only had the school authored a rapid rise from "Tumbleweed Tech," but Tarkanian took risks on players with grades and personal troubles that left them unrecruited by other prominent programs. Both the university and its players were underdogs; they just happened to be better than everyone else.

The year prior to UNLV's run, the University of Michigan won the NCAA tournament. The Wolverines were a third regional seed and not a traditional underdog in any way, but prior to the tournament, word leaked that the team's coach, Bill Frieder, had agreed to take a job at Arizona State following the season, so university athletic director Bo Schembechler fired Frieder, replacing him with interim coach Steve Fisher. Under the helm of an interim coach, the Wolverines won six consecutive games and the national championship. It was a Cinderella coaching tale that provided a compelling comeback narrative and earned Fisher a full-time job.

Then there were the Cinderella stories that captured national attention despite not reaching the NCAA Championship. On their way to the title in the 1990 season, for example, the Runnin' Rebels won an Elite Eight matchup against Loyola Marymount University, champions of the West Coast Conference. Marymount, coached by Paul Westhead, was led by two All-American players, Hank Gathers and Bo Kimble, transfers from USC and friends who had played together since their high school days in Philadelphia, who brought the small Catholic college in southern California a national profile and Associated Press ranking. During the team's conference tournament run, however, Gathers, who suffered from exercise-induced ventricular tachycardia, collapsed on the court and died of hypertrophic cardiomyopathy. Coverage of the incident ran on ESPN's SportsCenter and brought the tragedy to a national audience. A crestfallen Kimble played in the NCAA tournament in honor of his friend, a right-handed player who shot his first free throw of each game in the tournament left-handed in a memorial to Gathers. Though Loyola Marymount lost to UNLV in the Elite Eight, the Gathers-Kimble story captivated fans across the country, providing a Cinderella story that was undiminished by the defeat.

Though CBS was the broadcast network for the NCAA tournament, the story's power was exacerbated by constant highlights and commentary on ESPN. With the metastasizing of athlete marketing and the inordinate growth of cable television as the principal method of American entertainment, it was a virtual inevitability that channels dedicated to sports would soon arise. Thus it was that on September 7, 1979, the Entertainment and Sports Programming Network was launched by Bill and Scott Rasmussen. Both had been involved in hockey promotion in New England, and in 1977 they began planning the beginnings of a sports-related cable channel. The Rasmussens were from Connecticut and envisioned a sports network dedicated to Connecticut athletic teams like the Hartford Whalers hockey team and the University of Connecticut football and basketball teams. In the early days of cable television, however, maintaining a twenty-four-hour feed was cheaper than leasing a few hours every night. And so the Rasmussens decided to create a national coverage sports channel. Their first show on the channel's debut was called SportsCenter. In an effort to fill twenty-four hours a day, they broadcast a variety of sports, including tennis, boxing, Australian rules football, and others. ESPN also featured collegiate football and basketball from its inception, DePaul and Wisconsin playing the first televised college basketball game on the channel in December 1979. Color commentator Dick Vitale, former coach of the University of Detroit and the Detroit Pistons, proved a sensation with his flamboyant commentary and enthusiasm, calling games across the country for ESPN. As the years progressed, college basketball became more and more prominent on the network, as the number of teams, the easily digestible two-hour contests, and the low overhead and few necessary cameras made the games cost effective.

Meanwhile, ESPN's coverage bolstered the collegiate game's popularity, growing it from a game into a spectacle. Building on the success of the broadcasts, the channel parlayed its viewership and advertising revenue into a new network, ESPN2, in 1993. Three years later, it created ESPNews. The year after that, 1997, it purchased the Classic Sports Network and renamed it ESPN Classic. ESPN also took advantage of satellite technology and began broadcasting all over the world, in Asia, Africa, and South America, before finally entering Europe in 2004. But the growth wasn't facilitated by just the Rasmussens. In 1984, ABC bought an 80 percent stake in ESPN, with the other 20 percent going to Nabisco, who then sold their shares to Hearst Media. In 1995, Disney bought ABC, and thus ESPN, bringing over Disney marketing models. The change was significant and damaging to American sports, as Disney, concerned more with marketing than with sports journalism, turned ESPN's shows and commentary into advertising vehicles for ESPN, ABC, and Disney programming, limiting the role of hard journalism in the process.

And sports proved inordinately susceptible to such predatory advertising techniques. ESPN's massive control of the sports market share made it inordinately influential as an arbiter of value. The network's interest in certain teams and conferences exacerbated the division between the haves and have-nots in college basketball. The game thus moved away from the parity model in the 1990s as traditionally dominant programs took advantage of increased television exposure to recruit the best high school players to their universities. In the year following UNLV's championship, for example, Mike Krzyzewski's Duke Blue Devils won the first of two consecutive championships, led by Christian Laettner, Bobby Hurley, and Grant Hill.

In the second of Duke's championship contests, the team defeated a group of five freshmen who fundamentally altered the culture of college basketball, despite not winning a national title. The University of Michigan's Steve Fisher managed in 1991 to recruit five of the top high school recruits in the nation. Chris Webber, Jalen Rose, Juwan Howard, and Jimmy King were all McDonald's All-Americans, and Ray Jackson was also on the list of the country's top one hundred recruits. Nicknamed the Fab Five, the Michigan freshmen not only played with style and dominated their opponents, but they also bucked tradition by wearing black shoes, black socks, and baggy shorts. They were a group tailor-made for the ESPN era of sports. The Fab Five's brash demeanor earned them infamy from traditionalists but a devoted following among a new generation of college basketball fans. They would make the championship game in two consecutive seasons. After losing to Duke in 1992, the Fab Five lost to North Carolina in a game known for Webber calling a phantom timeout in the waning moments of the game, earning him a technical foul and putting the contest out of reach for the Wolverines. Even had they won, however, the championship would have been voided years later when it was discovered that several Michigan players received loans and payments from a booster. It was the inherent danger of collegiate basketball's new popularity, driving influential fans to literally invest themselves in the games by paying players in violation of NCAA rules.

Much of the corruption invading college basketball was a product of the Amateur Athletic Union (AAU). Though the AAU began as an outgrowth of the early muscular Christian impetus to promote the value of amateurism in athletics, it transmogrified over the next century into a controversial gatekeeper for young basketball players seeking to become the next Michael Jordan. Independent traveling teams became the main recruiting outlet for college programs, professional scouts, and potential advertising sponsors, creating a breeding ground for potential controversy. Nike, Jordan's sponsor, initiated the growth in AAU programs in the 1980s, signing coaches to shoe deals that mirrored similar deals for collegiate coaches, turning certain AAU teams into pipelines for college programs who wore the same company's gear. It was a synergy that enabled a variety of corruptions that gave lie to the amateurism that the AAU was supposed to promote. Even when corruption was not in play, the system led the AAU and the corporations that sponsored its teams to hold the keys to the kingdom of basketball exposure and opportunity, regulating which players would be given the best opportunities. Universities formed relationships with certain teams, creating a feeder system similar to that of minor league baseball, with the exception that high school players jumped AAU teams strategically to associate themselves with certain coaches, brands, or universities in an effort to become noticed or to earn a scholarship to the school of their choice. It placed demands on high school players that deemphasized schoolwork in an effort to chase what for most was an unlikely ambition.

It was a gamble made all the more stark when the players came from impoverished backgrounds. The problems inherent in such negotiations were introduced to a national audience in 1994, when Steve James's *Hoop Dreams* made its debut. Roundly considered one of the best movies of the year and one of the most important documentaries of the twentieth century, *Hoop Dreams* follows two Chicago teenagers from impoverished neighborhoods recruited to play for a private predominantly White high school in suburban Westchester. The combination of travel, practices, and acclimating to a new social environment make it difficult to excel in their studies while simultaneously attempting to excel as players in a saturated market for talented athletes hoping to make their way to a career in the game. The film is a stark depiction of the intersection of race and class with education and athletics in the late twentieth century, of the hope provided by private schools and AAU teams that prey on the dreams of the impoverished, promising basketball as a palliative to domestic difficulty and a path out of poverty for children and their families. They were promises that sometimes legitimately paid off for young players, but far more often robbed them of other opportunities generated by academic achievement. The media played a powerful role as the conduit metal that transmitted such dreams to impoverished, often Black students. The same companies that advertised the sneakers named for their favorite players were sponsoring their AAU teams and acting as agents for collegiate coaches who had the ability to take them out of housing projects like Chicago's Cabrini-Green, where one of the players featured in *Hoop Dreams* lived. The commercials for those companies ran constantly on cable networks like ESPN during the timeouts of games featuring teams like Michigan's Fab Five. The media created a self-replicating cycle, a machine that consumed young players hoping for the glory celebrated on television and paraded in SportsCenter special interest pieces about athletes who pulled themselves out of poverty through sports. It was as far from muscular Christianity as amateur basketball had ever been.

For high school players who found themselves at the top of that particular heap, many solved the problem of poor academic performance in the face of unreasonable basketball demands on their time by foregoing college and moving straight from high school to the NBA. The template for the move happened in 1974, when Moses Malone jumped from his Virginia high school to the ABA. The following year, Darryl Dawkins, nicknamed "Chocolate Thunder," and Bill Willoughby made a similar jump, demonstrating the risks of the endeavor. Malone was one of the best professional players of his era. Dawkins was a supremely talented athlete with a successful career, and Willoughby became a professional journeyman. The risks involved in the process kept it from happening again for another twenty years. Indiana high school star Shawn Kemp began his professional career in 1989 without playing in college, but only because low SAT scores kept him out of play for his freshman season at the University of Kentucky. But in 1995, high schooler Kevin Garnett skipped college and directly jumped to the NBA, beginning a trend that continued for the rest of the decade. In 1996, Philadelphia guard Kobe Bryant and Columbia, South Carolina, center Jermaine O'Neal forewent college careers. The next year, Tracy McGrady skipped college. Amar'e Stoudemire did the same in 2002, as did Dwight Howard in 2004. In between them, in 2003, LeBron James made the jump. For every great player who chose against college basketball, however, there were several others who went directly to the NBA from high school and failed, overwhelmed by the association's talent and an inability at a young age to adapt to the demands of professional life. Most notoriously, Kwame Brown was a high school player selected with the first overall draft choice in 2001 who failed to live up to the potential expected of a number one pick.

Brown was representative of many high school busts in the professional ranks, and league management worried about the maturity of players entrusted with so much responsibility and money. During negotiations for the 2005 collective bargaining agreement, David Stern proposed a twenty-year age limit for incoming signees, and the Players Association compromised by agreeing to an age limit of nineteen years after being one year removed from high school, creating what became known as the one-and-done rule, wherein talented high school players would attend collegiate programs for one season before jumping to the professional ranks.

The rule was a product of collective bargaining in the NBA, but perhaps its greatest effect was on the college game, changing recruiting strategies and play, as the best freshman players were assumed to be available for one brief season. The team cohesion and senior-laden championship teams that came prior to the one-and-done rule were replaced with younger squads that more closely resembled the early years of Michigan's Fab Five. The changes to recruiting and freshman assumptions that they would not remain in college for the full four years led to a variety of problems related to financial inducements to high school players and a failure of collegiate freshmen to attend or even enroll in classes. It only further separated the players from the rest of the student body, making many of them functional guns for hire with no real intention of participating in the academic mission of the institutions for which they played.

Such is not to say that controversy and young championship teams were new in the post–one-and-done era. In 1994, for example, coach Nolan Richardson's Arkansas Razorbacks won the team's only national championship led by sophomores Scotty Thurman and Corliss Williamson. The Hogs were one of the winningest teams of the decade with a program that had participated in Final Fours since the 1940s. Two years prior to its championship season, the Razorback team had star senior guards Todd Day and Lee Mayberry but only made the round of thirty-two. It was a squad that included no senior starters that actually won the national championship. As with other teams, however, success bred controversy. Richardson was open about the racism he experienced at a southern school and willingly criticized the university's administration and fans when they expressed it. When his accusations bred recriminations from a largely White fan base, Arkansas athletic director Frank Broyles fired him in February 2002.

The reputation of collegiate basketball was fraught in the 1990s, but there were moments of unabashed pathos that maintained its popularity through scandal and change. Two years prior to the Razorbacks' championship season, for example, in June 1992, months after Todd Day and Lee Mayberry failed in a similar endeavor, former North Carolina State coach Jim Valvano was diagnosed with metastatic adenocarcinoma. With his cancer prognosis becoming more dire as the months passed, he was named the recipient of the inaugural Arthur Ashe Courage and Humanitarian Award by ESPN and invited to give an acceptance speech at its first ESPY Awards in March 1993, just prior to the NCAA tournament. Valvano's health was fading rapidly, but he appeared at the awards program and gave one of the most iconic speeches in American sports history. He announced the creation of the V Foundation for Cancer Research and encouraged those suffering with the disease, "Don't give up, don't ever give up." He told his audience that everyone should do three things every day. "Number one is laugh. You should laugh every day. Number two is think. You should spend some time in thought. And number three is, you should have your emotions moved to tears, could be happiness or joy. But think about it. If you laugh, you think, and you cry, that's a full day. That's a heck of a day. You do that seven days a week, you're going to have something special." As he closed, he expressed his courage in the face of almost certain death. "Cancer can take away all of my physical abilities. It cannot touch my mind, it cannot touch my heart, and it cannot touch my soul. And those three things are going to carry on forever."

Valvano died less than two months later, but the V Foundation remained to raise money for cancer research, ESPN annually using its college basketball coverage to replay Valvano's speech and encourage viewers to donate to the cause, raising tens of millions of dollars that it presents as grants to cancer research labs around the world. It was an example of the good the game could do, and Valvano's message reached beyond the cloistered world of collegiate basketball and in the process grew a new fan base interested in the game.

That growth, in turn, grew the tournament that culminated its season and represented to many the public face of college basketball. Throughout the 1980s and 1990s, the NCAA hosted several of its Final Four tournaments in large football stadiums, building on the attendance success of the Michael Jordan tournament final in 1982. In 1997, the association mandated such stadiums for the Final Four, requiring of applicants petitioning to bring the event to their city venues with seating for at least 40,000 spectators. It was a controversial requirement, as it demonstrated the profitability and demand for a game that forced its players to play for free. But there were also no venues that fit NCAA requirements on either of the nation's coasts; it ensured that the tournament final would stay in the middle of the country rather than in the regions where the game originally grew.

The NCAA was able to look past such criticism because its leaders framed the tournament's primary function as a television miniseries. The association wanted spectacle more than anything else. Such thinking wasn't new. Professional football's championship game appeared with the rise of television, as well, and as such scheduled its Super Bowl game at neutral sites. Though sports like baseball with championships that developed prior to the dominance of television played on the local draw of teams to host championships in the parks of the competitors, local constituencies mattered less to the NFL. The Super Bowl was less an event intended to draw fans to a stadium and more an overly produced television show intended to draw viewers and advertising revenue. The NCAA viewed its tournament, and the last two rounds in particular, as a similar program.

It was a framing encouraged by growing television contracts for the event. In the 1980s, ESPN covered early rounds of the tournament before CBS took over coverage for the late rounds. In 1991, CBS signed a contract with the NCAA to broadcast the tournament in its entirety, as its popularity continued to grow through the decade. That popularity would only increase revenue for both the NCAA and CBS, ensuring that the spectacle would metastasize and that the next broadcast contract would be larger and more expensive. In 2009, the NCAA upped its seating requirement for Final Four applicants to 70,000. The following year, the association signed a new CBS deal that also included Turner cable networks TNT, TBS, and TruTV. The fourteen-year, $11 billion contract laid bare the revenue generated from a game played by those not included in the windfall. Though in 2013 the NCAA eliminated its Final Four seating requirement, allowing all venues to apply to host the event, the concession was no sign of concern about attendance or viewership. Three years later, CBS and its Turner partners signed an $8.8 billion extension of their original deal that would carry the broadcast contract through 2032.

But the popularity of the collegiate game would continue against a backdrop of scandal, which had been part of the sport since it began generating revenue without sharing it with those who drew the crowds. Point shaving, for example, continued into the late twentieth century. In 1979, players at Boston College agreed to a scheme prompted by local gamblers and facilitated by members of the Lucchese crime syndicate, one of New York's notorious "Five Families" of organized crime. Rick Kuhn and Jim Sweeney agreed to shave points in return for a portion of the gambling profits they created. The operation was discovered in 1980 when a member of the Lucchese family turned state's evidence in a robbery case at New York's Kennedy Airport, known as the Lufthansa heist, in which more than $5 million was stolen. The Boston College scandal did not traffic in such large sums, but the contours of the scheme were uncovered in the Lufthansa investigation. Five conspirators, including Kuhn, were indicted in a RICO case that sent all of them to prison for different lengths of time.

Several years later, in 1985, players at Tulane University were discovered to have shaved points, and in the process of that investigation, the team's coach, Ned Fowler, was shown to have paid players himself. The scandal led Tulane administrators to end its basketball program until 1990. In 1994, Arizona State players Stevin Smith and Isaac Burton were found to have shaved points in exchange for tens of thousands of dollars. Smith was roped in because of existing gambling debts, using his profits from tanking to pay gamblers he owed. Both players and their handler, former Arizona State player Benny Silman, served time in prison for their roles in the scandal. In 1998, it was discovered that while Smith and Burton were shaving points in Arizona, Kenneth Lee and Dewey Williams were shaving points at Northwestern University. Their efforts in 1994 and 1995 did not come to light until after their time at the school, but both would eventually serve prison time, as well.

It was clear from the continued schemes of gamblers and collegiate players that using an unpaid workforce to generate revenue for universities created a willingness among some to monetize their play in other, more nefarious ways, leading some to call for a revenue-sharing system wherein players would receive more than tuition, room, and board as part of their agreement to play for high-profile college teams. The calls, however, went unheeded. The mythos of amateurism that had grown from the gymnasium in Springfield and had been codified in the early century efforts of the YMCA and AAU held a power over its adherents that disallowed them from considering any possible benefit to acknowledging the clear professionalization of every aspect of the collegiate game except for paying those who played it.

Scandal as part of college basketball, however, was broader than simple game fixing. Five years after the 1998 prosecution of the Northwestern University point-shavers, Baylor University forward Patrick Dennehy went missing. His decomposing body was discovered in a gravel pit near Waco, Texas, in July 2005, and his teammate Carlton Dotson was charged with his murder. The horrifying event rocked the college basketball world and evinced an outpouring of sympathy for Dennehy's family. At the same time, the murder laid bare problems within the Baylor program that had been fomenting for years. Baylor coach Dave Bliss, it was discovered, had paid Dennehy's tuition and that of another player when no scholarships were available. Drug and alcohol abuse was common among the team, known by the athletic staff but not reported. Bliss had also engaged in a variety of other recruiting violations. As all of the program's dirty laundry began to be aired, Bliss compounded his problems by attempting to cover-up his role in payments to players, even falsely attempting to scapegoat the murdered Dennehy as a drug dealer responsible for masterminding the Baylor team's improprieties. Bliss finally admitted his wrongdoing and resigned, but that did not stop the NCAA from imposing harsh penalties on his former school. In addition, the association imposed a ten-year show-cause penalty on Bliss, ostensibly barring him from coaching in an NCAA-affiliated institution for the next decade.

Part of the shock deriving from the Baylor scandal was the profile of the school itself, a conservative, private institution in Texas affiliated with the Southern Baptist Convention. But Baylor wasn't the only university involved in financially motivated corruption. The rot undergirding much of the game was exposed in 2017. The year prior, the Securities and Exchange Commission charged financier Marty Blazer with wire fraud and embezzlement after taking millions of dollars from professional athletes, convincing them to invest in a variety of Ponzi schemes. In response, Blazer turned state's evidence, helping the FBI unravel a vast network of malfeasance in the men's college game. Ten assistant coaches and shoe company executives were originally arrested for paying recruits and using the AAU system to bankroll young athletes and push them to certain collegiate programs for the marketing benefit they provided to the schools and to the companies, Adidas in particular. In all, players at twenty-five different major universities were implicated in the scandal, demonstrating the systemic nature of the corruption in the game. Arizona, Auburn, Kentucky, North Carolina State, Michigan State, Texas, USC, and even Naismith's Kansas played a role in a broad-based pay-for-play scheme that gave lie to the amateurism defended by so many in college basketball.

The most high-profile victim of the investigation, however, was the University of Louisville and its coach, Rick Pitino. Louisville was the flagship program that played in Adidas apparel, part of a system initiated between all collegiate athletic programs and athletic clothing manufacturers like Nike and Under Armor, wherein companies provided branded uniforms for teams. The schools got necessary supplies and the manufacturers got association with the programs and the rights to sell branded merchandise featuring team logos and trademarks. It was a system that prompted a variety of concerns about the independence of university basketball teams and led various programs to be labeled as "Nike schools" or "Under Armor schools." Louisville was an Adidas school, and to ensure that the team remained strong, and the brand stayed on television, Adidas funneled money to potential recruits to steer them to the school. Many of the facilitators were youth basketball coaches who helped broker such deals. "No one swings a bigger dick than [Pitino] at [Adidas]," one of them explained. "All [Pitino] has to do is pick up the phone and call somebody [and say], 'These are my guys.' [And then] they're taking care of us." Most immediately, at Pitino's direction, Adidas paid Louisville recruit Brian Bowen $10,000 to play for the Cardinals.

When details of the investigation appeared, in September 2017 Louisville placed Pitino and athletic director Tom Jurich on administrative leave. The following month the school fired both, though Jurich was later cleared of wrongdoing.

It was the inevitable consequence of the move away from Naismith's original ideal, the pressure of competition for demanding spectators driving corruption in service to the cause of pleasing them. As a check against such difficulties, however, there were the games themselves, which continued to draw the passion of fans despite the corruption that constantly marked the topography of the sport. In 2006, for example, George Mason University from the Colonial Athletic Association began the tournament as an eleventh regional seed but managed to make its way to the Final Four, captivating the nation as a recapitulation of the Cinderella story and making the Patriots' coach, Jim Larranaga, a celebrity. It was the first time since Tarkanian's UNLV Runnin' Rebels won the title in 1990 that a school outside of the major conferences made it to the tournament's semifinal round. George Mason lost to the eventual champion, the University of Florida Gators, but its run demonstrated the inherent draw of the NCAA tournament.

To exacerbate that draw and create further revenue, in 2011 the NCAA tournament added four play-in games and expanded its field to sixty-eight teams. In the first year of the new format, the Rams of Virginia Commonwealth University were slotted to compete in the play-in rounds. Like George Mason before them, the Rams were members of the Colonial Athletic Association and an eleventh regional seed. Unlike George Mason, Virginia Commonwealth was required to play in one of the qualifying games. There they bested the University of Southern California before moving into the tournament's main field. Surprising the pundits, however, VCU continued to win, making the Final Four, as had George Mason five years prior. Again, the team's coach, Shaka Smart, became a celebrity in the process. Again, the team lost in the semifinal round, this time to Indiana's Butler University, who made the tournament's final game for the second year in a row.

The success of the Patriots and the Rams demonstrated that the appeal of the NCAA tournament served as a salve against the game's larger problems. Their runs were temporary, but other small schools like Spokane, Washington's Gonzaga University would use similar tournament runs to become perennial powers in the collegiate game. While such ascendancies benefited those who enjoyed the games, the tournament also created in them a kind of willful ignorance, allowing many to overlook the corruption generated by the corporatism that governed the sport and the unwillingness of its leaders to cut in the players who drove its popularity. There was little amateur about twenty-first-century collegiate basketball, but the long shadow of the YMCA still kept many in darkness about its pseudo-professional corporate profile. The inherent contradictions in the game were generated by its attendance and television ratings. Meanwhile, the women's collegiate game and the professional efforts that developed from it struggled with different contradictions, building a smaller but devoted audience while fostering a competitive ethos that cut against modern gendered assumptions and sloughed off the legacy of physical education leaders like Senda Berenson.

14

The Rise of Women's Basketball

WHILE THE IMMEDIATE post–World War II decades witnessed the creation of the NBA and the exponential growth of college basketball, the women's game suffered a sharp decline in the same period, the middle-class conservative suburbanism promoted by both media and government agencies fostering a retrenchment from the reliance on women's work and service during the war. The constantly promoted vision of American prosperity featured a wife and mother who remained in the home, devoting herself to cooking, cleaning, and childcare in a one-income household that symbolized the American Dream. It was an image unrepresentative of what women had done during the war, and it was unrepresentative of what they were doing in the 1950s, but it created in the minds of many an expectation that cut against competitive competition, reinforcing a new version of the Victorian ideal that limited the popularity of women's basketball. Instead, girls hoping to engage in athletic activity were encouraged to become cheerleaders for men's teams, an athletic version of the supportive role of housewifery mapped onto the basketball court.

Changing that paradigm was difficult, but progress, however slow, was happening. In the late 1950s, the Nashville Business College negotiated with the city's George Peabody College for Teachers of Vanderbilt University to allow its women's players to enroll there if they wanted a liberal arts education. In the early 1960s, schools like the University of Maryland began sponsoring women's basketball club teams on campus. Chris Weller, who was part of that original club cohort and would later go on to coach Maryland's women's varsity, took a philosophy course on the value of sports. "I would argue if these values are so good, why aren't the girls having these opportunities?" she remembered. "We had to stand up and say, 'Look—we're participating very seriously with sports and we believe in the values of sports, too.'"

The women pushing for that change were aided by a broader movement in the era to reform the patriarchal relationship between men and women in American public life. In 1963, for example, Betty Friedan published *The Feminine Mystique*, which detailed a broad disaffection among American women. She called that disaffection the "problem that has no name," an emptiness felt by women who weren't able to live the lives they imagined for themselves. Most of the women Friedan interviewed had material possessions and a middle-class life. But marriage and children—the things the media always told them they were supposed to want—left them feeling unfulfilled. The book was a sensation, and it generated a new, legitimate movement for women's rights, a second-wave feminism that provided momentum for new laws like the first Equal Pay Act later that year. The Civil Rights Act of 1964 also included a gender equality provision. In turn, the new women's rights movement emboldened women to take a more active role in civil rights and anti-Vietnam protests. In 1966, Friedan joined a group of twenty-four women and two men to form the National Organization for Women (NOW), which argued that sexism, though it looked different in practice, had similar catastrophic effects to racism. The group's lobbying efforts ensured that gender rights would be included in affirmative action provisions under Lyndon Johnson's Great Society initiatives. The year after its founding, NOW issued a Women's Bill of Rights that called for equal education, job training, federally supported daycare, childcare tax credits, and federally mandated maternity leave.

Advocates of women's sports were also aided by the Cold War, as the American rivalry with Russia made besting the USSR in international competition a priority, and strong women's athletic teams could bolster medal counts. With the successful Soviet showings in the Olympics, for example, Eisenhower established the President's Council on Youth Fitness in 1956, which found that millions of American children were less fit than their foreign counterparts. Eisenhower's successor, John Kennedy, argued, "Our Olympic team and athletes play a significant role in preserving our way of life," and inherent in his argument was a promotion of women's Olympic competition. While many men did not have the same respect for women's sports as they did for men's, they still hated and feared communism and wanted to beat it back in whatever way they could. The Amateur Athletic Association (AAU) responded by placing more resources into women's athletics. The opposition of women's physical educators to elite, competitive women's sports all but dissipated. In 1958, the United States Olympic Committee (USOC) created the Women's Advisory Board. Two years later, in 1960, Doris Duke Cromwell, heiress of the Duke tobacco fortune, donated a half million dollars to the USOC to promote women's athletics. In 1966, the principal organization of physical educators, the Division of Girls and Women's Sports, created its Commission on Intercollegiate Athletics for Women, which became the Association for Intercollegiate Athletics for Women (AIAW) in 1971 to organize and regulate collegiate competition for female students.

The most immediate development building from the changes was the creation of intercollegiate women's basketball teams. Though they moved from club to varsity status in the late 1960s, women's teams had a decidedly diminished role in the hierarchy of college athletic departments. As Jody Conradt, coach of the University of Texas Longhorns, explained, "Back then, the only reason to be a female college athlete was that you loved it." Sue Gunter, who would go on to fame as the coach of the Louisiana State University Tigers women's basketball program, began her career as the coach of Stephen F. Austin University in the 1960s and 1970s. There she struggled to get uniforms and basic supplies to field her team, finding that university administrators cared little about women's basketball and had no desire to fund it.

Gunter didn't experience a glass ceiling; she experienced one made of iron, the disdain that kept it in place unapologetically paraded in front of those who simply wanted an opportunity to play. In the face of such intransigence, the Commission on Intercollegiate Athletics for Women began organizing a series of national championships for collegiate women's sports in 1969, intent on keeping the programs out of the hands of the men who ran the NCAA and the athletic departments that had proved so hostile.

Also that year, Bernice Sandler worked with the Women's Equity Action League to file a class action lawsuit against the Department of Labor. She had been passed over for tenure-track jobs in the University of Maryland's psychology department, despite her qualifications. Members of the department were openly hostile to the idea of a female colleague, and in response an indignant Sandler began collecting similar stories of women who found themselves in similar positions. Their class action described "an industry-wide pattern of discrimination against women in the academic community." A resulting investigation by several female members of Congress ultimately led to Title IX of the Educational Amendments Act of 1972, aided by a variety of women's lobbying groups and pushed through the legislature by Representative Edith Green of Oregon and Senator Birch Bayh of Indiana. "No person in the United States shall, on the basis of sex, be excluded from participation in, be denied the benefits of, or be subjected to discrimination under any education program or activity receiving Federal financial assistance," the title mandated. It never mentioned collegiate athletics, but if interpreted literally, the title would require revolutionary changes in school sports. Sue Gunter immediately went to her students at Stephen F. Austin. "I told my kids they could be on scholarship the next year." The players were shocked and elated. They asked what had changed to give them the possibility of scholarships when the university had proven so hostile to treating them as a full part of the athletic program. "Because of Title IX," she told them.

The title created enthusiasm among advocates of women's collegiate play, but it also raised a dilemma. Some wondered whether women should support the principle of sexual integration in sports or a separate but equal doctrine, a doctrine considered anathema to the smoldering civil rights movement. The desire for equal opportunity in varsity athletics led most to defend the latter position, but Title IX also encouraged sexually integrated physical education classes and integrated intramural sports programs. The AIAW supported Title IX, for example, but was adamantly opposed to women's sports following a men's sports model. The group actually presented an original opposition to athletic scholarships for women, seeing the corruption of the men's game as an inevitable and undesirable consequence of the potential practice. In 1973, a lawsuit successfully charged that the AIAW's practice of not allowing athletic scholarships was discriminatory. Soon afterward, all major university athletic programs began awarding women athletic scholarships. By the late 1970s, the number and monetary value of women's scholarships as compared to men's became a principal test for compliance with Title IX. By the onset of the 1980s, the number of women playing intercollegiate sports had doubled, and nearly two million girls participated in varsity high school sports, promising the further growth of college basketball in the coming years.

Title IX was a watershed, but it was only the largest example of a series of gains made by women in the 1970s. Though its direct effects were limited to schools, its principle of sexual equity set a precedent throughout the world of sports. Even before Title IX, lawyers had been filing suits on behalf of girls who wanted to play on boy's teams, cases that would lead, for example, to the sexual integration of Little League Baseball. In 1973, *Sports Illustrated* presented a three-part series that indicted sexism in sports and advocated for the further development of games like women's college basketball. In 1976, women's basketball became an official Olympic sport. In 1978, *Time* magazine concluded that "the revolution in women's athletics is at full, running tide, bringing with it a sea change— not just in activities but in attitudes as well."

The most public outgrowth of the revolution in 1978 was the creation of the first women's professional league. The Women's Professional Basketball League (WPBL) was organized the previous year, the brain-child of entrepreneur Bill Byrne, who sought to take advantage of the interest in women's basketball bred by Title IX by creating a pro league. He teamed with principal investors David Almstead and Carew Smith, incorporating the venture the following year. Then they went searching for potential teams and team owners and were able to begin the league's inaugural season in December 1978. Original teams were in NBA cities like Chicago, Houston, Milwaukee, and New York, but also in Dayton, Minnesota; Elizabeth, New Jersey; and Cedar Rapids, Iowa. On December 9, the Chicago Hustle traveled to play the Milwaukee Does in the league's first game in front of more than seven thousand fans. It was even covered by Walter Cronkite on the CBS Evening News. Attendance would not usually be so robust, but the league was able to survive with all its teams intact at the end of its first season, the Houston Angels defeating the Iowa Cornets to win the first championship. UCLA's Ann Myers, the league's first draft choice, was named a co-MVP of the season.

In its second campaign, the league added teams in New Orleans, Dallas, St. Louis, and San Francisco. Grand View University's Molly Bolin, the first player to sign a contract with the new organization, starred for the Iowa Cornets and was a co-MVP for 1979–1980. Despite her performance in the Cornets' second Finals appearance, the team was again bested, this time by the New York Stars. Foreshadowing things to come, however, the champion Stars announced a two-year hiatus shortly after their title run. The women earned comparatively small salaries, but even those often went unpaid in a league constantly struggling for financial solvency. In a March 1981 game in the league's third and final season, the Minnesota Fillies and Chicago Hustle walked off the court in a scheduled Minneapolis game to protest unpaid salaries. The teams were averaging roughly one thousand fans per game, and owners pleaded poverty in breach of player contracts, but the women were unmoved. The upstart Nebraska Wranglers won the league's final championship, but the WPBL had amassed more than $14 million in debt over its troubled three seasons and collapsed soon afterward.

Meanwhile, the feeder system for would-be professional organizations experienced resistance to the growth of women's college basketball. The chief critic of the new push was the NCAA. It lobbied for Title IX's repeal immediately after it passed, fearing that women's athletic scholarships would diminish schools' ability to offer existing scholarships for men's sports, driving less popular programs to abandon competition entirely. It was a straw man built by a century of paternalism in basketball, and its effort to repeal Title IX was unsuccessful. So in 1980, the NCAA developed a new strategy, one that it had used when creating the Sanity Code years prior: it decided to sponsor women's national championships. The decision led to a head-on collision with the AIAW, which already managed more than 750 state, regional, and national championships for 970 member schools. The NCAA, however, had as leverage more money and television coverage, and the vast majority of colleges abandoned the AIAW as a result. The AIAW responded by filing an antitrust lawsuit against the NCAA. The courts, however, sided with the older organization, and the AIAW collapsed in 1984.

And with its collapse, women no longer exercised predominant control over the direction of women's sports at the collegiate level. That same year, the Supreme Court hurt Title IX by arguing that it only applied to those specific programs that received federal funds. Since few women's sports programs obtained any of their funding directly from the federal government, the ruling threatened to end Title IX as an arbiter of value in women's college basketball. In 1988, however, a Democratic congress passed the Civil Rights Restoration Act over the veto of Ronald Reagan. The act barred any institution that received federal aid from discriminating in any of their programs on the grounds of race, age, disability, or gender, regardless of whether or not the specific program benefited directly from federal money. In the process, the new law saved Title IX. Still, in 1992, four years after its passage, the number of varsity male athletes outnumbered females two to one at NCAA Division 1A schools. There were also massive discrepancies in budgets and scholarship monies. Women held less than half the coaching positions in women's collegiate sports and only about one-third of the administrative posts that helped govern them. Coaches of women's teams received far less pay than did their male counterparts. Thus it was that in 1993 President Bill Clinton's Office of Civil Rights set a revolutionary set of new guidelines. One of its most controversial provisions was "proportionality," requiring the number of varsity male or female athletes to approximate their proportions of the general student body. The only way to achieve that goal was to either reduce the size of football programs, which provided eighty-five individual scholarships, or to include more women's sports in collegiate athletic departments.

The most immediate beneficiary of Title IX and its troubled defenses was women's basketball, the most prominent women's collegiate game. And the interest such controversies drew, as had been the case in a variety of men's sports, including college and professional basketball, generated star players and teams, dynasties that rose to dominate play. Because of the paternalism inherent in both the collegiate project and in basketball's history, however, the pseudo-Victorian retrenchment left over from the 1950s would invade even its most stalwart representatives.

It was in 1974, for example, that Louisiana Tech University established a women's athletic program, hiring a young Ruston High School PE teacher named Sonja Hogg as the basketball team's first head coach. Hogg was a leader in the tradition of the early century physical educators like Senda Berenson who carried women's sports from exercise to competition. Those women dealt with the Victorian sexist critiques that basketball grew women's muscles, and thereby reduced the differences in body shapes between men and women, that it could damage the reproductive organs and unleash uncontrollable female passions. Hogg, inheritor of that tradition, insisted that her players conduct themselves like ladies. She outfitted them in shirts with sleeves and didn't allow elbow and knee pads. She refused to call them Bulldogs, the traditional mascot of Louisiana Tech, because a female bulldog was a bitch. Instead, they became the "Techsters." A 1986 *Sports Illustrated* feature described the move as fitting perfectly with the small-town north Louisiana conservatism of Ruston. "A Lady Techster is likely to be a good student and a devout Christian," the article claimed, "probably favors needlepoint over Madonna tapes on airplanes and fears a drug test about as much as she does an airport metal detector." Along with its air of proper Victorian femininity, the move also served to soften blackness to a largely White alumni base watching a sport historically associated with race.

But the easiest way to ingratiate a basketball program into a community was to win. And Hogg's teams did, building successful seasons throughout the 1970s until Final Fours in 1979 and 1980 gave way to national championships in 1981 and 1982. "What we did was right for Ruston," Hogg later explained. "It's a very conservative town, and it was important that we have a team who looked nice and conducted themselves like young ladies. Now we wanted to be competitive too— ready to knock somebody's head off. But it was also important how they presented themselves." Hogg's teams also presented themselves as winners, making the Final Four in 1983, 1984, and 1987. The program would remain dominant after Leon Barmore took over from Hogg, winning a third national championship in 1988, the sport's first legitimate dynasty.

And it was a sport that would be defined by its dynasties and its star players. In 1983 and 1984, for example, the University of Southern California (USC) had a brief run as a championship power, winning back-to-back titles led by forward Cheryl Miller, named Naismith Player of the Year three times and tournament MVP for both of the Trojans' title runs. Miller was one of the most talented players in history, but she was not alone. Her teammate Cynthia Cooper was probably the second-best player in the game during those years and would go on to become one of the best professional players of all time. They were joined by All-American twins Pamela and Paula McGee to create a team whose dominance of the game was brief but all-encompassing. While USC wouldn't win any further championships, it would remain a powerhouse program through the rest of the century.

While Louisiana Tech and USC were dominating the early years of the NCAA tournament, however, there was another dynasty beginning its nascent development in Knoxville, Tennessee. Patricia Head was born in nearby Clarksville in 1952. Obsessed with basketball from an early age, her family was forced to move to Cheatham County, Tennessee, because Clarksville's high school did not have a girls' basketball team. After school, Head attended the University of Tennessee at Martin, where she played for Nadine Gearin. There was no Title IX when she enrolled, and though her brothers received athletic scholarships, Head had to pay her own way. With no professional league available to her after graduation, she began coaching, but two years later was able to return to play on the US women's national team in the 1976 Olympics in the first year that basketball was included.

After her senior season at Martin, Head joined the staff at the University of Tennessee as a graduate assistant, but when the team's head coach resigned, the twenty-two-year-old was elevated to the position. The game she coached was different than the one that her success would help create. "I had to drive the van when I first started coaching," she remembered. "One time, for a road game, we actually slept in the other team's gym the night before. We had mats, we had our little sleeping bags. When I was a player at the University of Tennessee at Martin, we played at Tennessee Tech for three straight games, and we didn't wash our uniforms. We only had one set. We played because we loved the game. We didn't think anything about it." Her Volunteers team raised money for uniforms by selling doughnuts. Head washed them after games. She was virtually the same age as her players. And yet she was able to build a winning program from scratch. By 1979, Tennessee made its first Final Four, repeating the feat the following season. After her 1980 marriage, she became known as Pat Summitt.

Summitt took her teams to three additional Final Fours between 1982 and 1986 before finally winning the NCAA Championship in 1987, defeating nemesis Louisiana Tech in the championship game. Summitt's Lady Vols would be the standard-bearer for women's collegiate basketball for the next two decades, winning eight national titles and playing in twenty-two Final Fours. Tennessee won the Southeastern Conference championship sixteen times and Summitt was named the NCAA's coach of the year seven times. Each of her players who completed her eligibility earned a college degree and played in an Elite Eight. She also coached the 1984 Olympic team to a gold medal.

Tennessee's dominance was unprecedented, but the university was not the only one to have a talented team in the century's waning decades. Stanford University, for example, had played the first women's intercollegiate game in the nineteenth century, but in the modern era its program was built by coach Dotty McCrea. Her success in the 1970s and early 1980s was mixed, but the team grew into a powerhouse under the leadership of McCrea's replacement, Tara VanDerveer, who took over in 1985. VanDerveer led the program to its two national championships in 1990 and 1992, but the consistent success of the Cardinal was laid bare by its thirteen Final Four appearances and twenty-six Sweet Sixteens.

Her championship teams had a variety of great players, but transcendent talents did not always opt for one of the game's traditional powers. During Stanford's 1991–1992 championship season, for example, a junior college transfer at Texas Tech University captured the country's imagination. Sheryl Swoopes had originally committed to the University of Texas before attending South Plains College for two seasons. From there it was on to Texas Tech, where she began regularly breaking school and national records. In her 1992–1993 senior season, Swoopes averaged more than 28 points, 9 rebounds, and 4 assists per game. She scored 53 points against the University of Texas, averaged more than 35 in the NCAA tournament that season, and scored 47 points in the championship game, winning Texas Tech its only national championship. Her success came at the same time as that of the Chicago Bulls, and thus invited comparisons between Swoopes and Michael Jordan, an individual dominance of the game not witnessed since Cheryl Miller's time at USC.

After her graduation, however, there was no professional league in the United States, so Swoopes, like so many other women's collegiate stars, had to travel overseas to play professionally. The WPBL had folded in 1981, but other attempts had been made in the intervening years. Hoping to take advantage of the success of Pat Summit's 1984 Olympic team, for example, Bill Byrne attempted another promotion, the Women's American Basketball Association, though the upstart organization only lasted for one brief season. Almost a decade later, in 1992, promoter Lightning Mitchell created the Women's Basketball Association, a fifteen-game summer league that placed teams in WPBL strongholds like Kansas,

Nebraska, Iowa, and Missouri. As was necessary for any sports league in the late twentieth century, the organization had a television contract with Liberty Sports, a small cable channel based in Dallas, Texas. The league survived for three summers until 1995 and planned a reformation in 1997 before Fox Sports purchased Liberty Sports and proved uninterested in the project. In 1996, a new full-season effort, the American Basketball League (ABL), began play, founded by Steve Hams, Anne Cribbs, and Gary Cavalli. The group hoped to capitalize on the popularity of women's basketball deriving from the success of the gold medal–winning team at the 1996 Olympics in Atlanta. Franchises in Columbus, Ohio, and Richmond, Virginia, joined others in Seattle, Portland, San Jose, and Atlanta. The Columbus Quest won both the league's championships and was the best team entering its third season, but the league folded before the Quest had the opportunity to defend its titles. Poor financing decisions played a role in the ABL's demise, as did another new association that had behind it the organizational and marketing power of the NBA.

In April 1996, the NBA's board of governors approved the creation of a Women's National Basketball Association (WNBA) and held a press conference announcing the new venture that featured Sheryl Swoopes, Lisa Leslie, and Rebecca Lobo, who would become the faces of the early association, the core around which it was marketed. Swoopes, of course, had been a larger-than-life presence at Texas Tech. Leslie, meanwhile, had been a standout center at USC from 1990 to 1994 and a fashion model when she wasn't playing. Her beauty and its mention when male commentators discussed her play exposed a double standard that women had faced since the earliest days of the game, physical appearance becoming part of the story in a way that it never would have for her male counterparts like Shaquille O'Neal.

At the same time, the sexualization of female athletes also led to discussions of lesbianism in women's basketball, as if, in the tradition of early twentieth-century commentators, the game itself somehow drove players away from a given sexual orientation. As social scientist Susannah Dolance has observed, "The lesbian athlete stereotype (female athlete equals lesbian) has served as a form of social control to limit women's participation in sports and to denigrate women's sports in comparison to men's." When the players were open and unapologetic about their sexuality, however, attempts at denigration lost their power. Leslie was straight, but several of her competitors in the new association weren't, and the burgeoning gay rights movement and the supportive community built around a game that had always suffered from gender discrimination allowed players to be open about who they were in a way that was unavailable to male players in similar situations. That openness, in turn, grew a new fan base, as, again in the words of Dolance, "the (perceived) large lesbian attendance at WNBA games enables the construction of a lesbian community by lesbian and bisexual fans in a site qualitatively different from traditional locations of lesbian community."

While Rebecca Lobo wasn't part of the lesbian community, she was a member of a group even more influential to the trajectory of the women's game: the University of Connecticut. UConn, as the school's athletic teams were known, founded its women's basketball team in 1974, and it struggled through its first decade with only one winning season. In 1985, hoping to spark interest in its moribund program, Connecticut hired Geno Auriemma, an Italian-born immigrant who had moved to the United States as a child and had served as an assistant coach at several different universities before landing the head coaching job with the Huskies. Two years after he arrived, Auriemma landed his first major recruit, Kerry Bascom, who won the conference Player of the Year award for three consecutive seasons and led UConn to its first two NCAA tournament appearances and, in her 1991 senior year, the Final Four. The next season, Auriemma added Lobo, who would take the team to even greater heights. In her 1994–1995 senior season, Lobo and the Huskies would go undefeated and win the school's first national championship. They were the only team in collegiate history to win thirty-five games without a loss and drove unprecedented interest in the women's college game, helping to convince the NBA of the potential viability of a women's professional association. The University of Connecticut would go on to win ten more titles in the first two decades of the twenty-first century, led by players like Nykesha Sales, Swin Cash, Tamika Williams, Sue Bird, and Asjha Jones, all of whom would later star in the WNBA, as well. In 2001, Auriemma added Chico, California's Diana Taurasi, who won three national championships in her sophomore, junior, and senior seasons. Maya Moore, who committed to Connecticut after a bitter recruiting battle between Auriemma and Tennessee's Pat Summit, would lead the Huskies to two undefeated seasons and a streak of ninety consecutive wins. Breanna Stewart arrived on campus in 2012, the top recruit in the nation, and proceeded to lead UConn to four consecutive NCAA Championships. Stewart was named the tournament's most outstanding player four years in a row, the NCAA's Player of the Year in her final three seasons.

Along with Summit's Volunteers, Connecticut's chief rivals for NCAA power in those years came from Muffet McGraw's Notre Dame and the Baylor Bears of Kim Mulkey, who had starred as a player for the earlier Louisiana Tech dynasty. The high-level competition that had developed in a comparatively short amount of time ensured that the women's collegiate game would remain incredibly popular, and that the growing professional association would have a strong pool of talent from which to draw.

Lobo was the first essential piece of UConn's contribution to that pool, and she stood with Leslie and Swoopes as David Stern announced the creation of the WNBA. "Without his vision and engagement, the league wouldn't have gotten off the ground," said Val Ackerman, the WNBA's president, who had previously served as an attorney with the men's NBA. "He was the mastermind, and the WNBA was really in line with his vision about how sports and society are intertwined." Ackerman portrayed Stern as an immovable force who convinced a reluctant board of governors that women's professional basketball was a good idea. "He saw which way the winds were blowing and put the NBA's full resources behind it," Ackerman said. The man who would originally become Stern's replacement, Associate Commissioner Adam Silver, helped write the WNBA's original business plan and also saw its creation as both a social and economic benefit to the association.

The WNBA began with eight teams, all in NBA cities. Houston, Cleveland, Charlotte, and New York comprised an eastern division, and Salt Lake City, Sacramento, Phoenix, and Los Angeles represented the west. Following the lead of the ABL before it, the WNBA would play its season during the summer, hoping to capitalize on the interest of basketball fans while the NBA wasn't playing. NBC, who held the NBA television license at the time, would broadcast select games, as would ESPN and the Lifetime network. Leslie would compete for the Los Angeles Sparks, Lobo for the New York Liberty, and Swoopes with the Houston Comets. The first game of the association's first season commenced on

June 21, 1997, a nationally televised contest between Lobo's Liberty and Leslie's Sparks, played in Los Angeles and won by New York. Swoopes, meanwhile, wouldn't play much that first season, sitting out during a pregnancy and thus allowing Cynthia Cooper, who had been a core part of the USC championships of the early 1980s, to star over her younger opponents. Cooper was named the association's Most Valuable Player during that first season and led the Comets to the WNBA's inaugural championship, defeating the Liberty in the playoff finals.

Perhaps more importantly, the games that first season averaged roughly 10,000 fans and appeared regularly on national television. In 1998, the association added two more teams, in 1999 two more. In 2000, the WNBA expanded again, adding four more franchises and doubling the total from its maiden season. The new teams, however, proved little competition for the association's original dynasty. Led by coach Van Chancellor and a playing combination of Sheryl Swoopes, Cynthia Cooper, and Tina Thompson, another former USC standout, the Houston Comets won the first four WNBA titles. Average attendance hovered around 10,000 during the last two years of the 1990s, but never reached such heights again, steadily declining in the proceeding years, moving to 9,000, then 8,000, then 7,000, to roughly 6,500.

The association's waning attendance in the stands, however, did not affect the quality of play on the court. In 2001 and 2002, for example, Lisa Leslie was able to break through against Houston and led the Sparks to two consecutive titles of their own. Originally, teams like the Comets and the Sparks were owned collectively by the NBA, but after the second Sparks championship, the association divested, selling teams to the NBA franchise owners in member cities. The Orlando Miracle were an exception to that general rule, sold to a third party, the Mohegan Indian tribe, who moved the team to Connecticut, where they would be renamed the Connecticut Sun and play home games at the Mohegan Sun Casino. It was a significant move for several reasons. The Mohegans were the first American Indian group to own a professional sports franchise in the United States. The fraught relationship between basketball and gamblers over the game's history also made the move to a casino particularly relevant. Major men's professional sports leagues, for example, had refrained from placing teams in Las Vegas to avoid the appearance of impropriety, but the WNBA led the way in making the case that proximity to institutions of legal gambling did not necessarily augur an intrinsic susceptibility to illegal gambling. Eventually, leagues like the NHL and NFL would follow the WNBA's lead and move teams to the formerly taboo Nevada city. Even the NBA would hold its All-Star festivities in Las Vegas. Finally, the Sun represented the first team in the WNBA not dependent on an NBA organization, city, and fan base to support the franchise. Instead, the Mohegan tribe understood that fanaticism surrounding the successful University of Connecticut women's basketball team would serve much the same function.

The Sun would find success in their new home, reaching the WNBA Finals in both their second and third seasons. The team wasn't able to win a championship in the decade, however, often finding themselves behind the decade's most dominant team, the Detroit Shock, coached by former Pistons' Bad Boy Bill Laimbeer. The Shock's principal western rival was the Phoenix Mercury, who rose to prominence after drafting UConn's Diana Taurasi, winning championships in 2007, 2009, and again in 2014. By the century's second decade, however, Phoenix's success would be overshadowed by a new dominant franchise, the Minnesota Lynx, who featured star center Seimone Augustus and began winning championships after drafting UConn's Maya Moore, who led the Lynx to a title in her first season and three more by 2017. The other change for the Lynx was a new coach, Cheryl Reeve, who arrived in 2010 and amassed one of the best winning percentages in history.

Reeve was an embodiment of the game's development. A graduate of La Salle University in 1988, there was no professional league for her upon graduation, so Reeve turned to coaching, first in the collegiate ranks, then with the pros, rising from an assistant at several WNBA teams to become one of the most successful head coaches in the game's history. Of course, the organized league and collegiate history that she represented was not as long as that of the men, stanched for so many decades by patriarchal if not misogynistic assumptions by leaders who doubted both women's ability and their biological fitness for the game. The legacy of such paternalism still appears in women's playing and coaching salaries, and in comparatively small arena attendance and television ratings, but the talent of the players and the competition it generates have given lie to the gendered assumptions that limited the women's game through much of the twentieth century.

15

The NBA in the Twenty-First Century

KOBE BEAN BRYANT was born in August 1978 in Philadelphia, the son of former NBA player Joe "Jellybean" Bryant. After the elder's time in the NBA was complete, when Kobe was six years old, he moved his family to Italy to continue his professional career. For seven years, Bryant lived in Italy, developing a global outlook while learning basketball from his father and from VHS tapes sent from family back home, before returning to Philadelphia at age thirteen. There he starred at Lower Merion High School, in his senior year becoming a McDonald's All American, the Naismith High School Player of the Year, and Gatorade Men's National Basketball Player of the Year. Though his academic success was comparable to that of his athletic accomplishments, Bryant chose to forego college and enter the 1996 NBA Draft.

Shaquille O'Neal was born in March 1972 in Newark, New Jersey, and raised by his mother and stepfather, a career army officer, who took the family with him to bases in Germany, giving O'Neal a similar if less pronounced international experience in childhood. Early in his high school career, the family moved back to the States, where O'Neal attended Cole High School in San Antonio, Texas, overwhelming his basketball competition, setting a state record for rebounds, and leading his team to a state championship in his senior year. While in Europe, he met Louisiana State University coach Dale Brown, who convinced him after his high school career to attend college in Baton Rouge. In his three seasons with the Tigers, he averaged almost 22 points and 14 rebounds per game, led the program to a Southeastern Conference championship, and was named National Player of the Year. After his junior season, O'Neal left college for the NBA Draft, where he was taken with the first overall choice by the Orlando Magic. In his first three seasons with the team, he proved overwhelming to opponents, averaging more than 27 points and 13 rebounds per game and leading the Magic to the NBA Finals in 1995.

In 1996, O'Neal entered free agency as Bryant entered the draft. He had clashed with Magic head coach Brian Hill and resented the public belief among fans that the asking price for keeping him would be too high. He was a large man in a small market, and he wanted to leave Orlando. The Los Angeles Lakers coveted O'Neal but needed to clear financial space under the league's salary cap to be able to afford the heavy remuneration he would command. At the same time, Lakers general manager Jerry West was also interested in the young high school star from Philadelphia, but the Lakers had a low draft choice and he worried that acquiring him would be difficult. West understood talent. The former West Virginia University standout had been one of the Lakers' best players in the pre–Magic Johnson era and had annually battled Russell's Celtics, winning one championship and one Finals Most Valuable Player award. His image became the logo of the NBA. And now, as general manager, he needed to score a different kind of victory, acquiring a superstar veteran and a potential superstar rookie at the same time. To do so, he traded Lakers center Vlade Divac to the Charlotte Hornets for the thirteenth choice in the 1996 draft, using the collectively bargained rookie wage scale to ensure that the trade would save the team enough money to sign O'Neal and give them the ability to draft Bryant.

The ingredients for a dynastic reign were set, but it would take several years for the young player just out of high school to adapt to NBA play. His first signs of greatness came in the lockout-shortened season of 1999, and the team added former Bulls coach Phil Jackson after its completion, demonstrating to many that the turn of the century would augur a similar turn for the Lakers franchise. It did. The Lakers began the new millennium by winning three consecutive championships, reviving the team's success of the 1980s. The combination of O'Neal and Bryant proved a force beyond the control of the association's other teams, with Kobe becoming a legitimate superstar and Shaq winning one regular season and three Finals Most Valuable Player awards. Behind the curtain, however, there was turmoil, as the team's two stars were often at odds, their interteam rivalry included in most reports of their on-court dominance. But there were also other problems afoot.

A year after the Lakers' third consecutive title, on July 1, 2003, Bryant was in Colorado to have an off-season surgery. That night he had a sexual encounter with a nineteen-year-old White hotel employee, and the next day, she reported the incident as rape. Officials interviewed the Lakers' star, confronting him with evidence of a violent struggle and bruises around the woman's neck. At first, Bryant denied even knowing her, but after seeing the results of her rape kit, he reluctantly admitted to having consensual sex with her. He claimed that he enjoyed strangling as part of the sexual act, that he had another extramarital partner who allowed him to choke her, and that the hotel employee's body language seemed to him to indicate consent. After the interview, Bryant returned to Los Angeles, but came back to Eagle, Colorado, two days later to surrender himself after a warrant was issued for his arrest. He posted bond and was immediately released, but the story of the arrest broke nationally two days later. After a formal charge on July 18, Bryant held a press conference with his wife by his side admitting to infidelity but adamantly denying that he committed sexual assault. Bryant's lawyers defended him by attacking the victim, leading Bryant's fans to send her a variety of death threats after her name was leaked to the press. The threats and character destruction ultimately left the victim unwilling to testify publicly, and thus the district attorney dropped the criminal charge. In a civil suit, however, Bryant settled financially with the woman in what many interpreted as a tacit admission of guilt.

The case was, perhaps, the apotheosis of the troubled intersection of race and gender in basketball. Even the most charitable version of the events in Colorado presented a man who assaulted a woman without overt verbal consent, a man of power and popularity who took advantage of a woman with no such power, and a Black man committing an act of violence against a White woman. The behavior of men's basketball fans who defended Bryant despite the clear evidence against him demonstrated the disconnect between adherents of the men's and women's games, the performance of masculinity engendered by male fandom manifesting itself as cruelty to the victim of sexual assault. Others outside of that particularly rabid subset of fandom noted the overt power and race differences among accuser and accused, complaining about the ability of the rich to secure a double standard in the justice system and pointing to historical White fears demonstrated in basketball by reactions to the Kermit Washington punch and in America writ large by the long history of the animalization of Black male sexuality and the supposed protection of White womanhood that generated thousands of lynchings at the turn of a previous century.

The response to Bryant's trouble in Colorado was exacerbated by controversies within the game itself, controversies that also hinged on similar concerns that echoed the history of the racial disparities embedded in the game. When Michael Jordan retired and the century turned, for example, many players began to shed that corporate image, embracing the fashion and culture of hip-hop. Again, White fans worried about what some saw as problematic performative blackness. It was common fare outside of sports for commentators to associate hip-hop and rap culture with criminality and vice, and the behavior of a small segment of the league's athletes played into the hands of those propagating such narratives, allowing some White fans to assume cornrows and tattoos as signposts of deviance. The team that symbolized the new version of racialized negative associations with professional basketball more than any other was the Portland Trailblazers. Known as the "Jailblazers" for the first several years of the twenty-first century, the club witnessed several of its players in legal jeopardy. Stars Rasheed Wallace and Damion Stoudamire were arrested for marijuana use. Role-player Qyntel Woods suffered animal abuse charges for staging dog fights in his house. The team also signed registered sex offender Reuben Patterson to a contract. On the court, things were not much better. Wallace was suspended for threatening a referee. Fights in practice were common. The "Jailblazers" alienated the White fan base in Portland and many White fans across the country.

The reputation of the Jailblazers hung like a cloud over much of the association's reputation in the early century, but more specific bolts of lightning proved even more dangerous. On November 19, 2004, an early season game between the Indiana Pacers and Detroit Pistons became one of the NBA's most infamous contests, rivaling the 1977 game between the Lakers and Rockets in which Washington almost killed Rudy Tomjanovich. The Pacers and Pistons had competed against one another in the playoffs the previous season, and the return engagement had a national audience on ESPN. Held in Detroit's Palace at Auburn Hills, Indiana was winning the game comfortably with forty-six seconds remaining. After Pacer forward Ron Artest fouled Detroit center Ben Wallace on a layup attempt, Wallace shoved Artest in the face, sparking what in the moment seemed a brief altercation. Artest lay dramatically on the scorer's table while officials sorted out the various fouls to be assessed. After Wallace walked by and threw a towel at him, Artest briefly stood up and a fan threw his drink at him. In response, Artest turned and charged into the stands. A nearby Pacers radio broadcaster attempted to hold him back, falling and fracturing several vertebrae in the process. Artest grabbed a fan he thought to be his original assailant, causing others in the crowd to throw more concessions at him. Pacers' teammate Stephen Jackson also entered the stands in response and punched another fan who had poured a drink. Multiple players and personnel rushed into the crowd in response, and some fans began running onto the court. Meanwhile, as Artest began leaving the stands, several fans rushed him, and he punched one of them in a combination of anger and self-defense. Another fell onto the court and upon standing was punched particularly violently by Pacers' center Jermaine O'Neal in a blow reminiscent of Washington's years prior. Chaos ensued, and security found it difficult to quell the disorder around them. Pacers assistant Chuck Person, who would later become an assistant coach at Auburn and would be indicted in the 2017 Adidas bribery scandal, compared the tumult on the court to being "trapped in a gladiator-type scene where the fans were the lions and we were just trying to escape with our lives. That's how it felt. That there was no exit. That you had to fight your way out."

The event became known as the "Malice at the Palace," and punishments for the players were swift and harsh. Artest was suspended for the rest of the season, seventy-three regular season games and another thirteen in the playoffs. Jackson was suspended for thirty, O'Neal for twenty-five, though his suspension was reduced to fifteen games upon appeal. Two other Pacers and four Pistons players also received suspensions. In addition, five Pacers players and five Pistons fans were charged with assault, each given various fines and probationary periods.

The incident stood as a metaphorical scarlet letter for a league whose reputation had diminished substantially under the weight of a decidedly racialized narrative in the early 2000s. To try to counter the White backlash, David Stern attempted what many saw as a racialized solution, instituting a player dress code in 2005. In a reification of Walter Kennedy's sanitation efforts of 1963, players were required to dress in business attire to and from arenas or at any event representing the NBA. Do-rags, gaudy jewelry, and Timberland boots were banned, as were T-shirts and blue jeans. The policy seemed directed at representations of hip-hop culture, and Black hip-hop culture in particular. It was the modern personification of the concern expressed in *Sport* magazine's infamous 1966 article about the league's "hidden fear," though in the early twenty-first century that fear was not so hidden.

There were also lingering over the sport echoes of basketball's other most pressing historical vice: gambling. Tim Donaghey was the son of a referee who began his officiating career in the NBA in 1994. In the early twenty-first century, he was part of the Jailblazers devolution, the recipient of a postgame tirade by Rasheed Wallace after calling a technical foul on the Portland star for throwing a ball in anger at a fellow referee. The upheaval earned Wallace a seven-game suspension. Donaghey was also one of the officials for the Malice at the Palace. In the years following those incidents, however, Donaghey began gambling heavily on basketball games and was approached by bookmakers to shave points to affect betting lines. As in so many earlier point-shaving scandals, the referee's crimes were discovered by the FBI during a tangential investigation of organized crime. They were reported publicly in July 2007, prompting immediate concern from an NBA clearly aware of the game's historical association with the problem. "We would like to assure our fans that no amount of effort, time or personnel is being spared to assist in this investigation," said Stern, "to bring to justice an individual who has betrayed the most sacred trust in professional sports, and to take the necessary steps to protect against this ever happening again."

Donaghey pleaded guilty to wire fraud and interstate commerce violations, admitting that he had passed information on player injuries and referee relations to gamblers, allowing them to predict game winners more easily. While the indictment only referenced a small number of fixed games, a kind of moral panic developed among teams and fans about other games in which he participated, cratering the trust that many had in the legitimacy of NBA outcomes. Only compounding the problems, Donaghey filed court documents the following year alleging that he was not the only one affecting game results. He claimed, for example, that the association had a financial interest in seeing O'Neal and Bryant's Lakers win their third consecutive title. In the 2002 Western Conference

Finals, the Lakers faced elimination in the sixth game of the series, but officials awarded them eighteen more free throws than their opposition, the Sacramento Kings, and the Lakers won the game. "It was in the NBA's interest to add another game to the series," Donaghey's filing claimed, so the association used officials to control outcomes to benefit its financial bottom line. And it wasn't the only time. "Top executives of the NBA sought to manipulate games using referees," the brief alleged. Stern adamantly denied the claims, and federal officials never found evidence to corroborate them, but they played on long-held assumptions by disgruntled fans that referees had robbed their teams of victories and on the institutional history of corruption in the game, dating to the 1951 collegiate gambling scandal. Donaghey's sentencing to fifteen months in federal prison did little to quell such fears.

Recovery from the association's problems with race and corruption would draw from the same well from which it always did, team dynasties and individual stars. The team who won the 2007 championship just prior to the tumult of the Donaghey scandal was the San Antonio Spurs, one of the American Basketball Association arrivals from 1976. The team had achieved a measure of success in the late 1970s and early 1980s but hadn't reached the pinnacle of the NBA until the lockout season of 1999, led by coach Gregg Popovich and star forward Tim Duncan. The Spurs' title in 2007 was the team's fourth in eight seasons, a different kind of dynasty in the era of free agency, wherein dominance over an extended period did not necessarily translate into consecutive titles. The Spurs' pseudo-dynasty, however impressive, corresponded with a steady diminishing of television ratings. Duncan was known colloquially as "The Big Fundamental," and the Spurs' team game was interpreted by many as a more boring form of basketball compared to the flashy and ferocious play of stars like Bryant and O'Neal. The real reason for the ratings decline, however, was the controversy created by the race, violence, and gambling scandals that ravaged the association in the first decade of the twenty-first century.

History demonstrated that the game's recovery from such controversies depended upon the play of star athletes and legacy teams that drew increased attendance and larger ratings. In the last three seasons of the decade, the NBA witnessed the ascendancy of both legacy teams and star players that helped revive the popularity of the association. In 2008, the

Celtics won Boston's first championship since 1986. In 2009 and 2010, Kobe Bryant, this time without Shaquille O'Neal, led the Lakers to two additional titles. The principal story of 2010, however, occurred after the confetti and parades, far away from the glamour of Los Angeles in northeastern Ohio.

LeBron James was born on December 30, 1984, in Akron, Ohio, to a sixteen-year-old mother who struggled tirelessly to make ends meet. When James was nine years old, he moved into the home of a local youth football coach who fostered his interest in basketball. At an early age, James starred on an Amateur Athletic Union team and chose to attend St. Vincent-St. Mary High School, a private, predominantly White parochial academy. It was, in one sense, a recapitulation of Magic Johnson's move to a White high school in the 1970s, but unlike Johnson, James had a choice. Also like Johnson, James became the most celebrated high school player in the country. He was named Ohio's Mr. Basketball, the state's highest scholastic honor, and the National Player of the Year, in both his junior and senior years. James was a phenomenon unlike any other in the history of high school basketball. In his junior season, *Sports Illustrated* featured him on the magazine's cover, calling him "The Chosen One."

With the history of corruption in amateur basketball and the chronic exploitation of young players for financial gain, James's status led to inevitable controversies in his scholastic career. After his junior year, he petitioned the NBA to change its eligibility rules to allow him to enter the draft early, an unsuccessful effort that forced him to return to St. Vincent-St. Mary for his senior season. There he ran afoul of amateur rules when his mother bought him a Hummer for his eighteenth birthday, borrowing the money against her son's potential earning power. He also received clothing in return for posing for pictures at an Akron apparel store. The Ohio High School Athletic Association responded by stripping him of his eligibility, though an appeal ended in a brief two-game suspension. With his eligibility reinstated, James led his team to a third state championship in four seasons, averaging more than 31 points, 9 rebounds, 4 assists, and 3 steals per game in his senior year and ensuring that the high school star would become the first choice in the 2003 NBA Draft.

In another draft lottery that led many to suspect some form of conspiracy, the winner of the first selection that year was Cleveland, a franchise that played its games thirty-nine short miles from the St. Vincent-St. Mary gymnasium. Thus it was that LeBron James became a Cleveland Cavalier; a young man who had endured more notoriety and pressure than most at his young age was now saddled with the additional pressure of playing for a moribund franchise that had never won a championship in a city whose other professional teams, the NFL's Cleveland Browns and Major League Baseball's Cleveland Indians, had not won championships since 1964 and 1948, respectively. James, however, showed little effects of the pressure placed on his teenaged shoulders. In his rookie season, he averaged 21 points, 6 assists, and 5.5 rebounds, winning the association's Rookie of the Year award and improving the Cavaliers' record by eighteen games over that of its previous season. The team missed the playoffs, but James was a phenomenon and the future of the franchise appeared bright for the first time since the 1990s, providing hope for a disillusioned coterie of Cleveland sports fans who hadn't witnessed a championship season since running back Jim Brown led the city's football team in the months following the Civil Rights Act of 1964.

In the ensuing seasons, James's star would continue to rise. In his sophomore campaign, he set the Cavaliers' single-game scoring record with 56 points against Toronto. The season after that, James led his team to the playoffs for the first time in the new century, scoring a triple-double in his postseason debut and finishing second in the association's voting for Most Valuable Player. During the 2006–2007 season, James's fourth, he carried Cleveland to the NBA Finals. In the fifth game of the penultimate series of the playoffs, James scored 29 of his team's final 30 points, including the game-winning layup, in a performance that commentator Marv Albert called "one of the greatest moments in postseason history." The Cavaliers lost in the Finals to Tim Duncan's Spurs, but James's improvement continued the following season. In only his fifth year in the association, he became Cleveland's all-time leading scorer and followed that accomplishment in the 2008–2009 and 2009–2010 seasons by winning consecutive Most Valuable Player awards.

Still, there were concerns. The Cavaliers were unable to reach the NBA Finals in those seasons and James expressed visible frustration about the team's lack of playoff success. In 2010, he was a free agent and despite being marketed as the savior of Cleveland, there was concern among the fan base that he might choose to leave the team for a franchise better able to surround him with complementary stars. Worry only mounted when James signed a deal with ESPN to broadcast his choice of teams in a televised program titled "The Decision." James would sell commercial advertisements for the show, and the proceeds would be distributed to charity. It was there, in front of a live television audience, that James announced, "I'm going to take my talents to South Beach," indicating that he would join fellow free agents Chris Bosh and Dwayne Wade to play for the Miami Heat.

Reaction to "The Decision" in Cleveland was swift and devastating, with fans burning James jerseys in the streets. Dan Gilbert, owner of the Cavaliers, called James selfish and his decision a "cowardly betrayal" of the team and city. Gilbert was White, as were the bulk of jersey-burners, and like so many controversies surrounding the NBA, the wrath of those upset with James's decision was racially coded. Civil rights activist and former presidential candidate Jesse Jackson described Gilbert's attack as personifying "a slave master mentality," the owner treating a player who had fulfilled a signed contract as "a runaway slave." When asked later if he thought race played a role in the backlash from "The Decision," James said that he believed it did. "There's always, you know, a race factor." Still, other Black commentators downplayed any racial role in the backlash, claiming instead that "The Decision" itself was a poor tactical decision.

Despite concerns about the presentation of "The Decision," however, James was correct in his analysis. There had always been "a race factor" in basketball, and particularly in the professional game. A White team owner belittling a Black player for "cowardly betrayal" carried the racial baggage of the NBA's history, regardless of whether the statement was racially motivated or not.

When the smoke cleared, however, James was part of the Miami Heat, surrounded with other stars and complementary players that Cleveland was never able to provide. In his four seasons with Miami, James made the NBA Finals four times, winning two championships and two additional awards as the association's Most Valuable Player. Criticism followed him to South Beach, however, as many complained that a team featuring stars like James, Bosh, and Wade should have won more. It was clear that no matter where James played and no matter how much success he had, criticism would continue. Thus it was that after his fourth season with Miami, he left the team and returned to Cleveland, understanding that winning a championship for the beleaguered city would be an important piece of his legacy.

By that time, Cleveland had far better complementary players than it had fielded during James's initial run with the team. Duke University's Kyrie Irving was a legitimate star in his own right, drafted two years prior with another of the Cavaliers' first draft choices. At the same time, leadership traded players to Minnesota in exchange for All-Star center Kevin Love. With a new structure in place, James led the team back to the 2015 NBA Finals in his first return season, where Cleveland lost to the Golden State Warriors. In his second season back with the Cavaliers, the franchise again faced the Warriors in the Finals. Golden State had won seventy-three games in the regular season, breaking the record of Jordan's Chicago Bulls for most victories in a single season, but James led the Cavaliers to an upset victory with a triple-double in the seventh and final game of the series. He led all Finals players in points, assists, rebounds, steals, and blocks, the only time in history a player had ever dominated a playoff series in such a manner. And he did it in Cleveland, which finally had a championship after more than half a century.

After two more seasons in his hometown, where the Cavaliers returned to the Finals in consecutive campaigns, only to lose in the Finals, James again departed the city for warmer climes, this time taking his talents to Hollywood and the Los Angeles Lakers. There was less consternation about his second move, partly because it didn't come with a televised spectacle, partly because he had won Cleveland its coveted championship, and partly because it was difficult to stay angry at LeBron James. If "The Decision" had brought with it a recapitulation of internal league worries, those worries would be matched by a recapitulation of Bill Russell–style activism. James entered the NBA two years prior to Stern's dress code and inaugurated a new willingness of superstars to participate in protest, combining the league dominance, corporate presence, and unthreatening persona of Michael Jordan with the radicalism of Russell and Baylor. James understood that his talent and popularity were larger than whatever backlash might accrue to him for using his platform for racial justice advocacy. James spoke passionately about the Sudanese War in Darfur. He participated in the national hoodie campaign after the murder of Trayvon Martin and championed the protests in Ferguson, Missouri, after the police killing of Michael Brown. After New York police killed Eric Garner with an illegal chokehold, he wore a shirt with the phrase "I Can't Breathe" in warm-ups before a game. He spoke publicly against racist rallies like that in Charlottesville, Virginia, and in support of the national anthem protests of quarterback Colin Kaepernick. His philanthropy supported a variety of causes, many centering around educating underprivileged youth. In another mimic of the experiences of his forebears, White racists and conservatives used his activism as a cudgel against the player and the game, the most famous incident coming from right wing television host Laura Ingraham telling James in 2018 to "shut up and dribble."

He also, like Russell and Elgin Baylor before him, was willing to take on the league that gave him his platform. In 2014, for example, he publicly called for the removal of Los Angeles Clippers owner Donald Sterling. "There is no room for Donald Sterling in our league," he told reporters, urging the commissioner to take action against him. The Sterling controversy was a lived renewal of pro basketball's hidden fear of race, played out far from the boardroom of the association's governor's meetings. In April, TMZ released an audio recording of Sterling berating his mistress after seeing a photo of her with Magic Johnson. "It bothers me a lot that you want to broadcast that you're associating with black people," he told her. "You can sleep with them. You can bring them in, you can do whatever you want," he said, but he wanted her "not to bring them to my games." After his private racism became public, players across the association expressed their anger and frustration, and Clippers players discussed boycotting their playoff game scheduled for two days after the tape's release. While the team chose to play, the players entered the court with their warm-up shirts turned inside out to hide the Clippers logo in protest. The Los Angeles NAACP cancelled a ceremony in which it had planned to give Sterling an award. President Barack Obama, a fan of the game, also denounced his "incredibly offensive racist statements."

Adding to the controversy, the association was in a period of transition. Two months prior, in February 2014, longtime commissioner David Stern retired, replaced by his deputy Adam Silver. The new commissioner, a former attorney who had served in a variety of NBA roles since 1992, showed none of the racial equivocation of his predecessor. Four days after the tape was released, Silver banned Sterling from the NBA for life, stripped him of his authority over the Clippers, and banned him from team facilities and games. He fined Sterling $2.5 million and promised to pressure him to sell the team. It was an unprecedented response to racism in the game and demonstrated a decided change in leadership that would commit itself to racial equity. One month later, former Microsoft CEO Steve Balmer purchased the Clippers for a record $2 billion.

It was a controversial conclusion to the ordeal, as many worried over Sterling being rewarded for his racism with a $2 billion windfall, and the worry was only exacerbated by further racial controversy in its wake. The Atlanta Hawks, for example, had a long history of their own racial issues. Later in 2014, the team's general manager, Danny Ferry, was forced to resign after making racial remarks about a player the Hawks were considering acquiring. In 2015, the team's then-owner Bruce Levenson sent a racist email to employees complaining that the team's fan base was "overwhelmingly black" and that Black fans were "scaring away whites." Levenson eventually sold the team in response to the resulting scandal, and the Hawks ultimately hired a chief diversity and inclusion officer to regulate their racial policies and racial publicity, but the racist legacy of the incident lingered. In July 2017, the Hawks faced a racial discrimination lawsuit by a former manager of security operations who claimed that White celebrities were given preferential treatment by the team, while Black celebrities were not, and that he was fired for complaining about the discrepancy.

For all of the racial controversy that remained, other association intersections were witnessing marked improvement. In 2014, former Colorado State University and WNBA star Becky Hammon was hired as an assistant coach for the San Antonio Spurs, and the skill she demonstrated over the course of that first season proved that the effort was decidedly more than a paean to inclusivity. In 2015, she coached the Spurs' summer league team to a championship. The following season, she was an assistant coach in the All-Star Game, and the season after that she interviewed for the general manager position with the Minnesota Timberwolves. Most importantly, her success started a trend; by 2020, thirteen women were coaching men's basketball in the NBA.

Even before Hammon's success in the sport's major league, coach Nancy Lieberman had served as a head coach in the NBA's developmental organization. Both the association's minor league and its summer league were products of David Stern, who sought to create an infrastructure to develop talent for future play in the NBA and to make franchises better and more complete. In the process, he unwittingly provided a staging ground for another kind of completion in the process.

Others, however, were attempting to use a decidedly different process to make teams worse. Sam Hinkie, general manager of the Philadelphia 76ers, made the case that under the structure of the association's salary cap and wage scale, the only way to build a team's success was either to entice All-Star free agents to a given franchise or to lose so consistently that building through high draft choices would be possible. Without a principal draw to bring free agents to Philadelphia, Hinkie decided that his best option was the latter, selling off talented players and making little secret of the team's desire to lose. "The Process," as Hinkie's plan came to be known, was a controversial strategy, cutting against the association's longtime effort to prevent tanking by openly embracing it, calling into question the legitimacy of the records of divisional opponents who played multiple games against Philadelphia, and leaving many fans of the team unwilling to buy tickets to contests played by a group of players intentionally formed to lose. At least at first. "The Process" did bring the 76ers star players and improved the team's chances, demonstrating the pitfalls in the NBA's collective bargaining structure and reminding many fans outside large markets that championships for their teams were unlikely in an association built on star players and dynasties.

The last of those dynasties in the second decade of the twenty-first century was the Golden State Warriors, a team that had originally started its life in Philadelphia. The Warriors were led by Davidson College's Stephen Curry, whose shooting ability from beyond the 3-point line enraptured fans, provided him two awards for the association's Most Valuable Player, and led the team to five consecutive Finals appearances and three championships. As had other dynasties in prior generations, the Warriors' success grew a new popularity in the game, driving higher ratings for a sport on a seeming upward trajectory. In 2019, Golden State lost its bid for another title to the Toronto Raptors, bringing a championship to the home of the NBA's first game on November 1, 1946. The association had come full circle and appeared poised for further growth in the coming years.

But then came 2020.

Epilogue

K OBE B RYANT had devoted himself to a variety of philan-
thropic causes in the years since his rape trial and had only increased
his involvement since his retirement from basketball in April 2016. He
helped create programs for American after-school programs across the
country. His Kobe Bryant China Fund raised money for health and education programs in East Asia. Together with his wife, he founded the
Kobe and Vanessa Bryant Family Foundation to battle homelessness,
particularly in Southern California. He also worked with the Make-
A-Wish Foundation and was a founding donor to the Smithsonian's
National Museum of African American History and Culture. Among
his many other ventures, he also founded the Mamba Sports Academy in
Thousand Oaks, California, to help train and promote the next generation of sports stars.

On the morning of January 26, 2020, Bryant left an airport in Orange
County with his daughter Gianna and six friends, en route to the academy for a Sunday basketball game. The rain and fog made for difficult
travel, leading the pilot to circle over the Los Angeles Zoo before heading
south, attempting to rise above the fog before crashing into a mountain
in Calabasas, thirty miles from the arena where Kobe had starred for so
many years. Everyone on the helicopter died.

Bryant's death sparked a wave of grief and tributes to the fallen star
while at the same time prompting many to come to a difficult reckoning
with his legacy, one that included stellar play and championships, but
also the assault settlement from the events in Colorado. Every team in
the NBA presented a tribute to Bryant prior to a home game. The night
of the crash, the Grammy Awards, held in the Staples Center, home of
the Lakers, continued as scheduled but featured myriad tributes from a
variety of entertainers. Commissioner Adam Silver announced in February that the association's All-Star Game Most Valuable Player award

would be named for its fallen star. Still, several commentators struggled to remind those celebrating of the trauma experienced by many victims of sexual assault at seeing the valorization of the goodness and decency of someone credibly accused of rape, who had, in fact, settled a civil suit in the case. It was a necessary reckoning, but one that was largely drowned out by celebratory memorials uninterested in critical reexaminations of Bryant's complicated legacy.

Bryant was buried on February 7. Just over a month later, on March 11, the Utah Jazz were scheduled to play a game against the Oklahoma City Thunder. The players had taken the court for warm-ups; fans were filling the stands. And then a message on the arena's video board announced that the game had been cancelled. The players left the floor, the fans filed out of the arena. One of the Jazz players, Rudy Gobert, had tested positive for COVID-19, a virus that had recently arrived in the United States and had begun wreaking havoc on the country. The night prior, Gobert attempted to joke about the national paranoia concerning the virus, making a point to touch all the microphones at the Jazz press conference and the belongings of his teammates in the locker room. Though he didn't know that he had COVID at the time, his behavior appeared inordinately careless in hindsight and led to the infection of one of his teammates, Donovan Mitchell. Later that night, the NBA announced the cancellation of the rest of the season. Frustrated owners asked for a reconsideration after thirty days in the hopes that things would get better and play could be resumed.

Things did not get better. The next day, March 12, the NCAA announced the cancellation of the rest of the men's and women's basketball seasons, including the culminating tournaments that generated so much revenue for the association and its member universities. April passed, as did May, but in June, Silver and the NBA created a protocol that would allow professional games to resume. Players from the top twenty-two teams at the time of the season's suspension were tested at the facilities of their home team, cleared of the virus, then taken to an isolation zone, known as "The Bubble," at Orlando's Walt Disney World, where players would be quarantined, playing games in specially fitted gymnasiums that would allow fans to appear digitally on boards behind the scorer's table. The teams would play a series of seeding games for the first two weeks of August, with those qualifying for the playoffs continuing after that, culminating in a championship series running from late September to October. It was a plan that allowed the association to conduct play without fear of viral infection.

Between the season's original cancellation and the association's bubble plan, however, the country had another virus with which to reckon. On May 25, George Floyd was being arrested in Minneapolis, the original home of George Mikan's Lakers and the current home of the Minnesota Timberwolves. Floyd had been accused by a local store clerk of passing a counterfeit $20 bill, and police officers originally tasked with taking him into custody began physically abusing him. Officer Derek Chauvin wrestled Floyd to the ground, where he put his knee on the suspect's neck for eight minutes and forty-six seconds. Protests from bystanders begged Chauvin to stop, but Floyd died as a result.

Protests erupted around the country and throughout the world as activists spilled into the streets and police in tactical gear responded. Months earlier, in March, Louisville police killed Breonna Taylor while executing a no-knock warrant, and while the case originally received little national attention, the uprisings beginning in May called new attention to her case, as well. Ahmaud Arbery was killed before Taylor in February by three White vigilantes in Brunswick, Georgia. That murder, too, received little media attention until a video of the assault was released in May. Protests around the nation in response to police assaults on Black lives and the rights and freedoms of peaceful protestors threw the country into chaos, dividing along racial lines.

It was an uprising to which NBA players were particularly sensitive. The association that had once worried about the role of its blackening found itself with record television ratings and a player composition that was 75 percent Black. After the video of Ahmaud Arbery's killing appeared, LeBron James took to Instagram. "We're literally hunted EVERYDAY/EVERYTIME we step foot outside the comfort of our homes!" he wrote. "Can't even go for a damn jog man! Like WTF man are you kidding me?!?!?!?!?! No man fr ARE YOU KIDDING ME!!!!! I'm sorry Ahmaud (Rest In Paradise) and my prayers and blessings sent to the heavens above to your family!!" When George Floyd was killed, James asked his followers, "Do you understand NOW!!??!!?? Or is it still blurred to you??" James had proven in a variety of instances over his playing career that he was unafraid to use his status and position to argue for a change in the country's racial politics, and the summer uprisings provided another opportunity for him to use his platform. He would not, despite further criticism from conservative critics, shut up and dribble.

But he would, under the right circumstances, dribble. The bubble concept was outside the bounds of the traditional season and therefore had to be negotiated with the Players Association, the organization that had long stood for players' rights. James spearheaded the negotiating effort to ensure that the players would be allowed to express their political concerns about racial justice and that the league would not only support those concerns but magnify them. Adam Silver had demonstrated none of the racial equivocation of his predecessor and readily agreed to the players' terms. Each was allowed to include a social justice phrase on the back of their jersey. Kneeling protests were staged for the national anthem. The court itself was emblazoned with the phrase "Black Lives Matter." In addition, both the NBA and its sponsors crafted commercial advertisements that highlighted racial justice causes.

Then, as if a continuation of a terrible nightmare, an unarmed Black man named Jacob Blake was shot in the back seven times by police officers in Kenosha, Wisconsin, while his children watched from his car. The incident validated the necessity of much of the summer's protests and led the Milwaukee Bucks, who played their home games forty miles north of Kenosha, to boycott a first-round playoff game against the Orlando Magic on August 26, three days after the shooting. Soon, the rest of the teams scheduled to play decided to postpone their games, as well, prompting Major League Baseball, the National Hockey League, and Major League Soccer to also postpone games in protest. It was a demonstration of the power and popularity that professional basketball had accrued since the doldrums of tape-delayed finals, but it was also a demonstration of the deep scars left by the cyclical racial reckoning faced by the league and the nation in which it operated.

Another league with similar scars was the WNBA. As early as 2016, players in the women's professional association had been at the forefront of protesting racial injustice. In response to the police killings of Minnesota's Philando Castile and Louisiana's Alton Sterling, players on the Minnesota Lynx wore warm-up shirts saying, "Change Starts With Us: Justice & Accountability." The New York Liberty and Phoenix Mercury wore #BlackLivesMatter shirts. All the players were fined in violation of the association's collective bargaining agreement but refused to stop. The Liberty's Tina Charles won the WNBA's award for player of the month in July 2016 and turned her officially approved warm-up shirt inside out to accept the prize in protest. Indiana Fever players took a collective knee during the national anthem at a 2016 playoff game. Prior to the 2020 season, the players established a WNBA Social Justice Council, devoted to increasing awareness about women's voting, police violence against Black women and girls, and Black- and female-owned businesses.

So when the protests against police brutality in 2020 began, the players of the WNBA were poised to continue their activism. Like the men, they initiated concessions from association officials to include similar iconography on their uniforms and on the court, with similar league and commercial advertising. After Jacob Blake's murder in Kenosha, they, too, cancelled games. "When most of us go home, we still are Black and our families matter. We got this little guy with us that we see every day. His life matters," said Washington Mystics guard Ariel Atkins, referring to the son of her teammate Tiana Hawkins. The effort of Atkins and the players of the NBA and WNBA were, in their way, a recapitulation of the muscular Christianity that prompted the game's creation in the first place, a public use of basketball for moral ends. Though so many of its developments over the previous 130 years would likely have disappointed James Naismith, basketball's role as a conduit of moral concern would surely have pleased a nineteenth-century theology student concerned with the ethics of physical activity.

The players' strike in both the men's and women's leagues was the first organized, racially motivated work stoppage since the effort of Harry Edwards to convince Black athletes to boycott the 1968 Olympics, keeping athletes like UCLA's Lew Alcindor from the games. The notoriety of the protest and continued trauma of police shootings on a predominantly Black workforce led many in both leagues to suggest cancelling the rest of the makeshift bubble seasons. Ultimately, however, the players decided to play, realizing that their ability to present their message to a large audience hinged on them staying in the public spotlight provided by the bubble.

Of course, as LeBron James had learned when speaking out on a variety of social justice issues over the preceding years, White conservative critics would necessarily find fault with Black protest. Donald Trump's son-in-law and special advisor Jared Kushner criticized the players for the strike, arguing that a group of wealthy, entitled athletes were only making things worse and referred to their protest as "tak[ing] a night off from work." Kelly Loeffler, Republican senator from Georgia, targeted the WNBA players in particular as part of her reelection campaign, even encouraging her supporters to boycott the league despite her own financial interest in the Atlanta Dream. WNBA players, unbowed by such criticism, responded by actively campaigning for her opponent, Rafael Warnock, participating in public videoconferences with the candidate and wearing "Vote Warnock" shirts. White conservative pundit Charlie Kirk tweeted his own racist criticism. "Hilarious to see Black NBA players who make millions a year take a knee to try and tell us black people can't succeed in America," he wrote. "Kick them out of the league. Done watching the NBA." Republican Missouri senator Josh Hawley wrote a public letter to the association, engaging in a disingenuous critique of the NBA's economic ties to China, home of a substantial basketball fan base, and arguing that such ties delegitimized player messages about social justice. In a completely tone-deaf request, he asked that jersey slogans include "Back the Blue," a common racist trope for supporting police violence.

It was a predictable response from those who derived the core of their popularity from the bigotry that they propagated, and it was a refrain that White conservative critics had leveled at the predominantly Black organization for generations, since early Black college players at predominantly White universities heard jeers from the stands, since Elgin Baylor refused to play his exhibition game in West Virginia, and since Laura Ingraham told James to "shut up and dribble." While White tone policing of Black voices was nothing new, however, neither was the activism that prompted it. Basketball's blackness and its negotiation with that blackness has defined the game since the early twentieth century. No other sport has carried the racial coding that basketball carried since the first introduction of Black teams in 1904, and that coding provided both opportunities for protest and hindrances to it, as White powerbrokers and Black players engaged in a call-and-response dialogue about the role of protest in sports. It was a dialogue that fundamentally shaped the posture of the NBA and allowed its players to serve as powerful voices for civil rights outside of the boundary lines that separated the athletes from the nation that watched them play. Basketball may have been "originally invented as a white man's game," but it became, through racial activism, a Black man's theater, a woman's theater, and a Black woman's theater, one for both play and protest.

And the game only benefited as a result. It continues to do so today.

Bibliographic Essay

THE HISTORIOGRAPHICAL TOPOGRAPHY of basketball is dotted with myriad autobiographies and ghostwritten tell-alls from the game's great players and coaches. If there is an important name in collegiate or professional basketball, there is likely an autobiography available to provide a first-person accounting of his or her career. This essay will, for the most part, veer from those publications, not because they don't provide important primary source material for any study of the game, but instead because a search of any prominent player or coach will reveal an available autobiography. That work, while valuable, does not, for the most part, provide the kind of historical analysis that sports historians expect from comprehensive argumentative accounts. Not including them here is a way of distinguishing between them and more analytical historical monographs. In all sports history, but particularly in the history of basketball, there are three distinct tiers of extant accounts. Those autobiographical works, sometimes referred to as vanity publications, make up a large percentage of basketball books because the game has been given less attention by American sports historians than have baseball and football. The work by historians, however, has been important, incomplete though it may be. Accompanying the effort of historians, and comprising the third tier of basketball scholarship, is a series of books by sports journalists who cover the game. This essay will emphasize the historical and journalistic tiers of basketball studies. It is, therefore, by no means a comprehensive historiography of American basketball, but instead seeks to provide readers with a road map to find that historiography in a variety of areas related to the given subject.

While the book you have just read is the first comprehensive account of the game that takes both college and professional, men's and women's, Black and White basketball into consideration, there are a variety of books that examine basketball through a relatively wide lens and provide a measure of comprehensivity in the process. It was, for example, in 1975, that Boston sportswriter Bob Ryan authored *The Pro Game: The World of Professional Basketball* (New York: McGraw-Hill, 1975). While it only focused on professionals, Ryan's work served as one of the first efforts to view basketball as a broad-based phenomenon.

More than two decades later, Peter C. Bjarkman published *The Biographical History of Basketball* (New York: McGraw-Hill, 1999), which, as the title suggests, uses the game's personalities to chronicle its history. Bjarkman's emphasis on individuals allows him to give a general narrative of the game's progression but keeps him from a more critical analysis. Ten years after Bjarkman, ESPN released *The ESPN College Basketball Encyclopedia: The Complete History of the Men's Game* (New York: Ballantine Books, 2009). Its limitations come from its sole focus on men's collegiate basketball and its encyclopedic structure that disallows broader analytical framing, but with those exceptions, the book is one of the most complete basketball offerings ever produced. In 2010, the website Free Darko.com produced *FreeDarko Presents: The Undisputed Guide to Pro Basketball History* (New York: Bloomsbury, 2010). Fitting the emphasis of the blog site, the book rates professional basketball's fights and players' mustaches, but it also gives a solid accounting of the men's pro game.

FreeDarko's cheeky publication was dwarfed that year by another blogger's monograph, *The Book of Basketball: The NBA According to the Sports Guy* (New York: Ballantine Books, 2010) by Bill Simmons. The commentator organizes his work through biography and statistical analysis, but in the process manages to provide a witty and helpful analysis of the NBA's progression. The following year, John Grasso's *Historical Dictionary of Basketball* (Lanham, MD: Scarecrow Press, 2011) and Frank P. Jozsa Jr.'s *The National Basketball Association: Business, Organization and Strategy* (Hackensack, NJ: World Scientific Publishing Co., 2011) provided more academic accounts of the game. Sports journalist Dave Zarum accomplished a similar feat nine years later with his *NBA 75: The Definitive History* (Richmond Hill, ON: Firefly Books, 2020), a comprehensive accounting of the professional association on the occasion of its seventy-fifth anniversary. Again, the sweep of such studies is limited by their sole focus on men's professional basketball. A different kind of limitation comes in Robert D. Bradley's *The Basketball Draft Fact Book: A History of Professional Basketball's College Drafts* (Lanham, MD:

Scarecrow Press, 2013), which is a comprehensive retelling and statistical collection of every collegiate draft.

One of the most interesting attempts at comprehensivity within a limited paradigm is *Basketball: A Love Story* (New York: Crown Archetype, 2018), by Jackie MacMullan, Rafe Bartholomew, and Dan Klores, based on ESPN's documentary series of the same name. The book allows basketball's influential players and coaches to tell the story of the game in their own words, using a style imitative of the oral histories of Studs Terkel to make its case. Two years later, Fred Van Lente and Joe Cooper published *The Comic Book Story of Basketball: A Fast-Break History of Hoops* (Berkeley, CA: Ten Speed Press, 2020), another unique account that attempts a comprehensive story of the game in an entertaining comic book form.

Other basketball books manage to capture the broad swath of the game's history through studies that focus not on college or professional organization, or on unique storytelling design, but on tackling the game through tangential lenses. *Basketball and Philosophy: Thinking Outside the Paint* (Lexington: University Press of Kentucky, 2007), edited by Jerry L. Walls and Gregory Bassham, uses basketball to prompt philosophical debates. Yago Colás's *Ball Don't Lie: Myth, Genealogy, and Invention in the Cultures of Basketball* (Philadelphia: Temple University Press, 2016) traces power relations in the game and their perpetuation through uses of language and discourse, showing a flexible, culturally relevant event that both reflects the culture that watches and provides a theater for that culture's dominant controversies.

Shawn Fury's *Rise and Fire: The Origins, Science, and Evolution of the Jump Shot—And How It Transformed Basketball Forever* (New York: Flatiron Books, 2017), and Yago Colás's *Numbers Don't Lie: New Adventures in Counting and What Counts in Basketball Analytics* (Lincoln: University of Nebraska Press, 2020), his follow-up to *Ball Don't Lie*, use science to contextualize the history of the game. The former builds on the pioneering work of John Christgau's *The Origins of the Jump Shot: Eight Men Who Shook the World of Basketball* (Lincoln, NE: Bison Books, 1999), and the latter builds on Ben Taylor's *Thinking Basketball* (New York: CreateSpace, 2016), both demonstrating that studies with a more narrow focus can be expanded into a more comprehensive frame.

Finally, Nick Greene's *How to Watch Basketball Like a Genius* (New York: Harry N. Abrams, 2021) takes the most unique approach to giving an overview of the game, recruiting wine critics, cartographers, magicians, psychologists, and game theorists to deconstruct basketball through a variety of disparate perspectives. All these comprehensive or pseudocomprehensive efforts provide a relatively distant view of the game, as does the volume you have just completed, but all of them are supplemented by the historical work of those narrowing their focus to certain events, figures, or points of cultural difference. The rest of this essay will organize those works within the context of the chapters of this book. The sources included for each chapter do not compose a full accounting of every avenue of American basketball history but are instead groupings of accessible, comprehensive, and historiographically significant accounts to guide readers to further exploration of individual subjects necessarily given cursory coverage in a book such as this with a broad temporal sweep.

CHAPTER 1

The best account of muscular Christianity as the principal driver of the ideology that created conditions for basketball's invention is Clifford Putney, *Muscular Christianity: Manhood and Sports in Protestant America, 1880–1920* (Cambridge, MA: Harvard University Press, 2001). Putney built on that original pioneering work a decade later with his "Luther Gulick: His Contributions to Springfield College, the YMCA, and 'Muscular Christianity,'" *Historical Journal of Massachusetts* 39 (Summer 2011): 144–69. David P. Setran's "Following the Broad-Shouldered Jesus: The College YMCA and the Culture of Muscular Christianity in American Campus Life, 1890–1914," *American Educational History Journal* 32 (Spring 2005): 59–67, spreads his analysis beyond the bounds of Springfield College to the rest of the United States. Paul W. Bennett examines the conditions muscular Christianity created in Naismith's Canada in "Training 'Blue-Blooded' Canadian Boys: Athleticism, Muscular Christianity, and Sports in Ontario's 'Little Big Four' Schools, 1829–1930," *Journal of Sport History* 43 (Fall 2016): 253–71. Linda J. Borish expands the analysis to include women in "The Robust Woman and the Muscular Christian: Catharine Beecher, Thomas Higginson, and Their Vision of American Society, Health and Physical Activities," *International Journal of the History of Sport* 4 (September 1987): 139–54.

The YMCA itself is a central figure in basketball's creation. An early study of the group that still remains an important foundation of the historiography is C. Howard Hopkins, *A History of the YMCA in North America* (New York: Association Press, 1951). Jeffrey C. Copeland and Yan Xu edit *The YMCA at War: Collaboration and Conflict during the World Wars* (Lanham, MD: Lexington Books, 2018). Much of the literature on the YMCA focuses on the group's activities around the world. For an exemplary study that provides a comparative analysis that better contextualizes the group's efforts in North America, see Harald Fischer-Tiné, "Fitness for Modernity? The YMCA and Physical-Education Schemes in Late-Colonial South Asia (circa 1900–40)," *Modern Asian Studies* 53 (March 2019): 512–59.

Of course, the centerpiece of the chapter is the founding of basketball itself. Yago Colás's "Our Myth of Creation: The Politics of Narrating Basketball's Origin," *Journal of Sport History* 43 (Spring 2016): 37–54, describes the inherent problem of origin stories in the mythmaking about sports foundings. For studies of Naismith himself, the original book-length account was Bernice Larson Webb's *The Basketball Man: James Naismith* (Lawrence: University Press of Kansas, 1973), followed in the twenty-first century by Rob Rains and Helen Carpenter's *James Naismith: The Man Who Invented Basketball* (Philadelphia: Temple University Press, 2009). And despite this essay's early caveat that it would not include autobiographies, Naismith's is an exception for its importance in the creation of that mythmaking and its value to this book's account. His *Basketball: Its Origin and Development* (originally published 1941; Lincoln: University of Nebraska Press, 1996) remains one of basketball's important precedent documents.

CHAPTER 2

As with many team sports in the United States, it wasn't long after the game's founding before efforts at professionalization sought to monetize it. For an early history of the sports culture in which basketball came of age, see Michael K. Bohn, *Heroes & Ballyhoo: How the Golden Age of the 1920s Transformed American Sports* (Washington, DC: Potomac Books, 2009). Robert W. Peterson's *Cages to Jump Shots: Pro Basketball's Early*

Years (Lincoln: University of Nebraska Press, 1990) takes that early context and narrows its focus to the game's early, fledgling attempts at creating a professional product.

The most successful early professional team was the barnstorming Original Celtics, chronicled most deftly by Murry R. Nelson, *The Originals: The New York Celtics Invent Modern Basketball* (Bowling Green, KY: Bowling Green State University Popular Press, 1999). The Celtics obviously emphasized their Irish heritage, but other ethnic groups also found success in the pro game. Douglas Stark's *When Basketball Was Jewish: Voices of Those Who Played the Game* (Lincoln: University of Nebraska Press, 2017) describes the Jewish influence on the early game, focusing on the players who made at least a partial living in the sport. Charley Rosen's *The Chosen Game: A Jewish Basketball History* (Lincoln: University of Nebraska Press, 2017) does much the same thing in a more traditional historical narrative. Matthew Sherman's master's thesis, "Point Guarden of Eden: Philadelphia as a Cradle for Jewish Basketball in the 1920s and 1930s" (MA thesis: Haverford College, 2017) narrows that focus to one city. Philadelphia's most influential early team were the SPHAs, chronicled by Douglas Stark in *The SPHAs: The Life and Times of Basketball's Greatest Jewish Team* (Philadelphia: Temple University Press, 2011).

League organization would be the mechanism that solidified the possibility of success for professional basketball. Murry R. Nelson's "The Original Celtics and the 1926–27 American Basketball League," *Journal of Popular Culture* 30 (Fall 1996): 87–100, tells part of that story. His *The National Basketball League: A History, 1935–1949* (Jefferson, NC: McFarland, 2009) goes into more depth about the organization that followed the American Basketball League. It would be the National Basketball League that ultimately transitioned into the National Basketball Association, a transition that stabilized the various competing circuits. Donald M. Fisher's "The Rochester Royals and the Transformation of Professional Basketball, 1945–57," *International Journal of the History of Sport* 10 (April 1993): 20–48, describes one team's experience with that transition, for better or worse.

Charley Rosen's *The First Tip-Off: The Incredible Story of the Birth of the NBA* (New York: McGraw-Hill, 2009) broadens the story from one team, then shrinks it again by turning its focus to the original game in the new Basketball Association of America, which would eventually become

the National Basketball Association, a game between the New York
Knicks and the Toronto Huskies, played in a Canadian hockey rink in
the year following World War II. Michael Schumacher carries the story
of that founding game forward to the creation of the NBA by following the career of the game's most important star in the postwar period.
*Mr. Basketball: George Mikan, the Minneapolis Lakers, and the Birth of the
NBA* (Minneapolis: University of Minnesota Press, 2008) is a biography
of Mikan, which does important work on a variety of fronts, but among
that work is a deft accounting of the role Mikan played in the stabiliza-
tion of the professional game.

CHAPTER 3

The game described in the book's first two chapters was decidedly
White, but Black basketball thrived, as well, developing teams and organizations similar to baseball's Negro leagues. The chief repository of
information on early Black basketball comes from the Black Fives Foundation, https://www.blackfives.org/.

Understanding the Black game, particularly the version coming out
of New York in the 1920s, it is important to understand the Harlem
Renaissance that undergirded most of the interest in it. See David Lever-
ing Lewis, *When Harlem Was in Vogue* (New York: Alfred A. Knopf,
1981); Nathan Irvin Huggins, *Harlem Renaissance* (New York: Oxford
University Press, 1973); and Ann Douglas, *Terrible Honesty: Mongrel
Manhattan in the 1920s* (New York: Farrar, Straus and Giroux, 1995) for
a broader understanding of the culture that made room for basketball on
the dance floors of Harlem clubs after the jazz music stopped playing for
the evening.

That said, Black basketball in Harlem predated the neighborhood's
renaissance. Claude Johnson's *Black Fives: The Alpha Physical Culture
Club's Pioneering African American Basketball Team, 1904–1923* (New
York: Black Fives Publishing, 2012) describes an early representative
effort. The Alpha Physical Culture Club would then be replaced by perhaps the most influential Black basketball team in the first half of the
twentieth century, the New York Renaissance Five. Susan J. Rayl's dissertation, "The New York Renaissance Professional Black Basketball

Team, 1923–1950" (PhD diss: Pennsylvania State University, 1996) provides a comprehensive accounting of the team's brief life.

New York, however, was not the only urban center fostering the Black game. Bob Kuska's *Hot Potato: How Washington and New York Gave Birth to Black Basketball and Changed America's Game Forever* (Charlottesville: University of Virginia Press, 2004) and John McNamara, Andrea Chamblee, and David Elfin's *The Capital of Basketball: A History of DC Area High School Hoops* (Washington, DC: Georgetown University Press, 2019) tell the story of the game in Washington. John Schleppi's *Chicago's Showcase of Basketball: The World Tournament of Professional Basketball and the College All-Star Game* (Haworth, NJ: St. Johann Press, 2008) turns its focus west to Chicago.

The Black basketball team that would have the most resonance with both the Black and White public would be the result of a decided connection between Chicago and New York: the Harlem Globetrotters. Ben Green's *Spinning the Globe: The Rise, Fall, and Return to Greatness of the Harlem Globetrotters* (New York: Amistad, 2005) is, to this point, the definitive account of the team. John Christgau's *Tricksters in the Madhouse: Lakers vs. Globetrotters 1948* (Lincoln: University of Nebraska Press, 2004) centers on the team's performance against the all-White Minneapolis Lakers in the year following Jackie Robinson's desegregation of Major League Baseball and the role it played in bringing basketball's own integration.

Finally, there are books like Oceania Chalk's *Pioneers of Black Sport: The Early Days of the Black Professional Athlete in Baseball, Basketball, Boxing, and Football* (New York: Dodd, Mead, and Company, 1975) that include early Black basketball play within the broader African American sporting context.

CHAPTER 4

For all the early attempts at professionalization, basketball was designed as an amateur game, and high schools and colleges also early began fielding teams. Much of the early enthusiasm for the amateur game came from Indiana, as described in Todd Gould's *Pioneers of the Hardwood: Indiana and the Birth of Professional Basketball* (Bloomington: Indiana

University Press, 1998). Phillip Ellett's *The Franklin Wonder Five: A Complete History of the Legendary Basketball Team* (Indianapolis: RLE Enterprises, 1986) focuses on one of the state's most dominant teams in the early 1920s, one that began as a high school team, then moved to Franklin College to continue play.

It is worth mentioning again that the most important source for learning about the teams of the collegiate game is *The ESPN College Basketball Encyclopedia: The Complete History of the Men's Game* (New York: Balantine Books, 2009), which traces each team to its origins. Marvin Washington and Marc J. Ventresca, "Institutional Contradictions and Struggles in the Formation of US Collegiate Basketball, 1880–1938," *Journal of Sport Management* 22 (January 2008): 30–49, is able to give context to those early collegiate team formations by demonstrating how they organized against one another.

But much of those origins were the work of early coaches who became legends themselves, and studies of those lives can help illuminate the development of the early game. Blair Kerkhoff's *Phog Allen: The Father of Basketball Coaching* (Carollton, TX: Masters Press, 1998) and Scott Morrow Johnson's *Phog: The Most Influential Man in Basketball* (Lincoln: University of Nebraska Press, 2016) chronicle the life of the University of Kansas coach whose influence spread well beyond the bounds of the plains. Russell Rice's *Adolph Rupp: Kentucky's Basketball Baron* (Champaign, IL: Sagamore Publishing, 1994) and James Duane Bolin's *Adolph Rupp and the Rise of Kentucky Basketball* (Lexington: University Press of Kentucky, 2019) do much the same for one of Allen's proteges and one of the most influential minds and lives in the collegiate game. Gus Alfieri, *Lapchick: The Life of a Legendary Player and Coach in the Glory Days of Basketball* (Lanham, MD: Lyons Press, 2006) tells the story of Joe Lapchick, who played for the Original Celtics before coaching four national championship teams at St. John's University.

The success of those coaches and teams would lead to a desire from fans for championships. Chad R. Carlson's "A Tale of Two Tournaments: The Red Cross Games and the Early NCAA-NIT Relationship," *Journal of Intercollegiate Sport* 5, No. 2 (2012): 260–80, and his *Making March Madness: The Early Years of the NCAA, NIT, and College Basketball Championships, 1922–1951* (Fayetteville: University of Arkansas Press, 2017) describe early tournament efforts, as does Terry Frei's *March 1939:*

Before the Madness—The Story of the First NCAA Basketball Tournament Champions (Lanham, MD: Taylor Trade Publishing, 2014).

CHAPTER 5

The seminal account of women's basketball is Pamela Grundy and Susan Shackelford, *Shattering the Glass: The Remarkable History of Women's Basketball* (New York: The New Press, 2005), and the first section of its comprehensive account describes the early women's game. Similarly, *A Century of Women's Basketball: From Frailty to Final Four*, edited by Joan S. Hult and Marianna Trekell (Reston, VA: American Alliance for Health, Physical Education, Recreation and Dance, 1991) includes in its early pages the game's development at the onset of the twentieth century.

The most important name in the early game was Senda Berenson, whose papers are archived at Smith College. Her *Basket Ball for Women* (New York: American Sports Publishing, 1901) is also still readily available. Agnes Cora Ruth Stillman, "Senda Berenson Abbott, Her Life and Contributions to Smith College and the Physical Education Profession (MA thesis: Smith College, 1971) provided the first substantial treatment of Berenson's life and work. H. V. Pfitsch's "Senda Berenson and the Early Days of Women's Sports," *Melpomene Journal* 13 (Fall 1994): 6–9, began a published historical analysis of her career, and Ralph Melnick, *Senda Berenson: The Unlikely Founder of Women's Basketball* (Amherst: University of Massachusetts Press, 2007) broadened that analysis in a book-length treatment.

Arrayed against the vision of Berenson were the Amateur Athletics Union (AAU) and the semiprofessional company teams that spread the popularity of women's basketball while emphasizing competition and physical play. Robert W. Ikard, *Just for Fun: The Story of AAU Women's Basketball* (Fayetteville: University of Arkansas Press, 2005) describes the AAU's role in the women's game. Sylvia F. Nadler, "A Developmental History of the Wayland Hutcherson Flying Queens from 1910 to 1979" (PhD diss: East Texas State University, 1980) provided an early history of one Texas's early company teams. That story is broadened by Mac C. Kirkpatrick and Thomas K. Perry, *The Southern Textile Basketball*

Tournament (Jefferson, NC: McFarland, 1997) and Lydia Reeder, *Dust Bowl Girls: The Inspiring Story of the Team That Barnstormed Its Way to Basketball Glory* (New York: Algonquin Books, 2017).

The greatest star who came from that semiprofessional circuit was Babe Didrikson. Susan E. Cayleff, *Babe: The Life and Legend of Babe Didrikson Zaharias* (Urbana: University of Illinois Press, 1996) and Don Van Natta Jr., *Wonder Girl: The Magnificent Sporting Life of Babe Didrikson Zaharias* (New York: Little, Brown, 2011) analyze the life of the early women's game's most transcendent personality.

As with the men's game, the vast majority of such women's organizations, whether housed in colleges, amateur associations, or semiprofessional circuits, were restricted to White players. But Black women also played the early game. Stephanie Yvette Felix's dissertation, "Committed to Their Own: African American Women Leaders in the YWCA of Germantown, Philadelphia, Pennsylvania, 1870–1970" (PhD diss: Temple University, 1999) and Rita Liberti's article, "'We Were Ladies, We Just Played Basketball Like Boys': African American Womanhood and Competitive Basketball at Bennett College, 1928–1942," *Journal of Sport History* 26 (Fall 1999): 567–84, create the beginnings of a historical accounting of early African American women's basketball, though there is much more work to be done on the subject.

CHAPTER 6

The original historical accounting of the midcentury college basketball scandal that shook the sport so significantly was Stanley Cohen, *The Game They Played: The True Story of the Point-Shaving Scandal That Destroyed One of College Basketball's Greatest Teams* (New York: Carroll and Graf, 1977), followed the next year by Charley Rosen, *Scandals of '51: How the Gamblers Almost Killed College Basketball* (originally published 1978; New York: Seven Stories Press, 1999). Cohen's account is comprehensive but focuses most of its attention on the travails of City College; Rosen, meanwhile, emphasizes the gamblers who manufactured the scheme. A decade later, Humbert S. Nelli supplemented the work of Cohen and Rosen by emphasizing the role of and consequences for the University of Kentucky in "Adolph Rupp, the Kentucky Wildcats, and the Basketball Scandal of 1951," *The Register of the Kentucky Historical Society* 84 (Winter 1986): 51–75.

The mantle of scholarship on the scandals would be taken up later in the decade by Albert J. Figone. His "Gambling and College Basketball: The Scandal of 1951," *Journal of Sport History* 16 (Spring 1989): 44–61, reimagined the scandals and Figone's later *Cheating the Spread: Gamblers, Point Shavers, and Fixers in College Football and Basketball* (Urbana: University of Illinois Press, 2012) places the scandal within the larger context of collegiate athletic scandals, including those of the football programs at the United States Military Academy and Michigan State University, interpreting them as part of a post–World War II pattern of misconduct prompted by a weak and ineffective NCAA.

More recently, William F. Reed's "Hidden World," *Sports Illustrated* 127 (6 November 2017): 70–75, has translated the scandals for a nonacademic audience. Dennis Gildea discusses the scandals within the context of broader biography. *Hoop Crazy: The Lives of Clair Bee and Chip Hilton* (Fayetteville: University of Arkansas Press, 2013) tells the story of the coach of Long Island University who found his career derailed by the scandal and his attempt at redemption through the publication of a series of children's books about fictional athletic star Chip Hilton.

Long Island's star player, Sherman White, went to prison as a result of the scandal, but much of the attention in New York focused on City College, the basketball power brought to its knees by the scandal. Unlike Kentucky, for example, City College never recovered, leading to both mythmaking surrounding the program and the bulk of historical scrutiny when analyzing the scandal. Steven Stern's documentary, *City Dump: The 1951 CCNY Basketball Scandal* (Film, 60 minutes, Black Canyon Productions), like Reed's *Sports Illustrated* article, pushed the gambling scandal back into the twenty-first-century mainstream. Edward Shapiro, "The Shame of the City: CCNY Basketball, 1950–51," in *Jews, Sports, and the Rites of Citizenship*, Jack Kugelmass, ed., 175–192 (Urbana: University of Illinois Press, 2007) discusses the team's struggles through an academic lens. Finally, Matthew Goodman's *The City Game: Triumph, Scandal, and a Legendary Basketball Team* (New York: Random House, 2019) provides a nuanced, academic analysis of the scandal and its role at City College that is also easily accessible to a nonacademic audience.

CHAPTER 7

The bibliography in chapter 2 discusses the early growth of professional basketball, and includes books like Charley Rosen's *The First Tip-Off: The Incredible Story of the Birth of the NBA* (New York: McGraw-Hill, 2009), which tells the story of the association's first game in Toronto. So, too, does Michael Schumacher's *Mr. Basketball: George Mikan, the Minneapolis Lakers, and the Birth of the NBA* (Minneapolis: University of Minnesota Press, 2008), which describes the life of the postwar game's most influential player and, later, administrator, and in the process uses the life of Mikan to tell the story of the NBA's birth and development stemming from the Basketball Association of America. Because of the influence of the NBA in modern basketball, the genesis of that organization in particular has been the recipient of significant historical scrutiny. Many of the works that broadly interpret the game mentioned in the introductory section of this essay detail the association's beginnings. There are, however, others that merit attention.

Terry Pluto, who has proven himself the Studs Terkel of professional basketball, allowed the players, administrators, and coaches of the postwar period to describe the creation of the association in *Tall Tales: The Glory Years of the NBA, in the Words of the Men Who Played, Coached, and Built Pro Basketball* (Lincoln: University of Nebraska Press, 1992). In 1998, Donald F. Staffo published "The Development of Professional Basketball in the United States, with an Emphasis on the History of the NBA to Its 50th Anniversary Season in 1996–97," *The Physical Educator* 55 (late winter 1998): 9–18, taking those first-person accounts and using them to generate an academic essay detailing the association's founding. Also that year, Stephen R. Fox's *Big Leagues: Professional Baseball, Football, and Basketball in National Memory* (Lincoln: University of Nebraska Press, 1998) places the founding of the NBA within the context of the country's other major sports leagues, then examines the legacy of that founding in the way people interpret both the game and the professional association that organizes it. Nearly a decade later, Connie Kirchberg's *Hoop Lore: A History of the National Basketball Association* (Jefferson, NC: McFarland, 2007) begins at the association's creation and continues its story through the twentieth century and into the twenty-first, as does

David George Surdam's *The Rise of the National Basketball Association* (Urbana: University of Illinois Press, 2012).

Along with these studies are others that emphasize certain individuals in the rise of the NBA. Andrew Van Burren, *MPLS: The Minneapolis Lakers and the Dawn of Professional Basketball* (Adelaide, Australia: Fletcher Thomas, 2019) supplements Schumacher's Mikan biography a decade prior, evaluating the role of the early association's most dominant team. Bill Reynolds, *Cousy: His Life, Career, and the Birth of Bigtime Basketball* (New York: Simon & Schuster, 2005) tells the story of the most important early player and coach for another of the NBA's dominant franchises, the Boston Celtics. Dolph Grundman, *Dolph Schayes and the Rise of Professional Basketball* (Syracuse, NY: Syracuse University Press, 2014) does the same for the star of the Syracuse Nationals, who later moved to Philadelphia and became the 76ers. Finally, Bryan Smith frames a slightly different narrative in *The Breakaway: The Inside Story of the Wirtz Family Business and the Chicago Blackhawks* (Chicago: Northwestern University Press, 2018), which tells the story of the family who owned the Chicago Blackhawks hockey team of the NHL. The Wirtzes were also integral boosters for professional basketball in Chicago, as were many hockey owners seeking more events for their arenas. These stories, when taken as a whole, create a nexus in which readers can situate the role of various markets in producing the NBA's early popularity.

CHAPTER 8

The most prominent complicating factor in that early popularity was race and integration, and the consequences for basketball's theater of Black-White relations, and integration in particular, is one of the most analyzed elements of the historiography. The college game in particular has experienced much of that scholarship, the bulk of it emphasizing the NCAA tournament game between the Black starting five of Texas Western and the White starting five of Kentucky. Frank Fitzpatrick's *And the Walls Came Tumbling Down: The Basketball Game That Changed American Sports* (Lincoln: University of Nebraska Press, 1999) was the first book-length account of the contest and its consequences. Like many of the popular celebrations of the game that would appear in the twenty-first century, Fitzpatrick's narrative is largely positive, if not hagiographic, in its treatment of the racial situation surrounding the game. Phillip Hutchinson's "The Legend of Texas Western: Journalism and the Epic Sports Spectacle That Wasn't," *Critical Studies in Media Communication* 33, Issue 2 (2016): 154–67, is critical of Fitzpatrick's treatment and the general celebratory nature of coverage of the game and provides an important corrective that emphasizes the role of media in creating the mythology of the event.

The other individual game that receives substantial historical attention is the 1963 contest between Loyola Chicago and Mississippi State, wherein the Bulldogs snuck out of Mississippi to play against an integrated team against the wishes of the state's governor and legislators. Michael Lenehan's *Ramblers: Loyola Chicago 1963—The Team That Changed the Color of College Basketball* (Evanston, IL: Agate, 2013) tackles the racial consequences of the game from Loyola's perspective, while Jason A. Peterson's *Full Court Press: Mississippi State University, the Press, and the Battle to Integrate College Basketball* (Jackson: University Press of Mississippi, 2016) and Kyle Veazey's *Champions for Change: How the Mississippi State Bulldogs and Their Bold Coach Defied Segregation* (Charleston, SC: The History Press, 2012) treat it from the perspective of Mississippi State.

Other accounts of collegiate integration take a broader, if still focused, approach. Charles H. Martin's "Jim Crow in the Gymnasium: The Integration of College Basketball in the American South," *International Journal of the History of Sport* 10, No. 1 (1993): 68–86, evaluates efforts at southern colleges and universities more broadly. Tom Graham and Rachel Graham Cody describe the life and influence of Bill Garrett in *Getting Open: The Unknown Story of Bill Garrett and the Integration of College Basketball* (New York: Atria Books, 2006). Garrett integrated Indiana University's team and became the first Black player to regularly participate in Big Ten contests. Charlie Scott did much the same for another perennial power, the University of North Carolina, as described in Gregory J. Kaliss, "Un-Civil Discourse: Charlie Scott, the Integration of College Basketball, and the 'Progressive Mystique,'" *Journal of Sport History* 35 (Spring 2008): 98–117.

Programs themselves have also merited scrutiny. John Matthew Smith, *The Sons of Westwood: John Wooden, UCLA, and the Dynasty That*

Changed College Basketball (Urbana: University of Illinois Press, 2013) wrestles with the role of Wooden and UCLA in that process. Robert D. Jacobus, *Houston Cougars in the 1960s: Death Threats, the Veer Offense, and the Game of the Century* (College Station: Texas A&M University Press, 2015) also shows the role that a collegiate team can have in a community and in the country. In addition to these program studies, Gregory Bond, *Jim Crow at Play: Race, Manliness, and the Color Line in American Sports, 1876–1916* (Madison: University of Wisconsin Press, 2008) places the early integration of collegiate teams into the broader context of sports integration writ large.

For the professional game, the two studies most comprehensive in their approach to integration are Ron Thomas, *They Cleared the Lane: The NBA's Black Pioneers* (Lincoln: University of Nebraska Press, 2004) and Douglas Stark, *Breaking Barriers: A History of Integration in Professional Basketball* (Lanham, MD: Rowman & Littlefield, 2019).

CHAPTER 9

Accompanying studies of basketball's integration are those dealing with the racial consequences of a game that was increasingly identified with blackness as more and more African American players joined collegiate and professional teams. In colleges, with some exceptions, the presence of Black players did its own work. Lew Alcindor's activism at UCLA and Bill Russell's uncompromising stances at the University of San Francisco provided important activism at the college level, and both of them continued that work in the professional ranks, where the bulk of players' racial activism came from. James Haskins chronicles Alcindor's activism at both levels of play in *From Lew Alcindor to Kareem Abdul-Jabbar* (New York: Lothrop, Lee & Shepard, 1972). Aram Goudsouzian's *King of the Court: Bill Russell and the Basketball Revolution* (Berkeley: University of California Press, 2010) makes a similar, though more comprehensive, analysis of Russell in both college and the NBA.

Civil rights and its role in the lives and games of players, however, was a topic analyzed in real time. John Devaney's exposé, "Pro Basketball's Hidden Fear," *Sport* (February 1966): 32–33, 89–92, exposed many of the racial tensions within the professional game. That same year, Bill Russell published his own account, *Go Up for Glory* (New York: Coward-McCann, 1966), which described his life in the game, but also reckoned with race in both basketball and society, solidifying his position not only as the star center for the Boston Celtics, but also as a voice for change in society. Three years later, San Jose State sociologist Harry Edwards published *The Revolt of the Black Athlete* (New York: The Free Press, 1969), analyzing the role of Black athletes like Russell in political discussions and arguing for stars in sports like basketball to use their public voices for revolutionary action.

Elgin Baylor was another player, like Russell, who worked in the cause of civil rights while working on the court. Bijan C. Bayne, *Elgin Baylor: The Man Who Changed Basketball* (Lanham, MD: Rowman & Littlefield, 2015) tells the story of both his activism and his play. Murray R. Nelson's *Abe Saperstein and the American Basketball League, 1960–1963* (Jefferson, NC: McFarland, 2013) describes another racial pioneer in the game.

Other contemporary accounts focused on the nature of basketball as an urban game, as a refuge for Black athletes who had neither the profile nor the pocketbook of professional players. Pete Axthelm's *The City Game: Basketball from the Garden to the Playgrounds* (Lincoln: University of Nebraska Press, 1999) was originally published in 1970. Fourteen years later, Rick Telander published *Heaven Is a Playground* (New York: Skyhorse, 2013). Axthelm was an academic, Telander a photojournalist, and taken together, *The City Game* and *Heaven Is a Playground* provide a comprehensive accounting of urban basketball.

Nelson George touches on the urban game in his 1992 book, *Elevating the Game: Black Men and Basketball* (New York: HarperCollins, 1992), but moves beyond the playgrounds to the hard courts of colleges and professional stadiums. Damion L. Thomas moves even farther, placing the racial theater of basketball into an international context in *Globetrotting: African American Athletes and Cold War Politics* (Urbana: University of Illinois Press, 2012). Thomas Aiello then examines that theater through the lens of professional basketball in the South when leagues moved to the region in the wake of desegregation in *Dixieball: Race and Professional Basketball in the Deep South, 1947–1979* (Knoxville: University of Tennessee Press, 2019).

Then there are accounts that include basketball in contemporary analyses of the modern racial implications of sport. John Hoberman, *Darwin's Athletes: How Sport Has Damaged Black America and Preserved the Myth of Race* (New York: Mariner Books, 1997) includes basketball in its analysis, as does Kenneth L. Shropshire, *In Black and White: Race and Sports in America* (New York: New York University Press, 1998). Dave Zirin's *What's My Name, Fool? Sports and Resistance in the United States* (Chicago: Haymarket Books, 2005) spends even more of its time on the game in its analysis of race and protest in professional sports.

Jeffrey Lane's *Under the Boards: The Cultural Revolution in Basketball* (Lincoln: University of Nebraska Press, 2007) and Todd Boyd's "The Day the Niggaz Took Over: Basketball, Commodity Culture, and Black Masculinity," in *Out of Bounds: Sports, Media, and the Politics of Identity*, Aaron Baker and Todd Boyd, eds., 134–37 (Bloomington: Indiana University Press, 1997) use basketball as a vehicle for political and racial analysis of late twentieth-century minority relations.

CHAPTER 10

Of course, race also played a role in the creation of the NBA's rival, the American Basketball Association (ABA), in 1967, a league that promoted its Black players in a way that the NBA had been reluctant to do. Adam J. Criblez captures that tension in the decade of the ABA in his "White Men Playing a Black Man's Game: Basketball's 'Great White Hopes' of the 1970s," *Journal of Sport History* 42 (Fall 2015): 371–81. Meanwhile, in the NBA, racial tensions reached a boiling point in Kermit Washington's punch of Rudy Tomjanovich, which features prominently in this account. John Feinstein's *The Punch: One Night, Two Lives, and the Fight That Changed Basketball Forever* (New York: Back Bay Books, 2003) describes the incident in minute detail.

The ABA itself, its creation, play, and administrative machinations, have been the subject of several accounts. Gary Davidson, *Breaking the Game Wide Open* (New York: Atheneum, 1974) and Bob Netolicky, Richard Tinkham, and Robin Miller, *We Changed the Game* (Chicago: Hilton Publishing, 2017) provide insight from the league's founders on the negotiations and motivations that created the organization and the strategy for forcing a merger to include dissident teams in the NBA. Other voices from the league are featured in another Studs Terkel–esque account from Terry Pluto, *Loose Balls: The Short, Wild Life of the American Basketball Association* (New York: Simon & Schuster, 1990), which stands as the most comprehensive accounting of the group.

The effects of the league rivalry were also substantial for the players, and Pluto's work helps flesh that out, as do books like Vincent Mallozzi's *Doc: The Rise and Rise of Julius Erving* (New York: Wiley, 2008), which uses the ABA's most prominent player to demonstrate the league's role in his own career and on those he played with. Sarah K. Fields goes into more depth about the antitrust issues the NBA's rival created in "Odd Bedfellows: Spencer Haywood and Justice William O. Douglas," *Journal of Sport History* 34 (Summer 2007): 193–206.

The teams also felt those effects, and several accounts analyze the teams of the ABA. Thomas Aiello's *Dixieball: Race and Professional Basketball in the Deep South, 1947–1979* (Knoxville: University of Tennessee Press, 2019) goes into depth about the New Orleans Buccaneers, while Mark Montieth's *Reborn: The Pacers and the Return of Pro Basketball to Indianapolis* (Indianapolis: Halfcourt Press, 2017) discusses the Indianapolis Pacers. While the Buccaneers folded early and the Pacers became part of the merger that included them in the NBA, other teams found themselves financially viable but without a place in the combined organization. Gary West and Lloyd Gardner, *Kentucky Colonels of the American Basketball Association: The Real Story of a Team Left Behind* (Morley, MO: Acclaim Press, 2011) describes the most successful ABA team to be denied a place in the new NBA.

The most prominent work about professional basketball in the 1970s, however, is one that analyzes the state of the NBA after the merger. David Halberstam's *The Breaks of the Game* (New York: Knopf, 1981) is one of the most important sports books ever written. It examines the 1979–1980 season of the Portland Trailblazers, but uses that team to trace the organization's previous seasons, the role of race and the merger in the modern game, and the impact of both on players and administrators in what was becoming a new age of professional basketball.

CHAPTER 11

That new age was defined in particular by the rivalry between two transcendent players, Larry Bird and Magic Johnson, one White and one Black, both supremely talented, who encapsulated much of the passion and theater of basketball throughout the decade of the 1980s. But the rivalry, manufactured as it was, to some extent, actually began in the 1970s, as the professional game was going through a variety of growing pains. Seth Davis's *When March Went Mad: The Game That Transformed Basketball* (New York: Henry Holt, 2009) tells the story of the NCAA championship game between Magic's Michigan State Spartans and Bird's Indiana State Sycamores. Davis describes the meaning of the game to fans; to racial commentators; and to the NCAA, which profited from the event and used it as a springboard to greater popularity for the collegiate game in the decades to follow.

The most complete book-length treatment of the Bird-Magic rivalry, both in the collegiate and professional settings, is Larry Bird, Earvin "Magic" Johnson, and Jackie MacMullan, *When the Game Was Ours* (New York: Houghton Mifflin, 2009), a comprehensive account that helped ground a documentary the following year: Ezra Edelman, Rick Bernstein, Ross Greenburg, Joe Lavine, and Rahul Rohatgi, *Magic & Bird: A Courtship of Rivals* (Film, 85 minutes, Home Box Office, 2010). A more literary evaluation that brings its own unique perspective, one of a fan in the 1980s, is Chuck Klosterman's "Celtics vs. Lakers," included in his essay collection, *Sex, Drugs, and Cocoa Puffs* (New York: Simon & Schuster, 2010). In addition to such accounts, the rivalry was also made into a Broadway play: Eric Simonsen, *Magic/Bird*, Broadway Production (New York: Dramatists Play Service, 2013).

Magic and Bird both have their own individual interpretations on their lives and rivalry, both of which (despite this essay's early warning that autobiographies would not be included in this bibliography) can be found in their autobiographies: Larry Bird, *Drive: The Story of My Life* (New York: Bantam, 1990), and Earvin "Magic" Johnson, *My Life* (New York: Faucet Books, 1992). Another account that details the rivalry is Jeff Pearlman's book about the 1980s Showtime Lakers, *Showtime: Magic, Kareem, Riley and the Los Angeles Lakers Dynasty of the 1980s* (New York: Gotham Books, 2013).

While the rivalry between the Celtics and Lakers, driven by Bird and Magic, defined much of the era, there were dangers afoot within the association, particularly relating to the prevalence of cocaine in the 1980s. John Papanek's "There's an Ill Wind Blowing for the NBA," *Sports Illustrated* (26 February 1979): 20–27, provides a contemporary account of a burgeoning problem, and Fraser C. Smith's *Lenny, Lefty, and the Chancellor: The Len Bias Tragedy and the Search for Reform in Big-Time College Basketball* (New York: Bancroft, 1992) provides historical context filtered through a life of one of the drug's most prominent tragedies, the death of Celtics draft pick and University of Maryland All-American Len Bias.

CHAPTER 12

There were, of course, other controversies in basketball in the 1970s and 1980s. David A. F. Sweet, *Three Seconds in Munich: The Controversial 1972 Olympic Basketball Final* (Lincoln: University of Nebraska Press, 2019) describes the United States Olympic team's controversial loss to the Soviet Union and the effect it had on the Cold War and American thinking about its role in an increasingly international sport. The Olympic team in the 1970s comprised amateurs, but the professionals were also in turmoil. Grant M. Hayden, "Some Keys to the NBA Lockout," *Hofstra Labor and Employment Law Journal* 16, Issue 2 (1999): 453–68, parses the legal issues of labor relations in the association.

Meanwhile, racial concerns did not magically disappear. Kwame Agyemang and John N. Singer, "An Exploratory Study of Professional Black Male Athletes' Individual Social Responsibility (ISR)," in *The Ethics of Sport: Essential Readings*, Arthur L. Caplan and Brendan Parent, eds., 242–64 (New York: Oxford University Press, 2017) provides a sociological and ethical analysis of the willingness of Black athletes to engage in public protest for human and civil rights. It is an important study, particularly when viewing professional basketball in the late 1980s and early 1990s, because the era's most transcendent star largely avoided politics and cultivated a corporate image designed to translate his on-court success into advertising prowess off of it.

Walter LaFeber's *Michael Jordan and the New Global Capitalism* (New York: W. W. Norton, 2002) examines that advertising prowess in particular and how Michael Jordan became an unprecedented capitalist icon at the end of the twentieth century. David L. Andrews's *Michael Jordan, Inc.: Corporate Sport, Media Culture, and Late Modern America* (Albany, NY: SUNY Press, 2001) does much the same.

Michael Jordan, however, was more than the sum of his advertising revenue. Roland Lazenby, *Michael Jordan: The Life* (New York: Little, Brown and Co., 2014) provides a comprehensive biography of the star athlete. Sam Smith, *The Jordan Rules: The Inside Story of a Turbulent Season with Michael Jordan and the Chicago Bulls* (New York: Simon & Schuster, 1992) reduces its analysis to one season, analyzing the Chicago Bulls in the season of its first championship.

The year Smith's book appeared, Jordan only added to his legacy by participating in a second Olympic games, this time as a professional. The rules had been changed after substantial negotiations that were, at least in some measure, a legacy of American bitterness over the 1972 games. When the pros were included, the talent gap between the United States and the rest of the world's teams widened substantially, as demonstrated in Jack McCallum's *Dream Team: How Michael, Magic, Larry, Charles, and the Greatest Team of All Time Conquered the World and Changed the Game of Basketball Forever* (New York: Ballantine Books, 2012).

Perhaps the most prescient accounting of Jordan's role in basketball, capitalism, and global celebrity is presented by David Halberstam, author of *The Breaks of the Game* (New York: Knopf, 1981). Two decades after that achievement, Halberstam published *Playing for Keeps: Michael Jordan and the World He Made* (New York: Broadway Books, 2000), a disquisition on Jordan's outsized influence on society.

Finally, Jordan's legacy and the success of his Chicago Bulls teams have been popularly memorialized in a prominent documentary. Jason Hehir, *The Last Dance* (Miniseries, 491 minutes, ESPN Films, 2020), emphasizes the Bulls' last championship season in the waning days of Jordan's playing career.

CHAPTER 13

As the century turned and Michael Jordan's playing career came to a close, both collegiate and professional men's basketball found themselves at a series of crossroads. Jerry Parkinson's *Infractions: Rule Violations, Unethical Conduct, and Enforcement in the NCAA* (Lincoln: University of Nebraska Press, 2019) describes many problems endemic in the collegiate game, while David Porter's *Fixed: How Goodfellas Bought Boston College Basketball* (Lanham, MD: Taylor Trade Publishing, 2000) reminds readers that the sport's turn-of-the-century problems were not new, describing another infamous point-shaving scandal during the 1978–1979 season at Boston College.

But gambling and point shaving were not the only problems plaguing the NCAA. Much of the controversy involved the pipeline to both major universities and the professional ranks, facilitated by supposedly amateur organizations like the Amateur Athletic Union. George Dohrmann, *Play Their Hearts Out: A Coach, His Star Recruit, and the Youth Basketball Machine* (New York: Ballantine Books, 2012) and Jonathan P. D. Abrams, *Boys Among Men: How the Prep-to-Pro Generation Redefined the NBA and Sparked a Basketball Revolution* (New York: Crown Archetype, 2016) describe the corruption inherent in youth basketball and the problems such corruption pose to the NBA and NCAA.

For whatever its twenty-first-century problems, however, college basketball and its season-ending tournament continued to grow in popularity, led by players, coaches, and rivalries that made every season compelling. Barry Wilner and Ken Rappoport describe the growth of the NCAA tournament, its burgeoning popularity, and the revenue it generates in *The Big Dance: The Story of the NCAA Basketball Tournament* (Lanham, MD: Taylor Trade Publishing, 2012). Perhaps the most adept observer of the college game has been John Feinstein, who has written at length about the sport's coaches, players, and history. His *The Legends Club: Dean Smith, Mike Krzyzewski, Jim Valvano, and an Epic College Basketball Rivalry* (New York: Anchor Books, 2017) describes the development and legacy of the fierce collegiate rivalries among the schools of North Carolina. Feinstein followed that effort three years later with *The Back Roads to March: The Unsung, Unheralded, and Unknown Heroes of a College Basketball Season* (New York: Knopf, 2020), examining midmajor colleges perennially "on the bubble," hoping not necessarily to win the NCAA tournament, but to be included in the field.

Being included among the sixty-eight teams invited to the tournament drives notoriety and revenue for many smaller schools, and that revenue is largely the result of television, which fundamentally changed the game by keeping college basketball on television every winter night. The ubiquity of televised contests was driven largely by an upstart network from Connecticut developed in the early days of cable, with a mission to broadcast sports and sports news twenty-four hours a day. Tom Shales and James Andrew Miller, *Those Guys Have All the Fun: Inside the World of ESPN* (New York: Little, Brown, 2011) provides yet another first-person account in the style of Terry Pluto's work, allowing the employees of the network to describe its history with a comprehensivity and style that makes it both informative and easily accessible.

But as television gives, it also takes away, constant coverage driving a new wave of scandal as the twenty-first century progressed. Karen Weaver's "Covering Up Murder: The Death of Patrick Dennehy at Baylor University," in *Scandals in College Sports*, Shaun R. Harper and Jamel K. Donor, eds., 70–78 (New York: Routledge, 2017) tells the story of one of the most shocking of the game's scandals, the murder of a teammate by a Baylor University player in 2003. Less violent but equally shocking was the fall of legendary coach Rick Pitino, who had risen through the ranks of coaching in stops at Boston University, Providence, Kentucky, and Louisville before finding himself embroiled in a pay-for-play scandal that involved apparel deals and paid prostitutes in university dorms. Michael Sokolove's *The Last Temptation of Rick Pitino: A Story of Corruption, Scandal, and the Big Business of College Basketball* (New York: Penguin, 2019) not only examines the scandal, but also takes on the larger phenomenon of money in amateur sports, the same money that had appeared in the earlier accounts of Jerry Parkinson and David Porter.

CHAPTER 14

Studies of the women's game necessarily emphasize gendered struggles resulting from heteronormative patriarchal control of basketball. It is a control that appears in most sports, and so women's experiences in the broader athletic realm ultimately contextualize women's basketball experiences. Susan K. Cahn, *Coming on Strong: Gender and Sexuality in Twentieth-Century Women's Sport* (Cambridge, MA: Harvard University

Press, 1994) and J. A. Mangan, *From 'Fair Sex' to Feminism: Sport and the Socialization of Women in the Industrial and Post-Industrial Eras* (New York: Frank Cass, 1987) provide particularly helpful grounding in women's experiences in basketball and sport writ large. Deborah L. Brake, *Getting in the Game: Title IX and the Women's Sports Revolution* (New York: NYU Press, 2012) emphasizes the impact of Title IX of the Education Amendments of 1972, prohibiting sex discrimination in educational programs that receive federal funding.

Title IX, by definition, affects all women's scholastic and collegiate athletic programs, at least those receiving federal money, but other studies focus specifically on basketball. Christine A. Baker's *Why She Plays: The World of Women's Basketball* (Lincoln: University of Nebraska Press, 2008) provides a sweeping analysis of the game, while other studies serve as companions that emphasize particular aspects and events. Sara Corbett's *Venus to the Hoop: A Gold Medal Year in Women's Basketball* (New York: Anchor Books, 1998) does for the 1996 women's Olympic team what Jack McCallum's *Dream Team: How Michael, Magic, Larry, Charles, and the Greatest Team of All Time Conquered the World and Changed the Game of Basketball Forever* (New York: Ballantine Books, 2012) does for the 1992 men's Olympic team, describing the burden carried by stars like Rebecca Lobo, Sheryl Swoopes, and Lisa Leslie, as they carried both the expectations of the country and the dreams of millions of young girls on their shoulders one year before the founding of the WNBA.

The WNBA was vital to the success of the women's game, but also depended on the popularity of efforts like that of the 1996 women's Olympic team to drive its popularity. It was a fraught endeavor. Karra Porter's *Mad Seasons: The Story of the First Women's Professional Basketball League, 1978–1981* (Lincoln: University of Nebraska Press, 2006) shows the precarity that could come with efforts at professional organizations for female players. The WNBA, however, would survive, despite inherent gendered problems, described in legal detail by N. Jeremi Duru in "Hoop Dreams Deferred: The WNBA, the NBA, and the Long-Standing Gender Inequity at the Game's Highest Level," *Utah Law Review* No. 3 (2015): 559–603. Juliette Terzieff, *Women of the Court: Inside the WNBA* (Boston: Alyson Books, 2008) views the league with a wider scope, while still grappling with many of the inherent gender disparities present in the professional sport.

The women's pro game is a relatively new phenomenon. Most seeking to play after high school turned to the collegiate game, one that would grow to popularity in the late twentieth century and early twenty-first through a rivalry between two programs and coaches: Pat Summitt's University of Tennessee Lady Vols and Geno Auriemma's University of Connecticut Huskies. Bill Haltom and Amanda Swanson, *Full Court Press: How Pat Summitt, a High School Basketball Player, and a Legal Team Changed the Game* (Knoxville: University of Tennessee Press, 2018) lays the groundwork for understanding that rivalry by making the case for Summitt's transformative role in the development of women's collegiate basketball into a revenue-generating spectacle. Jeff Goldberg, then, drills down on the heated battles between Summitt's Vols and Auriemma's Huskies in *Unrivaled: UConn, Tennessee, and the Twelve Years That Transcended Women's Basketball* (Lincoln: University of Nebraska Press, 2015).

Throughout women's basketball, from the late nineteenth century to the early twenty-first, players have had to negotiate false charges and lived realities of homosexuality in the game. Several accounts deal directly with the thicket of issues raised by stereotypes in the sport. Mary Anne Case, "Heterosexuality as a Factor in the Long History of Women's Sports," *Law & Contemporary Problems* 80, Issue 4 (2017): 35–46; Michael A. Messner, "Studying Up on Sex," *Sociology of Sport Journal* 13, No. 3 (1996): 221–37; and Jennifer Waldron, "It's Complicated: Negotiations and Complexities of Being a Lesbian in Sport," *Sex Roles* 74 (April 2016): 335–46, all wrestle with those issues.

CHAPTER 15

The NBA of the twenty-first century has proven to be a microcosm of basketball's successes and failures over the course of its existence. The first years of the 2000s were dominated by the Los Angeles Lakers. Jeffrey Scott Shapiro and Jennifer Stevens first took on the team's success in *Kobe Bryant: The Game of His Life* (New York: Revolution Publishing, 2004). More recently, Jeff Pearlman, *Three-Ring Circus: Kobe, Shaq, Phil, and the Crazy Years of the Lakers Dynasty* (New York: Houghton Mifflin, 2020) tells the full story of the tumultuous but successful group of stars who continued to win despite a tense coexistence.

If the Lakers were on the top of the association in the early 2000s, the Portland Trailblazers were near the bottom. Gone were the halcyon days described by David Halberstam in *The Breaks of the Game* (New York: Knopf, 1981), replaced by a group that continued to find itself on the wrong end of the scoresheet and the wrong end of the law. Kerry Eggers, *Jail Blazers: How the Portland Trail Blazers Became the Bad Boys of Basketball* (New York: Simon & Schuster, 2018) explains the team's problems and the racial coding that came with them. Racial coding, of course, would always be part of the association, exacerbated by a 2004 fight between players and fans during a game between the Indiana Pacers and the Detroit Pistons. David J. Leonard's *After Artest: The NBA and the Assault on Blackness* (Albany, NY: SUNY Press, 2012) examines the racial context of the controversy, supplementing other works describing race as lived in a variety of professional sports such as William C. Rhoden's *Forty Million Dollar Slaves: The Rise, Fall, and Redemption of the Black Athlete* (New York: Crown Publishers, 2006).

Three years after what became known as the Malice at the Palace, another scandal would rock the NBA, as referee Tim Donaghy was discovered to be part of a gambling scandal. Sean Patrick Griffin, *Gaming the Game: The Story Behind the NBA Betting Scandal and the Gambler Who Made It Happen* (Abington, PA: Independently published, 2019) provides the most comprehensive accounting of the controversy to date.

In the decade that followed, one of the most prominent controversies involved not illegal activity, but a disputed strategy for building team success. The Philadelphia 76ers, realizing that draft picks led to quality players, began a planned series of losing seasons to acquire better young players. Yaron Weitzman, *Tanking to the Top: The Philadelphia 76ers and the Most Audacious Process in the History of Professional Sports* (New York: Grand Central Publishing, 2020) analyzes the strategy and the public reaction to it.

The professional game, however, has also experienced a surge in popularity, led largely by transcendent players and dynasties that have captured the popular imagination. Ian Thomsen, *The Soul of Basketball: The Epic Showdown between LeBron, Kobe, Doc, and Dirk That Saved the NBA* (New York: Houghton Mifflin, 2018); Brian Windhorst and Dave McMenamin, *Return of the King: LeBron James, the Cleveland Cavaliers and the Greatest Comeback in NBA History* (New York: Grand Central

Publishing, 2017); and Ethan Sherwood Strauss, *The Victory Machine: The Making and Unmaking of the Warriors Dynasty* (New York: PublicAffairs, 2020) all make the case that the modern incarnation of the NBA is currently thriving.

If history is any guide, however, new turmoil is sure to come, and a growing historiography is sure to examine basketball, men's and women's, college and pro, with new scrutiny as the years progress.

Index